The FREEDOM CHALLENGE FOR MEN

60 DAYS

to Untie the Cords that Bind You

The FREEDOM CHALLENGE FOR MEN

60 DAYS to Untie the Cords that Bind You

PAUL & DAWN SCOTT DAMON

Published by Redemption Press, PO Box 427, Enumclaw, WA 98022.

Toll-Free (844) 2REDEEM (273-3336)

Redemption Press is honored to present this title in partnership with the author. The views expressed or implied in this work are those of the author. Redemption Press provides our imprint seal representing design excellence, creative content, and high-quality production.

ISBN: 978-1-64645-110-4 (Paperback)
978-1-64645-111-1 (ePub)
978-1-64645-112-8 (Mobi)

Library of Congress Catalog Card Number: 2020914245

CONTENTS

INTRODUCTION

After Dawn finished her manuscript for *The Freedom Challenge*, we awaited the delivery of this promising book. As I always do, I read it to be supportive, but I was also curious. The title intrigued me. I'm usually up for a "challenge." The idea of freedom captured my attention, and I wanted to learn more.

But after reading the first chapter, I was convinced that *I needed* this book, and not only me, but every man and woman. So together, Dawn and I made this powerful resource available for men. We will guide you through eight areas of spiritual struggle—cords that bind many men and women—as you encounter sixty days that will change your life. I'm excited to play a part in creating and presenting this revised version of *The Freedom Challenge* for men.

Dawn's Story

In 1990 I was headed for the perfect storm. Life's challenges loomed like threatening rain clouds. I felt as if every area of my life was swirling out of control in an angry squall—poor health, financial strain, marital distress, three active children, and impoverished spiritual life. Anxiety and depression gripped me, the troubling symptoms of post-traumatic stress disorder, making matters worse and draining me of strength and motivation. I was headed for a breakthrough or a breakdown, and I needed help. I longed to—no—I *needed to* know the truth and find rest in that truth. Broken and battered, I did the only thing I knew to do. I fell on my knees and cried out for God to rescue me.

To find answers, I reached for my Bible and opened it.

Paul's Story

My journey to freedom came as a result of my own perfect storm. Between 2006 and 2009, a series of events rolled in like dark clouds, devastated my life, and left me gasping for air. My wife suddenly and wordlessly left our marriage. I had to seek out the reasons why she left. The financial markets had collapsed, leaving my business gutted, and my net worth reduced from seven figures to negative figures. Emotionally, I was clinging to the end of my rope. I discovered that when men think they have no options, they often turn to God. I hated to admit it, but I had become one of those men. I fell to my knees and cried out for God to rescue me.

My Christian upbringing compounded my guilt and struggle. I grew up in a wonderful family with strong Christian parents who lived out their faith every day. They gave generously of their time, talent, and treasure, often at great sacrifice. But unfortunately, my early faith walk focused on religion and tradition, not a relationship with Jesus. I soon discovered that religion wasn't helpful for the hole in my broken heart. I needed something more. Something real. I needed Someone.

My journey to find a relationship with Jesus took some time, and it involved several key experiences. The first occurred when my good friend Steve introduced me to *Experiencing God* by Henry Blackaby. This book helped me understand that practicing religion was different than enjoying a relationship with the God of the universe. As I read the book, I hungered to learn more.

I thought I knew what I wanted out of life, but God was changing my perspective. Working in the financial services industry, I'd developed a worldly life view. I had planned to make a lot of money and retire at fifty-five to a life of leisure and relaxation.

But as I battled interpersonal storms, I realized nothing I *thought* I'd wanted from life aligned with God's Word or mattered from an eternal viewpoint. Frustrated, I searched Scripture hoping to find a place where Jesus said to his disciples, "Now here's what I want you to do: get good jobs making lots of money, stash a bunch of it in your 401k, and retire as early as you can to lives of fun and relaxation."

Bummer. Instead, I discovered we're to steward all we have for God's kingdom, take up our cross (live out our purpose), and follow him. God doesn't promise lives of comfort, fun, and happiness. Instead, he promises joy—if we follow him.

As I began to understand my calling and purpose, I felt a growing sense of joy and peace, but I also felt apprehension. I wasn't sure I wanted the fullness of the gospel in my life. I wasn't sure if I wanted to give up my worldly desires to pursue God's plan. I was smart enough to know I couldn't continue to believe the lies of the Enemy *and* live out my purpose.

I remember a moment when I was sitting in my office with my friend Jerry, and with tears in my eyes said, "I want my life to count for something meaningful. I want to be a good steward of everything God's given me and use it for his purposes—eternal purposes. I want what I do to last!" The Holy Spirit had started God's work in me, and I took another transforming step that day.

Then I took a huge leap forward in my spiritual transformation when I met and married Dawn. As a Spirit-filled child of God, she helped me understand and step into my true identity in Christ. Words cannot convey how grateful I am for her spiritual influence on my life. Thank you, Dawn.

Faithful God

Throughout the storms of my life and Dawn's, God has proven faithful over and over again. This book is the result of my wife's life-changing journey to freedom, as well as mine that soon followed. As she saturated her thinking with the Word of God, she found contentment, peace, and joy that were more than concepts or temporary feelings; they were inner sustenance that transformed her life. I also began a journey that changed my mindset and my soul's desires. After reading *The Freedom Challenge* for women, God transformed me, stripping away layers of old, false thinking like peeling paint on a derelict building.

Dawn and I are praying for you—that as you traverse the pathway on this freedom journey, you will discover God's abundance. We pray that he will untangle the cords of death that suffocate your soul so you can soar into new life.

Paul and Dawn

To order Dawn's book for women, go to:
Amazon.com/author/dawnscottdamon.

SECTION I

PREPARATION: FREEDOM IN CHRIST

I love the LORD, for he heard my voice;
he heard my cry for mercy.
Because he turned his ear to me,
I will call on him as long as I live.

The cords of death entangled me,
the anguish of the grave came over me;
I was overcome by distress and sorrow.
Then I called on the name of the LORD:
"LORD, save me!"

The LORD is gracious and righteous;
our God is full of compassion.
The LORD protects the unwary;
when I was brought low, he saved me.

Return to your rest, my soul,
for the LORD has been good to you.

For you, LORD, have delivered me from death,
my eyes from tears,
my feet from stumbling,
that I may walk before the LORD
in the land of the living. (Psalm 116:1–9 NIV)

CHAPTER I

FREEDOM BOUND

As I (Paul) was reading a book in preparation to teach a men's class, an open letter struck me, and my heart instantly flooded with compassion:

> A Catholic priest sexually and physically molested me decades ago. . . . I remember the incident vividly. My abuser, or what I like to call perpetrator, was a priest who I was groomed to trust. My parents also trusted him. I chose to forgive him and think he has been punished enough with the consequences of his behavior. However, he left me to deal with the aftermath. It is good to forgive but, unfortunately, I can't forget. I have tried.
>
> I lost my innocence that night. I did not know it was possible for a man, let alone a priest, to do that to a young boy. There is nothing more innocent than a child. He had led me down this path by gaining my trust. I've felt violated ever since. There is not enough money to take away the pain, shame, thoughts, and guilt that I have endured. Young victims are too ashamed to come forward and too young to understand the damage that was done until decades go by.
>
> I did not realize the extent of the damage until a few years ago. It is always there. It took me years of therapy

and visits to psychiatrists and therapists before I even told them I was abused. I did not put the depression and bad thoughts together with the abuse, so I never mentioned it to my doctors or therapists for decades. It was my little ugly secret.[1]

As I read this man's story on the internet, I couldn't help but read between the lines, imagining words he hadn't written and tears he had wept. Self-destructive thinking, emotions, and behaviors bound this man. I understood his bondage because my wife had lived under the same captivity. The "abundant life" the Bible speaks about was a fairy tale to this letter writer. He believed that a life of freedom and happiness was impossible for him.

Sadly, the author of this letter is not alone in his pain. Thousands—perhaps millions—of men feel helplessly bound by past or present circumstances and restricted by invisible but very real cords. The psalmist describes their despair this way: "The cords of death entangled me" (Psalm 116:3 NIV).

Perhaps you've felt this way, too, and wondered: *Can I ever be free? Really free?* If you're certain the answer is no, but you long to believe that freedom is possible, keep reading.

I have good news in the pages to come.

The Promise of Freedom

Christian men often feel caught in a paradox. We know that Jesus Christ purchased our freedom through his gift of salvation and that we're born again. Yet we live in a place of brokenness and defeat, bound by cords that strangle life and vitality from our souls.

Is this the life Jesus envisioned for us when he came, as he said in John 10:10, to give us life more abundantly? I don't think so. Freedom *is* possible. Because I've personally experienced this transformation, I can say, *yes, freedom really is possible.*

Release from past hurts can be a reality for you too. You and

I can receive deliverance because a Deliverer exists, a Freedom Fighter who so craves our liberty that he gave his life's blood to purchase it for us. His name is Jesus Christ.

I can tell you this is true, not because God's Word assures us of freedom (the greatest reason of all), but because I've experienced that freedom—life-giving, purpose-producing, and abundant.

I know what it means to be emotionally and spiritually bound. I've wondered if I would ever see the morning dawn after fighting raging tempests through the night. I've spent days filled with pain and despair. But through the power of the Holy Spirit, I found that although sorrow may last for a night, joy *does* come in the morning (Psalm 30:5).

God healed my heart. Bondage fought hard to entrap me and threw powerful blows, but I won and experienced God's glorious freedom.

Now I want to help *you* find true freedom. God's healing is real and tangible—more than changed emotions or new circumstances. God promises to sever the cords that bind you—to loose you from defeat and set you free (Deuteronomy 31:6, 8).

My wife Dawn's and my journeys both required obedience and trust, and yours will too. By the power of God, we slipped free from the fears and lies that had tethered us to our past.

But first we had to battle the pirates.

Freedom Lost

Only those who glimpse the true inescapability of their imprisonment and who fight to escape can fully cherish freedom.

Take Edmond, for example. Nineteen-year-old Edmond Dantès, the main character in Alexandre Dumas's famous story *The Count of Monte Cristo*, was falsely accused and imprisoned. According to the novel, after twenty-one grueling years of captivity—seven years in solitary confinement and fourteen years learning from the abbot—Edmond escapes the *Chateau d'If,* a prison located on a virtually deserted island. After slipping into a body bag meant for a deceased inmate, Edmond is hurled over the island's edge by unsuspecting prison guards and crashes into the pounding ocean waters below, cocooned in a death bag. He battles his way out of the bag, then washes up on shore.

Tattered and exhausted, Edmond Dantès is finally free!

Splashing.

Laughing.

Jumping.

Rejoicing.

Up and down the water's edge, Edmond celebrates freedom like a madman.

This is a picture of freedom—joy and laughter, living lost in the "reckless love of God."

Unfortunately, Edmond's story doesn't end there. His new-found freedom is challenged. A pirate ship carrying a hungry band of thieves lurks in his future. And they want him.

Like Edmond, I (Dawn) experienced God's invigorating freedom. I testified to my healing and happiness, but as seasons of life shifted, I ran into "the pirates." A struggle ensued, and defeated once again, I was hurled into the midst of a dark storm. The hungry band of thieves tore at my heart. Intense pain and anger overtook my spirit and shackled my soul. The devastation was so immense, I believed I would never recover. I was lost in the gray space of life, my freedom gone.

What happened to my intimate relationship with God? How could this trial have decimated me? Did God leave me? Why had I slid back into despair—living gutted, devastated, and disconnected? Cocooned in a bag of death, I was tired of fighting.

I knew I had to find answers to those questions if I hoped not only to regain the freedom I'd once known but also discover how to keep it—permanently. Until I did, I would remain vulnerable to changing circumstances and unwanted emotions.

Like Dawn, when the relentless trials of life pounded me, I had to learn how to stand firm, deeply rooted in God's truth.

As God's Word says, "It is for freedom that Christ has set us free. Stand firm, then, and do not let yourselves be burdened again by a yoke of slavery" (Galatians 5:1 NIV).

Perhaps those words describe you too. You knew freedom at one time, you enjoyed God's rich salvation, and you found longed-for release from sin when you first surrendered your life to him.

That was then, at the beginning of your journey with God. Now you find yourself struggling with self-destructive behaviors that hold you in bondage. You're tangled in cords that are choking God's peace and joy from your life.

You may wonder, *How did I wind up here? How did I lose the joy of my salvation, my soul's first love?*

You may know exactly what nudged you toward the pit of despair. Perhaps tragedy, abuse, or injustice left you ravaged, angry, defeated, and asking, "How do I get up and keep running my race?"

Has God withdrawn his blessing from you? Has he deemed you disqualified from living the abundant life Jesus came to give you?

Not at all.

Whatever brought you to this place of despair (for Dawn and me it was painful divorces), you must be willing to admit that the life you're living is anything but free. Your experiences have been costly, and you're not sure how or where you will find the strength to endure.

It's time for a breakthrough. Your parched soul is thirsting for the freedom Jesus died to give you.

Envision yourself in this beautiful picture Jesus paints of a Christian living fully and freely:

If the Son gives you freedom, you are free! (John 8:36 CEV)

I have come in order that you might have life—life in all its fullness. (John 10:10 GNT)

And you will know the truth, and the truth will set you free. (John 8:32)

Crowds followed Jesus because they were curious about what he could do that would benefit them. They didn't recognize the true gift of life in him that he offered when he said, "And you shall know the truth, and the truth shall make you free" (John 8:32 NKJV).

They retorted, "How can you say we will be free? We've never been slaves to anyone." They were angry, unaware of their spiritual and emotional bondage. Unfortunately, their stubborn refusal to acknowledge their slavery to self and sin kept them bound by the cords of death, forever trapped by their self-delusion: "Ha! *I'm* not a slave!"

In finding her way back to wholeness, Dawn awakened to her desperate need for freedom and to her responsibility to take hold of God's amazing liberty. She had allowed herself to become "entangled again in a yoke of slavery" (Galatians 5:1 BLB) by neglecting her responsibility to know and apply God's truth. She reread Jesus's words to make sure she rightly understood: "And you shall know the truth, and the truth shall set you free" (John 8:32 NKJV).

We have a responsibility to know the truth.

Jesus was not scolding the people for their bondage but was giving them the key that would unlock their chains and set them free. This equation will revolutionize your life—*know* the truth, and then *use it* to unlock your shackles and live in freedom. Your source of freedom is knowing and believing God's truth—about who he is, what Jesus accomplished on the cross, and your identity in him. And if freedom comes from knowing the truth, then the opposite must be true: bondage comes from believing lies. Since all humanity has believed Satan's evil distortions, it stands to reason, then, that everyone needs this freedom.

God's Word Is Truth

The reality is that we must obtain spiritual and emotional freedom. When Dawn and I became followers of Christ, we weren't delivered in an instant from the lies that deceived us: lies from Satan, this broken world, and our thoughts. Our spirits became alive at salvation, but our souls—our minds, wills, and emotions—were still in desperate need of God's cleansing and healing touch.

This is true for you too. While freedom is available through Jesus's sacrifice and his indisputable victory over the Enemy, our inner healing and emotional freedom do not come in an instant or automatically. Everything Jesus accomplished for us through his death on the cross becomes our right, privilege, and benefit, but we must claim our spiritual inheritance and apply it to our lives. Freedom comes when we know the truth and *choose* to live, walk, and remain in the truth.

When we immerse our minds and hearts in the illuminating truth of God, the light shines into those dark places and exposes Satan's twisted lies. We see how lies control our thoughts and behaviors, and after we expose them, we expunge them from our belief system. They cannot hold us prisoner. The secret to obtaining and retaining freedom is to remain in God's truth.

Yes, life happens. Pirate ships await us. Trials and temptations come, and we're often catapulted into hellish tornados that make us feel like we're spinning out of control. The turbulence sweeps away our thoughts, feelings, and emotions. We look at our circumstances, focus on our pain, and have to admit, "I'm anything but free."

No wonder the Enemy wants us to focus on the negative. Troubles. Wounds and pains of life. Because we must interpret life's events, if Satan can blind us to God's truth, we will be captured again by defeat. Instead, when we gaze into the perfect Word of God, we can declare, "I know the truth and the truth makes me free" (John 8:32 NKJV).

You, too, have freedom despite these trials, because it's not *what* you go through but what you *believe* about what you're going through that counts. Bondage does not come because of life's trials but as a result of how you interpret those trials. If you suffer at the hands of those hungry thieves—Satan's attempts to buffet you—and say, "Oh, I'm such a failure! God doesn't love me, and he never comes through," then you have succumbed to the purpose of the attack. Satan's goal is to bind you with lies. But if you say, "God, this is painful, but I know you love me, and you work all things together for my good," then you have stood in the truth, and the truth has kept you free.

Have you surrendered to defeat? Have you given up, believing that you can never be free from disabling thoughts, destructive choices, and discouraging life habits, addictions, and patterns?

Well, take a deep breath and open your mind to the truth. Freedom is yours for the taking!

Out of the Shadows

Often when Dawn and I minister, we share our testimonies. Dawn talks about her childhood sexual abuse, knowing many women share similar experiences. I share my struggle with performance-based acceptance and accepting my true identity. Afterward, people approach us with their stories of grief and loss, trauma, or betrayal. These men and women often wait in the shadows to speak to us, afraid of being identified or overheard because their pain is deep, personal, and agonizing. They can't bear the thought of being exposed as someone who struggles with sexual sin, addiction, depression, suicidal thoughts, or compulsive behaviors.

But these precious people need to realize—as do we all—that we cannot find freedom until we step out of the shadows and into the light. Admitting that we're locked in a battle between truth and lies is our first step toward freedom.

Our battles may look different on the surface, but at the core, they are all the same: lies bind us.

One man's wife, who is an abuse survivor, confesses she attempts to cope by drinking too much. Another man is caught up in sexual addiction, and he admits through tears that he struggles with guilt and authentic intimacy. A young father who was molested as a child walls himself off from his emotions, and his wife and heads to the bar every night. A pastor haunted by childhood shame seeks comfort in food and porn. Men who appear to be strong, polished role models often confess, "I'm bound by guilt and shame that obliterate my self-esteem." God's leading men, influential pastors, teachers, leaders, and role models often feel silently trapped in spiritual and emotional defeat and are invisibly struggling.

This is where Satan loves to keep us—hiding in the shadows in shame—because he knows our real power, beauty, and value as God's children.

Untie the Cords

It's time to focus on *you*. Do you wonder if you'll ever laugh again or face another day without depression, bitterness, or resentment? Are you so wounded that it feels like you've lost your way? Do you cower in shame and lash yourself with negative self-talk? Do you contemplate who you are and what you're supposed to be doing in life?

Then this challenge is for you.

Over the next sixty days, Dawn and I will ask you to take important steps on your freedom journey. In the following weeks, you'll uncover lies regarding your value and worth, your identity, your emotions, and your mindset by learning to apply the power of God's Word to your life. Instead of embracing toxic messages and destructive beliefs, you'll be invited to choose to believe God and take him at his word.

Sometimes you won't feel like the Scriptures are true for you, but don't quit. If you sense resistance to God's Word, you may have discovered a binding lie or vow (an unconscious promise made to yourself in childhood) that Satan has successfully used in the past to deceive you. The resistance you feel can be Satan's tug to keep you bound to this lie and the defeat it brings. Allow God to use his Word and the power of the Holy Spirit to set you free.

Our prayer is that you will experience transformation. As Dawn and I share our story of finding true and lasting freedom, which this book relates throughout, we pray it will help you find the courage to take your first step out of the shadows. You are not alone. Thousands of men like you are silently suffering and afraid to ask for help.

I (Paul) know. I was one of them.

But today God is calling you—yes, *you*—to take your first step toward freedom. It's our honor and joy to encourage you along the way.

Explore

1. What lies concerning your identity have bound you? Can you think of experiences in your childhood/past where these lies may be rooted?
2. How has Satan used these lies to defeat you?
3. What lies do you feel are crucial for you to renounce? Why?
4. *Claim* is an active verb that involves possessing something as your own. What steps can you take to claim your true identity in Jesus?

CHAPTER 2

THE COUNTDOWN BEGINS

And do not follow the customs of the present age,
but be transformed by the entire renewal of your minds,
so that you may learn by experience what God's will is—
that will which is good and beautiful and perfect.
Romans 12:2 WNT

The Freedom Challenge

Welcome to the Challenge. You're about to be transformed in remarkable ways!

For the next sixty days, you'll experience a complete overhaul that will change the way you think, feel, and behave. This metamorphosis may be so radical that you will find everything in your life positively impacted. You'll gain a fresh perspective and, ultimately, a more empowered life.

A New Mindset

You may be asking, "Really? This deal sounds too good to be true." But remember, this amazing promise for total renewal didn't start with Dawn or me. God promised it, and he backs it up:

> Let God transform you inwardly by a complete change
> of your mind. (Romans 12:2 GNT)

> Anyone who belongs to Christ is a new person. The past is
> forgotten, and everything is new. (2 Corinthians 5:17 CEV)

In the Freedom Challenge, you'll examine your thoughts and take steps to renew and rewire your mind—not only *what* you think, but the *way* you think. With daily immersion in the Word of God, your brain will undergo a powerful renovation. The Bible talks about this renovation as the renewal of your mind (Romans 12:2), a process also known as *cognitive reconstruction*.

This process empowers us to do the following:

- Identify unhealthy patterns of thinking (negative, maladaptive, distorted, untrue, sinful, automatic thoughts)
- Interrupt those patterns
- Replace unhealthy thinking with healthy, positive thinking
- Reconstruct brain pathways and create new growth

The Science of Renewal

We shouldn't be surprised to find out that science proves true what God's Word teaches us. Still, it's exhilarating to understand that to "be transformed by the entire renewal of your minds" (Romans 12:2 WNT) is not only a biblical mandate but a scientific truth. Your brain can undergo a physical and biological transformation.

Yes. You can change! As Dr. Caroline Leaf explains:

> Our choices—the natural consequences of our thoughts and imagination—get "under the skin" of our DNA and can turn certain genes on and off, changing the structure of the neurons in our brains. So our thoughts, imagination, and choices can change the structure and function of our brains on every level.[2]

For years, conventional science thought the brain stopped developing after the first few years of life. But new research shows what God has always taught: the brain can form new neural pathways and create new neurons even in adulthood. This ability, called neuroplasticity, is the muscle-building part of the brain that allows it to rewire through the development of new pathways and the growth of new dendrites—the part of the brain that functions in both memory and problem-solving. In other words, our thoughts change our brain's chemistry. Therefore, we can choose a healthy brain, and a healthy brain creates a healthy body, soul, and spirit.

No wonder the Lord instructs his people to meditate day and night on his life-giving promises and plans. He wants us to be healthy and prosperous—spiritually, physically, and emotionally.

> Memorize these laws and think about them. Write down copies and tie them to your wrists and your foreheads to help you obey them. Teach them to your children. Talk about them all the time—whether you're at home or walking along the road or going to bed at night, or getting up in the morning. Write them on the door frames of your homes and on your town gates. (Deuteronomy 11:18–20 CEV)

With every repetitive meditation or emotion, we reinforce a neural pathway, and with each new thought, we begin to create a new way of being. We literally become what we think and do. As Acts 17:28 (NIV) tells us, "For in him we live and move and have our being."

Since the brain is pivotal to all we think and do, harnessing neuroplasticity—renewing the mind—can improve everything about our lives.

Sources of Negative Thinking

I hope you're convinced that we all need to renew our minds. As we learned in chapter 1, we all believe powerful and seductive lies. These distortions come to us in a variety of ways:

- Through the modeling of parents, teachers, and authorities
- Through life experiences, traumas, and interpretations of those experiences
- Through the influence of our temperaments and dispositions
- Through demonic influences and assaults against our minds

All of these variables shape our habits of thinking and our view of the world.

As you progress through the 60-day challenge, you'll begin to notice the emergence of fresh hope as your old mindset crumbles and a new mind, built and rewired by God's Word, is built. Your transformed mind will begin to discern and dismantle lethal beliefs and thought patterns that have kept you imprisoned. Freedom was once only a concept, but now you easily surrender to better, more positive thoughts. As your cognitive processes are recalibrated and you gain a new perspective, your life will flourish like a healthy tree, as thought by thought and decision by decision, freedom breaks open wide.

> Solidify the lifelong habit of thinking about the truth of God
> as a means of enjoying the God of truth.
> —John Piper

Here's How It Works

The Freedom Challenge is designed to disrupt automatic negative and destructive patterns of thought, talk, actions, and reactions that have been programmed into your mind and have unconsciously become part of your worldview. As you renew your mind with God's Word and daily focus on select meditations that bring truth and light, your metamorphosis will begin.

The Challenge consists of a 60-day immersion in Scripture, divided into weekly chapters. Each week we explore a deadly "cord" of bondage that needs untying. As we laser focus on that cord, we destroy associated lies and, thread by thread, burn away their hold through the Word of God, our agreement, and confession.

> The cords of death entangled me, the anguish of the grave came over me;
>
> I was overcome by distress and sorrow. Then I called on the name of the LORD: "LORD, save me!" (Psalm 116:3–4 NIV)

The Daily Challenge

The Daily Challenge consists of seven cord-breaking components. Each day we will explore and apply these elements, saturating our hearts and minds:

- *Today's Truth*: Here you will meditate on God's Word. Today's Truth provides a weekly focus taken from the Bible in the form of an absolute and eternal truth that applies to everyone.
- *Declare*: Speak aloud and agree that Today's Truth is true for you and that you're prepared to accept it and live by it, regardless of how you feel.
- *Meditate, Believe, Accept*: Meditating on God's truth confronts and breaks the power of the lies that have bound you. It also changes your brain and renews your thoughts— how you think and what you believe about that untruth.

This is the transformational part of the Challenge. Real-life change begins here! How exciting!

- *Confess*: Confessing to God means that you surrender your former beliefs and actions and choose to walk a new path—the Way of Truth. You renounce and release your former false belief systems because you choose to agree with God.
- *Affirm*: This is your commitment to believe God's truth from this day forward. You affirm, "I accept by faith that this truth is *my* truth and *my* reality."
- *Explore*: Here you will contemplate thought-provoking questions to help you make discoveries.
- *Extra Memory Challenge*: You can also choose to memorize a weekly Bible verse.

Power Up

Before you begin, it's essential to be powered-up with foundational biblical truths. Make sure you read them aloud and absorb them into your mind and heart at the onset of this challenge.

God's Eternal Truth

- God loves me. I am his son.
- Freedom is mine because Jesus paid for my release.
- It is God's will for me to be free.
- I have a choice and can set my mind to be transformed.
- The Word of God is alive. It renews my mind and always works. I am victorious.

Now take a moment to read the guiding principles. Treat them as guardrails for your decisions.

Guiding Principles

- I will remember that Satan is defeated and cannot hold me captive.
- I will align my words with God's Word.
- I choose to accept God's truth no matter how I feel.
- Small steps mean everything.

You're about to start a journey—a healing, transforming, and courageous journey. Recognize that along the way you're going to arrive at unknown destinations. You're going to have "aha" moments and "oh no!" ones too. You're going to encounter yourself in ways you've dared not look at before. You'll probably want to dismiss some of the things you learn about yourself, finding them difficult to believe. "No way can I be this selfish, this prideful, or even this bitter," you may say. You're going to make many new discoveries too.

Painful discoveries.

Unbelievable discoveries.

Brilliant discoveries.

Are you ready? Take one last look in the mirror. Tomorrow you will already be on the road toward being a new man.

Let's roll.

Explore

1. Every day this week, write about how one of the above Eternal Truths has influenced your life.
2. How can you make choices to "set" your mind?
3. How can small steps make a difference in setting you free?
4. Where has Satan held you captive in the past?

SECTION II

THE CHALLENGE: UNTYING THE CORDS THAT BIND US

CHAPTER 3

CORDS OF FALSE IDENTITIES

When I discover who I am, I'll be free.
—Ralph Ellison, *The Invisible Man*

Challenge Week 1

Weekly Reading: False Identities

> *For we know that our old self was crucified with him so*
> *that the body ruled by sin might be done away with, that*
> *we should no longer be slaves to sin.*
> Romans 6:6 NIV

If someone asked you who you are, how would you answer? Does the question make you feel uncomfortable because you think of yourself as an average Joe, or worse, a nobody? Are you confident about who you are, or do you feel shame because it's difficult to think positively about your identity? What criteria do use when you identify yourself?

Your occupation?

Marital status?

Family role?

Achievements and financial status?

Hobbies?

How do you speak to yourself, and what names do you call yourself in the privacy of your thoughts? Are you your own best coach, cheering yourself on, or are you a self-critic? What names rush to your mind when you make a mistake or fear failure?

Idiot?

Not good enough?

Failure?

Incompetent?

Stupid?

Have others told you that you're worthless, inept, inadequate, less than a man, ignorant, soft, or undeserving of happiness and success? These negative identities don't reflect the way God views you. The world shouted lies like these into your spirit. The hurt hollowed out your heart. Satan's goal is to sear deception into your soul and mind with flames of accusation, guilt, and suffering.

Satan knows that what we think about ourselves becomes the driving force behind how we treat ourselves. This simple truth is one of his most powerful weapons against us.

Dawn often used negative labels to describe herself. Her identity was tied up in what happened to her and how she felt it disqualified her in life. She describes it this way:

> As a child, I encountered repeated sexual abuse from my father. The assault was an attack on more than my body; he also molested my mind and my heart. Emotional scars remained that took years to heal. In fact, I'm still on the healing path. Compounding my pain was the fact that someone close to me—someone who said he loved me—referred to me as *damaged goods* and my wounds as *dysfunctional baggage.* As a result, I continually questioned my worth and value.
>
> *Who am I?* I wondered.
>
> *Am I worth loving?*
>
> *Do I matter at all?*
>
> I grappled with my identity because I, like most

post-traumatic women, weighed my worth on the scale of my degrading abuse, believing I needed to compensate for my lack of value. I sought value from what I could accomplish, who I could impress, and the opinions of other people—broken, hurting, sinful humans like me—instead of trusting what God said about me.

My story (Paul) is different, but the results were much the same. As a child, I never heard the words "I love you" from my father. His idea of love was limited to only those emotions he had for my mother. While I knew my dad loved and cared for me, I felt I had to measure up—to be the best at everything I did to earn love and acceptance.

But your identity is not what *happened* to you. It's not the roles you fulfill, the things you do, or what others think of you. Your identity is *who God says you are*, which is irrevocable truth anchored in God himself and your relationship to him. Claiming this simple truth can transform your life the way it did mine.

The truest thing about you and me is that we are who God says we are.

The measurement of our worth is not how we feel, what we do or don't do, how much we own, what we accomplish, or anyone's opinion about us. A straightforward fact quantifies our identity and value: God has redeemed us, and therefore, we are everything he says we are. Because God's Word reveals this, we can confidently declare the truth about ourselves by saying, "I am God's child. I am accepted. I am capable. I am holy. I am forgiven. I am valuable. I am victorious!"

These God-identities boldly confront and overrule the distorted and untrue identities we—or others—have assigned us.

Consider what God's Word teaches about our identity. When we come to Christ and place our lives in his hands, we receive a new identity. Jesus's death affords us a brand-new position in life and death. Not only are our sins completely forgiven because of the blood of Jesus, but we are the recipients of an incredible exchange expressly crafted for us. He takes our old shameful and sinful nature and gives us a new one.

He exchanges:

- Our old nature for his new identity and nature
- Our imperfections for his complete acceptance
- Our brokenness for his wholeness
- Our sickness for his healing
- Our confusion for his peace

Second Corinthians 5:17 (NKJV) tells us, "Therefore, if anyone is in Christ, he is a new creation; old things have passed away; behold, all things have become new." The footnotes of 2 Corinthians 5:17 in the Passion Translation say this:

> This would include our old identity, our life of sin, the power of Satan, the religious works of trying to please God, our old relationship with the world, and our old mindsets. We are not reformed or refurbished, we are made completely new by our union with Christ and the indwelling of the Holy Spirit.[3]

Wow! How mind-blowing! We are not reformed or refurbished, but we become brand new. These are God's words to us. How is it, then, that so many of us never take hold of what God gives us and claim our true identity in Christ?

Deception.

We hold on to false thinking because our minds have not been renewed. As a result, we remain trapped in cords of bondage, trying to live a brave and free life while we feed on guilt and condemnation.

Sadly, many of our struggles connect directly to our false identity: imperfect, broken, distorted, and damaged self-worth. We fail to understand, believe, or accept the finished work of Jesus Christ on the cross. Because we don't grasp our identity in Christ and live in the truth and freedom he gives, we try to feel good about ourselves, but satisfaction eludes us. We wrestle with inadequacy, insecurity, and fear. We feel unloved and defeated.

But back to the important role of our feelings. Yes, men, I'm talking about feelings because they play an important role in how we think and act. Sometimes we don't *feel* new or *feel* forgiven or redeemed. Our lives still *feel* tumultuous.

Even though we are a new creation, and our sin nature no longer has dominion over us—it has been crucified (see Galatians 2:20)—we can still sin. But we *choose* not to and live empowered through the Holy Spirit. We've been given authority to overcome through Christ. Our new nature inclines us in a new direction. Instead of being bent toward sin, we are bent toward God as we listen to his voice, love him, and live for him in freedom.

The root of your value is not *feelings* but a matter of *fact*. May you grasp the truth of who you are in Christ not because you *feel* valued or are working to be valued but because you *are* valued. This powerful truth is eternal and unwavering, and it remains true whether or not you believe or accept it. Your feelings don't change the fact that God's Word is eternal and all-surpassing truth and is true for you.

This week you'll look at God's path to true identity. But first, make this affirmation:

> *I choose to believe God's Word concerning my identity.* I will tell my heart and my mind to accept the Word to be true for me, and as a result, I will be transformed. I will not reject the insights God gives me as I read his Word, nor will I ignore them. They are for me, and through

Jesus, I am worthy to receive God's promises. Therefore, I *will* be transformed by his Word. In Jesus's name, I renounce lies that have deceived me about who I am, and I untie the cord of false identity.

Did you pray? Are you ready for change? Your transformation starts right now.

Week 1

Day 1

TODAY'S TRUTH: I AM GOD'S CHILD

See what great love the Father has lavished on us,
that we should be called children of God!
And that is what we are!
1 John 3:1 NIV

T hroughout the Bible, we see God's passion for us to claim our identity as his children. From Genesis to Revelation, he pursues us and makes provision for our sin, forgives us, and offers us second chances when we fail him. Once we receive Jesus Christ as Lord of our lives, God gives us the same rights, privileges, and spiritual inheritance as Jesus.

As God's children, we share an intimate relationship with our Father. We can go to him any time, ask for his wisdom, be assured of his constant love and protection, and talk to him about our pain, fears, and failures. He never turns us away. We're unconditionally loved in ways beyond our comprehension. Trying to understand God's limitless love is like trying to shovel all the sand from the world's seashores into a coffee cup—we cannot grasp how vast is his love for us.

God adopts us into his family as chosen sons. Think a moment about adoption through the eyes of parents you may know who waited long months—perhaps years—for their adopted child to join their family. Perhaps they even ventured to a foreign country to bring their son or daughter home. This is a picture of what God did for us, compelled by his great love. Through Jesus, he gave up the glories of heaven and came to a sin-filled earth to save us and make us his own.

God also gives his children an inheritance because we belong to him—we're part of his family. Our inheritance is worth far more than Bill Gates's wealth. Its value is so great that it cannot be measured, but too often, we devalue these gifts.

So what is our inheritance?

- God's wisdom
- God's trusted guidance
- God's forgiveness
- God's mercy
- Admonition (God's GPS assistance when we're headed toward things that will hurt us)
- Correction (God's instruction in how to correct our steps)
- The Holy Spirit (comfort, presence, and the power to grow more like Jesus)
- Eternal life
- Peace and joy

Those who have received this inheritance also experience an intimate relationship with God. He will never disappoint us or let us down. He is our Provider, our Hope, our Peace, our Comforter, and our Best Friend. He is everything we look for in earthly relationships and that friends, brothers, girlfriends, or wives cannot provide. God alone satisfies our deepest longings.

Declare

I am God's son. He loves me and has chosen me. I am not alone. I will accept, believe, and live as God's beloved son—chosen by him, lavished with his love, and valued as his very own child. I am God's child. I declare this in Jesus's name.

Meditate, Believe, Accept

I am God's son.

> The Spirit himself testifies with our spirit that we are God's children. (Romans 8:16 NIV)

> So you are no longer a slave, but God's son; and since you are his son, God has made you also an heir. (Galatians 4:7 NIV)

I am a coheir with Jesus.

> Now if we are children, then we are heirs—heirs of God and coheirs with Christ, if indeed we share in his sufferings in order that we may also share in his glory. (Romans 8:17 NIV)

I am chosen.

> In him we were also chosen, having been predestined according to the plan of him who works out everything in conformity with the purpose of his will. (Ephesians 1:11 NIV)

I am adopted.

> He predestined us for adoption through Jesus Christ, in accordance with his pleasure and will. (Ephesians 1:5 NIV)

> To all who did receive him, to those who believed in his name, he gave the right to become children of God. (John 1:12 NIV)

I am God's friend.

> I no longer call you servants, because a servant does not know his master's business. Instead, I have called you

> friends, for everything that I learned from my Father I
> have made known to you. You did not choose me, but
> I chose you and appointed you to go and bear fruit—
> fruit that will last. (John 15:15–16 NIV)

Confess

Lord, I confess I don't always live like I'm your chosen son. Today I choose to untie the cord of false identity and renounce my old ways of thinking. I accept your Word and tell myself to focus, meditate, and believe your truth. My heart and mind will become transformed as your Holy Spirit fills and renews me.

Affirm

I am God's child, and he loves me. God has lavishly poured out his love upon me without measure. I am not orphaned, nor am I alone in this life. I am safe as his child. I untie the cord of false identity.

Repeat "I am God's child" four times. Each time you read it, add special emphasis to the bolded word below:

I am God's child—yes, me. I have been chosen.

I **am** God's child—not could be, or someday might be; I am his child right now.

I am **God's** child—God's own. He has claimed me. He has redeemed me.

I am God's **child**. I belong to God. He is a good Father. He will provide for, protect, and care for me as his son.

Extra Memory Challenge

> See what great love the Father has lavished on us, that
> we should be called children of God! And that is what
> we are! (1 John 3:1 NIV)

Explore

1. How is God speaking to you about being his child? Listen to him now.
2. How does it feel to be called God's child?
3. How does knowing you are God's child change the way you view God? Yourself? Others?
4. Is it a comfort to know that God is your heavenly Father? Why or why not? In what ways is he a comfort?
5. What other things did you see in today's lesson?

Journal

Week 1

Day 2

Today's Truth: I Am Accepted

Accept one another, then, just as Christ accepted you,
in order to bring praise to God.
Romans 15:7 NIV

If you're like many of us, you've spent time and energy trying to earn acceptance from people: your parents, siblings, coaches, classmates, teachers, coworkers, friends, spouse, family members—and the list goes on. But no matter how hard we try through athletic abilities, educational degrees and awards, accomplishments and financial wins, we always fall short. Someone somewhere doesn't like something about us. Our efforts to earn acceptance can exhaust us.

People will always find reasons not to accept us because we all have prideful, judgmental hearts. Yes, that includes you and me.

But here's the good news: God loves us unconditionally. He knows our selfish hearts far better than we know them ourselves. He created us and watched as we rebelled against him and sinned over and over again, but he still loved us enough to redeem us. We are his twice: once by creation and a second time through redemption.

God accepted us—not once, but twice—and he will never give up on us or abandon us because we fall short or disappoint him. His love never fails and never runs out. He accepts us.

Past.

Present.

Future.

For eternity.

This is true security and freedom beyond our comprehension:

God's love for us will never run out. No matter how we fail him, he still loves us.

"But you don't know what I've done," you say. No, I don't, but I know what God's done, and his work is complete. Even though we've all sinned and missed the mark of God's standard, he devised the perfect plan to reconcile us to himself through Jesus. You are God's son. He wiped out your sin. You now possess Jesus's perfection, and forevermore God sees you only through the sinless perfection of his Son.

Because God formed every cell in your body in your mother's womb, you can trust that every detail about you is perfect.

Perfect? Really? you ask.

Yep! Because the God who formed you can do nothing apart from love, and his purposes are always loving. God's every move and act flow from love. He created every cell in your body from the outflow of his loving heart. He also loves you too much to allow any area in your life to remain less than he created it to be. He works in you to transform and shape you so you can experience the fullness of his presence and purpose in your life.

We are free from the weight of striving for acceptance. God, who created us and breathed every detail into the universe, calls you his own. You are a member of his family, with all the rights and privileges of Jesus himself. Claim your true identity.

Declare

I do not have to perform, plead, or strive for God to accept me or to earn his approval. He has made me loved, accepted, chosen, and worthy. I am valuable beyond comprehension. I am not rejected, disqualified, or cast out, but I am accepted and made worthy and worthwhile. Therefore, I can accept others and myself. I will live loved. I will live chosen. I will live accepted. I am accepted. I declare this in Jesus's name.

Meditate, Believe, Accept

God loves me. Nothing can separate me from his love.

> And I pray that you, being rooted and established in love, may have power, together with all the Lord's holy people, to grasp how wide and long and high and deep is the love of Christ, and to know this love that surpasses knowledge—that you may be filled to the measure of all the fullness of God. (Ephesians 3:17–19 NIV)

> Who shall separate us from the love of Christ? Shall trouble or hardship or persecution or famine or nakedness or danger or sword? As it is written: "For your sake we face death all day long; we are considered as sheep to be slaughtered." No, in all these things we are more than conquerors through him who loved us. For I am convinced that neither death nor life, neither angels nor demons, neither the present nor the future, nor any powers, neither height nor depth, nor anything else in all creation, will be able to separate us from the love of God that is in Christ Jesus our Lord. (Romans 8:35–39 NIV)

> As the Father has loved me, so have I loved you. Now remain in my love. (John 15:9 NIV)

> See what great love the Father has lavished on us, that we should be called children of God! And that is what we are! (1 John 3:1 NIV)

I am accepted by God. I am not unacceptable or rejected.

> Blessed be the God and Father of our Lord Jesus Christ, who has blessed us with every spiritual blessing in the heavenly places in Christ, just as He chose us in Him before the foundation of the world, that we should be holy and without blame before Him in love, having predestined us to adoption as sons by Jesus Christ to

Himself, according to the good pleasure of His will, to the praise of the glory of His grace, by which He made us accepted in the Beloved. (Ephesians 1:3–6 NKJV)

God supports me. I'm not alone, forsaken, or abandoned.

Never will I leave you; never will I forsake you. (Hebrews 13:5 NIV; see also Deuteronomy 31:6; Joshua 1:5; 1 Chronicles 28:20)

But now in Christ Jesus you who once were far away have been brought near by the blood of Christ. (Ephesians 2:13 NIV)

God chooses me. I am not unwanted.

Therefore, as God's chosen people, holy and dearly loved, clothe yourselves with compassion, kindness, humility, gentleness and patience. (Colossians 3:12 NIV)

For he chose us in him before the creation of the world to be holy and blameless in his sight. (Ephesians 1:4 NIV)

You did not choose me, but I chose you and appointed you so that you might go and bear fruit—fruit that will last—and so that whatever you ask in my name the Father will give you. (John 15:16 NIV)

God makes me worthy. I am not unworthy of his love or blessings.

But some of you were once like that but you were cleansed; you were made holy; you were made right with God by calling on the name of the Lord Jesus Christ and by the Spirit of our God. (1 Corinthians 6:11)

Our sins are washed away and we are made clean because Christ gave His own body as a gift to God. He did this once for all time. (Hebrews 10:10 NLV)

He gave himself for us so he might pay the price to free us from all evil and to make us pure people who belong only to him—people who are always wanting to do good deeds. (Titus 2:14 NCV)

Confess

Lord, sometimes I reject myself. I see things about myself I don't like, and I criticize and speak negatively about myself. I don't always honor and love myself the way I should. As a result, I have a difficult time accepting your love, and I often reject you. I also reject others and find fault in them to bolster my own self-worth. Today I renounce self-rejection, and I choose your acceptance and love.

Affirm

God loves me and accepts me the way he made me. Because God loves me so much, he will not neglect me, but he will continue to shape me and mold me into the image he has designed for me from the beginning. I untie the cord of false identity.

Repeat "I am accepted" three times. Each time you read it, add special emphasis to the bolded word.

I am accepted.

I **am** accepted.

I am **accepted**.

Extra Memory Challenge

Accept one another, then, just as Christ accepted you, in order to bring praise to God. (Romans 15:7 NIV)

Explore

1. How is God speaking to you about being accepted? Listen to him now.

2. How does knowing that God completely accepts you change the way you view yourself? Others?

3. How does knowing that God has accepted and chosen you change the way you approach him?

4. Have you experienced abandonment and rejection? How does it feel to know God will never forsake or abandon you?

5. What other truths did you see in today's lesson?

Journal

Week 1

Day 3

TODAY'S TRUTH: I AM CAPABLE

We have everything we need to live a life
that pleases God.
It was all given to us by God's own power,
when we learned that he had invited us
to share in his wonderful goodness.
2 Peter 1:3 CEV

This verse is power-packed! Think about it—he has given us everything we need to live this life with godliness. We are a fully loaded, one-of-a-kind creation, equipped with all we need to succeed. The New International Version of 2 Peter 1:3 says, "His divine power has given us everything we need for a godly life *through our knowledge of him*" (emphasis added). That means we don't have an ability problem, although sometimes we do have a knowledge problem. We are unaware of how richly God has endowed us and empowered us to flourish in this life.

Imagine how that truth can impact you. You are highly capable! Do you believe that? Do you feel capable to accomplish great things through God's power? Do you see every day as an opportunity to partner with him in accomplishing his eternal purposes here on earth? God created you to carry out specific tasks for his kingdom, and he equipped you with all you would ever need to succeed in that mission.

You are capable because the Lord gifts you with wisdom, talents, spiritual gifts, and abilities to use for his fame. He gives power and strength through the indwelling of his Holy Spirit. We often forget that the power available to us through the Holy Spirit is the same power Jesus received.

Since God equips you, how does that encourage you to dream? Hopefully you are ready to dream big, to accomplish great things, and to reach your destiny in him. Refuse to accept the negative thoughts that whisper inadequacies to you. God has you covered.

You are capable not because of yourself, but because God gives you what you need to accomplish everything he has called you to. Your inventory of skills and abilities does not limit you. God's abundance is yours.

So throw off the limitations that hold you back and jump into your purpose in God. It's there, neck-deep in faith, that you'll find your true capabilities. Your unique personality, talents, passions, and strengths become tools to fulfill your God-given destiny through the power of the Holy Spirit. You can do all things through Christ, who is your strength (see Philippians 4:13).

God provides every good thing we will ever need to live godly lives. This power comes through our growing knowledge of him as we come to know him more intimately and rely on the power of the Holy Spirit at work in us.

Declare

He has given me everything I need to live this life with purpose and passion. I do not lack gifts, abilities, or talents. Because the Holy Spirit dwells within me, I have wisdom, strength, and a sound mind. I am not inferior, substandard, or second rate. My heavenly Father supplies all my needs. I am capable. I declare this in Jesus's name.

Meditate, Believe, Accept

I am God's design, and he approves of me.

> For we are God's masterpiece. He has created us anew in Christ Jesus, so we can do the good things he planned for us long ago. (Ephesians 2:10)

I have all sufficiency. God supplies all my needs.

> God is able to make it up to you by giving you every-
> thing you need and more so that there will not only be
> enough for your own needs but plenty left over to give
> joyfully to others. (2 Corinthians 9:8 TLV)

I am competent. I am not inadequate.

> Not that we are competent in ourselves to claim any-
> thing for ourselves, but our competence comes from
> God. He has made us competent as ministers of a new
> covenant—not of the letter but of the Spirit; for the
> letter kills, but the Spirit gives life. (2 Corinthians 3:5–6
> NIV)

God is completing me and won't give up on me.

> Being confident of this, that he who began a good work
> in you will carry it on to completion until the day of
> Christ Jesus. (Philippians 1:6 NIV)

I am blessed. I am not lacking.

> Praise the God and Father of our Lord Jesus Christ!
> Through Christ, God has blessed us with every spiritual
> blessing that heaven has to offer. (Ephesians 1:3 GW)

I have a special future and destiny. God has a plan for my life.

> "For I know the plans I have for you," declares the
> LORD, "plans to prosper you and not to harm you, plans
> to give you hope and a future." (Jeremiah 29:11 NIV)

I am anointed. God uses me in powerful ways.

> All of God lives fully in Christ (even when Christ was
> on earth), and you have a full and true life in in Christ,

who is ruler over all rulers and powers. (Colossians 2:9–10 NCV)

As for you, the anointing you received from him remains in you, and you do not need anyone to teach you. But as his anointing teaches you about all things and as that anointing is real, not counterfeit—just as it has taught you, remain in him. (1 John 2:27 NIV)

Confess

Lord, I confess that by myself I am inadequate. I struggle and strive in my flesh when I live independently of your presence. But I thank you that I am not alone. You have wonderfully and fearfully created me and redeemed me. I am yours twice. You fill me with your Spirit and empower me by your presence, and I lack no good thing.

Affirm

I am more than adequate and competent in Christ. "I can do all things through him who strengthens me" (Philippians 4:13 ESV). I am not inferior or incapable of fulfilling God's call on my life. I untie the cord of false identity.

Repeat "I am capable" three times. Each time you read it, add special emphasis to the bolded word.

I am capable.

I **am** capable.

I am **capable**.

Extra Memory Challenge

His divine power has given us everything we need for a godly life through our knowledge of him who called us by his own glory and goodness. (2 Peter 1:3 NIV)

Explore

1. How is God speaking to you about being capable? Listen to him now.
2. Does knowing you are capable change the way you will face new challenges? Why or why not?
3. How does being capable differ from being self-sufficient?
4. What dreams or goals do you believe are part of your destiny?
5. What steps will you take to achieve your goals and dreams now as you trust God to use your capabilities?
6. What other truths did you see in today's lesson?

Journal

Week 1

Day 4

Today's Truth: I Am Holy

For he chose us in him before the creation of the world
to be holy and blameless in his sight.
Ephesians 1:4 NIV

It may be hard to believe, but you are holy. If you've accepted Jesus into your life, the Bible no longer refers to you as a sinner, but a saint. Salvation through Jesus Christ made you a new creation, repositioned you as righteous, and set you apart. That means you're holy. In fact, you're 100 percent righteous, 100 percent of the time.

Wait, you might think. *That can't be right. Don't I have to read my Bible more, pray, go to church more often, tithe, and fast to become holy?*

No. While those things may be beneficial and even important disciplines to incorporate into your life, they do not make you more holy. The truth is, you can't become more holy than you already are. (I know you want to reread that sentence!) This is because holiness is not based on anything we can do or anything we don't do. Remember, our identity—including our holiness—is founded on the finished and complete work that Jesus Christ accomplished on the cross. He alone is our holiness.

That doesn't mean, however, that our thoughts and actions don't need to catch up with our identity. We need to grow more and more in the expression of our holiness and reflect more of the true person we already are.

You see, through Jesus's substitutionary death, God made us holy so that he can enjoy deep personal fellowship with us. Our relationship and position as believers in Jesus Christ make this holiness a spiritual reality. God sees us as perfect. Blameless. Experientially, however, you and I are still *in the process* of acting holy. We are still pulled between the desire to live to please God and the desire to live to please ourselves.

The word *holy* means "to be separate or set apart from." God's holiness means that he is transcendent—above and beyond all creation in purity, wisdom, knowledge, beauty, and earthly goodness. He is inherently holy. We, on the other hand, become holy only through our relationship with Christ. "For God's will was for us to be made holy by the sacrifice of the body of Jesus Christ, once for all time" (Hebrews 10:10).

When we are in union with Jesus, God's holiness becomes our holiness. Today is a call to remember your identity and to live in his holiness.

Declare

I have been set apart and made holy by God. Because of the precious blood of his Son, Jesus Christ, I am washed clean, made pure, and put in right standing with God. I do not have to live in ungodliness or act in ways that are unholy. I am the righteousness of God in Christ Jesus. I am holy. I declare this in Jesus's name.

Meditate, Believe, Accept

I am made holy.

> It is because of him that you are in Christ Jesus, who has become for us wisdom from God—that is, our righteousness, holiness and redemption. (1 Corinthians 1:30 NIV)

> For by one sacrifice he has made perfect forever those who are being made holy. (Hebrews 10:14 NIV)

I am without blame in Christ.

> So that you may become blameless and pure, children of God without fault in a warped and crooked generation. Then you will shine among them like stars in the sky. (Philippians 2:15 NIV)

> For he chose us in him before the creation of the world to be holy and blameless in his sight. (Ephesians 1:4 NIV)

I am purified.

> If we confess our sins, he is faithful and just and will forgive us our sins and purify us from all unrighteousness. (1 John 1:9 NIV)

I am justified.

> And all are justified freely by his grace through the redemption that came by Christ Jesus. (Romans 3:24 NIV)

Confess

Lord, I confess that there are times I do not live as I am in you—holy. In those moments, I do not walk in the Spirit but choose to walk after the flesh. Today I remind myself that you bought me with a price and that I belong to you. I will be holy as you are holy.

Affirm

I am holy because of Jesus Christ and his shed blood. He has secured this standing for me by his death on the cross. Therefore, I am in right standing with God. I shine like the stars. I don't have to perform to earn my righteousness because I cannot earn it. However, because of the indwelling Holy Spirit, I will choose to act and live in holy ways. I untie the cord of false identity.

Repeat "I am holy" three times. Each time you read it, add special emphasis to the bolded word.

I am holy.

I **am** holy.

I am **holy.**

Extra Memory Challenge

> For he chose us in him before the creation of the world to be holy and blameless in his sight. (Ephesians 1:4 NIV)

Explore

1. How is God speaking to you about being made holy? Listen to him now.
2. Have you ever thought of yourself as holy and blameless? How did those thoughts make you feel?
3. How does knowing you are holy free you from shame and influence your attitude toward yourself?
4. Does knowing God has made you holy change the way you approach him in prayer?
5. What other truths did you see in today's lesson?

Journal

Week 1

Day 5

Today's Truth: I Am Forgiven

I am writing to you, dear children,
because your sins have been forgiven
on account of his name.
1 John 2:12 NIV

I don't know how God could ever forgive me. My sin is too big.
I don't deserve forgiveness; after all, I keep failing over and over again.

How can God forgive me when I can't even forgive myself?

Have you ever felt this way, caught in a quagmire of regret and defeat over your sin? Feeling unforgivable is common because this way of thinking is one weapon in Satan's arsenal of lies. He loves to use this pride-based deception to keep us tied with cords of bondage. The truth is that there is no sin so big that Jesus's forgiveness can't cover it. His blood is more than powerful enough to purge us.

Forgiveness is one of our heavenly Father's most expensive gifts to us. We don't deserve his forgiveness and could never do enough to earn it. He freely forgives our sins and washes us clean when we come to him with penitent hearts. The Word teaches us that God removes our sin far from us—"as far as the east is from the west" (Psalm 103:12 NIV), and that he "will cast all our sins into the depths of the sea" (Micah 7:19 NKJV). In Christ we are forgiven and are given a fresh beginning.

God knows we mess up. He knows we're going to fail people and make hurtful choices, so he created a way to forgive us, eradicate our sin, and maintain an unbroken relationship with us. And the most remarkable thing?

Micah 7:18 tells us that God delights in showing us mercy. He will never turn us away when we come to him and genuinely ask for forgiveness. Micah 7:18 was written during a time of history when God's people, Israel, were acting especially rebellious. Surprisingly, God doesn't say that he was *willing* to forgive them; he says that he *delighted* in forgiving them.

This is a shocking statement. Let's be honest: Is this the way we feel toward people who've turned their backs on us in vicious ways? No way. Yet God's unlimited love pursues the guilt-ridden cry of every person who lives under the crushing weight of unforgiven sin. He's always ready to purify the vilest of us all.

Today cry out to him for cleansing and receive his pardon. He delights in forgiving you!

Declare

There is nothing I could say or do that God would refuse to forgive. Because I confess my sin to him, God forgives me completely and releases me from my debt. I can forgive others and myself because God has forgiven me. I live free from condemnation as I accept God's forgiveness. I am forgiven. I declare this in Jesus's name.

Meditate, Believe, Accept

I am forgiven.

> So listen, friends! Through this Jesus, the forgiveness of sins is offered to you. (Acts 13:38 TPT)

> Be kind and compassionate to one another, forgiving each other, just as in Christ God forgave you. (Ephesians 4:32 NIV)

I am a new creation.

> Therefore, if anyone is in Christ, he is a new creation; the old has gone, the new has come! (2 Corinthians 5:17 NIV)

I am free from condemnation.

> Therefore, there is now no condemnation for those who are in Christ Jesus, because through Christ Jesus the law of the Spirit who gives life has set you free from the law of sin and death. (Romans 8:1–2 NIV)

I am washed clean.

> Some of you were once like that. But you were cleansed; you were made holy; you were made right with God by calling on the name of the Lord Jesus Christ and by the Spirit of our God. (1 Corinthians 6:11)

I am free from guilt.

> Let us draw near to God with a sincere heart and with the full assurance that faith brings, having our hearts sprinkled to cleanse us from a guilty conscience and having our bodies washed with pure water. (Hebrews 10:22 NIV)

Confess

Today I accept your forgiveness, God. At times I am tempted to replay the sins of my past and live in shame. I sometimes fail to walk in the freedom you have provided through your total forgiveness. I choose to fully accept your love and forgiveness and live free from guilt.

Affirm

Because I confess my sins before God, I am forgiven of all my sin. I am no longer a slave to sin, but I am made alive in Christ Jesus. Because I walk in his forgiveness, I forgive others and myself. I am free from condemnation and guilt. God has redeemed my life and set me free. I untie the cord of false identity.

Repeat "I am forgiven" three times. Each time you read it, add special emphasis to the bolded word.

I am forgiven.

I **am** forgiven.

I am **forgiven**.

Extra Memory Challenge

I am writing to you, dear children, because your sins have been forgiven on account of his name. (1 John 2:12 NIV)

Explore

1. How is God speaking to you about being forgiven? Listen to him now.
2. Have you been able to receive God's forgiveness?
3. How does being completely forgiven by God impact the way you should forgive others? Yourself? God?
4. When faced with guilt or condemnation from your past, how will knowing that God forgives you affect your response?
5. What other truths did you see in today's lesson?

Journal

Week 1

Day 6

TODAY'S TRUTH: I AM VALUABLE

I praise you because I am fearfully and wonderfully made;
your works are wonderful, I know that full well.
Psalm 139:14 NIV

I (Dawn) once heard a story about a family that held a garage sale. After years of accumulating hand-me-down furniture and household décor, kids' toys, clothes, family heirlooms, bikes, skis, and every kind of sports gear imaginable, it was time to purge. The family placed a measly fifty-cent price tag on most items in a hopeful attempt to sell them fast.

On the day of the sale, a slow but steady stream of bargain hunters rummaged through the "junk" looking for treasures. One shopper burrowed his way to the back corner of the garage and found a painting that intrigued him. His eyes grew wide as he studied it, then he abruptly paid the fifty cents to the homeowner and thrust the painting beneath his coat like a smuggler. Later it was discovered that the anonymous shopper had found an original Renoir painting. It now hangs in an art gallery with a price tag of hundreds of thousands of dollars.

Whether folklore or true, this story illustrates a point. In an instant, the painting was transformed from junk to priceless treasure because of the revelation of the famous creator's signature.

The same is true for us. We are often tossed to the dark corners of life and deemed worthless and of no value. Others fail to see our worth, and we, too, often believe there is nothing good in us. But we bear the signature of our Creator, the God of the universe, who says this about our value:

> I crafted you and infused your being with value, worth, and significance. While you were in your mother's womb, I knit you together using thread from my very own being. I weaved value and worth into you at creation. Your value does not come from your appearance—for this world can decimate the outward appearance—nor from your performance, self-assessment, or the flawed opinions of other human beings. Your human value is inherent. You're my daughter, created in my likeness. You carry my dignity and reflected value. As your Creator, I alone know your true value, and I placed a price tag—the life of my Son—upon you.

God has uniquely handcrafted you and made you a one-of-a-kind masterpiece. *You* are his treasure.

Declare

God created me, and I inspire wonder and awe. I am valuable, and my life is important to him and others. I am not defective beyond his ability to use me for his glory. God has crafted me perfectly, by him and for him. I am valuable. I declare this in Jesus's name.

Meditate, Believe, Accept

I am God's delight. (Yes, men, God delights in you.)

> For the Lord takes delight in his people; he crowns the humble with victory. (Psalm 149:4 NIV)

> Here is my servant, whom I uphold, my chosen one in whom I delight. (Isaiah 42:1 NIV)

I am the light of the world.

> You are the light of the world. A town built on a hill cannot be hidden. Neither do people light a lamp and

put it under a bowl. Instead they put it on its stand, and it gives light to everyone in the house. In the same way, let your light shine before others, that they may see your good deeds and glorify your Father in heaven. (Matthew 5:14–16 NIV)

I am God's extraordinary creation.

For we are the product of His hand, *heaven's poetry etched on lives*, created in the Anointed, Jesus, to accomplish the good works God arranged long ago. (Ephesians 2:10 VOICE).

I am beautiful in him. (Yes, men also reflect God's beauty.)

Those who look to him are radiant; their faces are never covered with shame. (Psalm 34:5 NIV)

I am created in God's image.

Then God said, "Let us make mankind in our image, in our likeness, so that they may rule over the fish in the sea and the birds in the sky, over the livestock and all the wild animals, and over all the creatures that move along the ground." So God created mankind in his own image, in the image of God he created them; male and female he created them. (Genesis 1:26–27 NIV)

I am included in Christ, sealed in him.

And you also were included in Christ when you heard the message of truth, the gospel of your salvation. When you believed, you were marked in him with a seal, the promised Holy Spirit. (Ephesians 1:13–14 NIV)

Confess

Distortions and lies have battered me. I have struggled with broken self-worth and acceptance. Satan has blinded my spiritual eyes to keep me from seeing and believing in the worth and value God has given me—first through creation and now through redemption. I have spoken words that agree with Satan's condemnation and not with God's valued truth. Today I choose to accept the truth—I am valuable!

Affirm

I have been made in God's image and likeness, and I am valuable. I am a one-of-a-kind masterpiece. I am unique and special, and God has gifted me. He loves me as he created me. My life is priceless. I untie the cord of false identity.

Repeat "I am valuable" three times. Each time you read it, add special emphasis to the bolded word.

I am valuable.

I **am** valuable.

I am **valuable**.

Extra Memory Challenge

> I praise you because you made me in an amazing and wonderful way. What you have done is wonderful. I know this very well. (Psalm 139:14 NCV)

Explore

1. How is God speaking to you about your value? Listen to him now.
2. How does knowing you are valuable, significant, and of great worth change your view of yourself?
3. Are you able to agree with God and confess that you are radiant and beautiful? Why or why not? How does your view of masculinity make it difficult to embrace this? What lies have held you back in the past?

4. How will knowing you are valuable change the way you esteem yourself?

5. What other truths did you see in today's lesson?

Journal

Week 1

Day 7

Today's Truth: I Am Victorious

But thanks be to God!
He gives us the victory through our Lord Jesus Christ.
1 Corinthians 15:57 NIV

Dawn and I both love to win. Scrabble competitions at our house get intense.

As a kid, Dawn took playing games seriously. She was competitive, and nothing felt better than hard-fought victory. After a satisfying win, she'd often jump up, snap her fingers, and like comedian Jackie Gleason, say, "How sweet it is!"

I agree. What is sweeter than victory?

When I think of victory, I'm reminded of the scene from the movie *Rocky* with Sylvester Stallone standing at the top of a challenging stretch of stairs waving his hands in anticipation of his hard-earned victory. Can you feel the exhilaration?

Jesus's death on the cross and resurrection defeated the powers of darkness, sin, and death. His victory required an agonizing battle in the garden of Gethsemane, where he *chose* to die for us. Jesus would suffer the greatest pain and sacrifice in the history of the world—death on a cross—but even more importantly, he would suffer the crushing horror of allowing the sin of the entire world to become *his* sin so he could claim victory for us. But his power didn't end there. Three days after his death, Jesus won the ultimate victory over the grave when God raised him from the dead!

Can you feel the exhilaration? Jesus won! He is the all-time Champion, but his victory is our victory.

How sweet it is!

The ultimate good news is that because we belong to Christ, we win too. No weapon formed against us can prevail (Isaiah 54:17). We're on the winning side because Jesus shares his victory with us, leading us in triumph over *all* the powers of the Enemy. We're bold conquerors through him, victorious in this life through the power of the Holy Spirit.

Snap your fingers here, men. Shout "Amen!" Can I get a witness? This is more than truth, more than facts—this is living hope.

Jesus spoke his final words on the cross with purpose: "It is finished."

Why? Because the powers of sin and death were demolished.

Obliterated.

Destroyed.

And we are the recipients of the power and freedom that flowed from the cross that day. We are victors over sin, and we are free.

Today remember *you* are victorious! The battle is the Lord's. You don't have to fight because Jesus won the fight for you. The victory is yours, and how sweet it is.

Congratulations! You've finished your first week! Go ahead—tell yourself you're an overcomer. The victory is yours because Jesus won the battle for you.

Savor the win.

Declare

I am victorious over sin. The battle is the Lord's. I don't have to fight because Jesus won the fight for me. No weapon formed against me can prevail.

Meditate, Believe, Accept

I am an overcomer. I am not defeated.

> But we have power over all these things through Jesus Who loves us so much. (Romans 8:37 NLV)

> For everyone born of God overcomes the world. This is

the victory that has overcome the world, even our faith.
(1 John 5:4 NIV)

I am dead to sin.

My old self has been crucified with Christ. It is no longer I who live, but Christ lives in me. So I live in this
earthly body by trusting in the Son of God, who loved
me and gave himself for me. (Galatians 2:20)

In the same way, count yourselves dead to sin but alive
to God in Christ Jesus. (Romans 6:11 NIV)

I am established, rooted, and strong.

Therefore, my dear brothers and sisters, stand firm. Let
nothing move you. (1 Corinthians 15:58 NIV)

And now, just as you accepted Christ Jesus as your Lord,
you must continue to follow him. Let your roots grow
down into him, and let your lives be built on him. Then
your faith will grow strong in the truth you were taught,
and you will overflow with thankfulness. (Colossians
2:6–7)

He will also keep you firm to the end, so that you will
be blameless on the day of our Lord Jesus Christ. God
is faithful, who has called you into fellowship with his
Son, Jesus Christ our Lord. (1 Corinthians 1:8–9 NIV)

I am delivered from the powers of darkness.

For he has rescued us from the dominion of darkness and brought us into the kingdom of the Son he
loves. (Colossians 1:13 NIV)

I am set free.

It is for freedom that Christ has set us free. Stand firm,

then, and do not let yourselves be burdened again by a yoke of slavery. (Galatians 5:1 NIV)

You, my brothers and sisters, were called to be free. But do not use your freedom to indulge the flesh; rather, serve one another humbly in love. (Galatians 5:13 NIV)

I walk in truth.

Then you will know the truth, and the truth will set you free. (John 8:32 NIV)

Some of the brothers traveling by have made me very happy by telling me that your life stays clean and true and that you are living by the standards of the Gospel. I could have no greater joy than to hear such things about my children. (3 John 3–4 TLB)

I am seated in heavenly places.

And God raised us up with Christ and seated us with him in the heavenly realms in Christ Jesus. (Ephesians 2:6 NIV)

I can do all things.

I can do everything through him who gives me strength. (Philippians 4:13 NIV)

Confess

Lord, you have not created me to be a victim, defeated by circumstances and difficulties. But sometimes I forget my identity, and I choose a lesser mindset than the overcoming, conquering mindset you call me to. Today I choose to shed a victim mindset and walk in victory!

Affirm

I am more than an overcomer. Whatever storms come my way in life, God will use them to strengthen, teach, and benefit me. They will not shake me from my faith. I will be triumphant. I am victorious! I untie the cord of false identity.

Repeat "I am victorious" three times. Each time you read it, add special emphasis to the bolded word.

I am victorious.

I **am** victorious.

I am **victorious**.

Extra Memory Challenge

> But thanks be to God! He gives us the victory through our Lord Jesus Christ. (1 Corinthians 15:57 NIV)

Explore

1. How is God speaking to you about being victorious? Listen to him now.
2. Does knowing that you are victorious in all things change the way you face the struggles in your life?
3. What strongholds in your life will you claim victory over, even though they presently seem to control you?
4. How does being rooted, established, and strong differ from being stubborn and headstrong?
5. What other truths did you see in today's lesson?

Free Thinking

You are free from the cord of false identity. Claim it. Although you may not fully see all these things in the natural realm, be confident that God is working in you. What is finished in the heavenlies will be accomplished on this earth—in you. He is transforming your negative mindset into a victoriously renewed mind.

All of God's truths are yours to claim.

Congratulations! You have completed week 1 and are on your way to a new life.

Journal

CHAPTER 4

CORDS OF DECEPTIVE SELF-TALK

What starts out as an intrusive thought can turn into an
overwhelming concept if we "feed" it with more
negative thinking.
—Eddie Capparucci, LPC, *Removing Your Shame Label*

Challenge Week 2

Weekly Reading: Deceptive Self-Talk

We demolish arguments and every pretension
that sets itself up against the that knowledge of God,
and we take captive every thought to make it obedient
to Christ.
2 Corinthians 10:5 NIV

This week we're examining the toxic self-talk that runs through our brains like the incessant hum of a refrigerator. Our self-talk plays an influential role in the way we feel and act. Dawn describes the conflicting influence of her self-talk at one point in her life:

> During the course of my divorce and in the months following, I often felt conflicted. The hurt part of me

wanted to lash out in defense. Another part of me felt angry and cried out for justice and revenge. Another part of me wanted someone to rise up and protect me. Yet another voice inside my head told me to act with justice, mercy, and in obedience to God. I found myself pulled between warring voices inside my head that advised me about the best answer, action, or solution to my situation. Subsequently, my emotions pinballed from guilt and shame to anger, then to godly repentance, and then back to a demanding spirit in a seemingly hopeless spiral.

Unfortunately, I didn't understand the role of self-talk at that time, and I felt confused and conflicted by the battle in my mind. But since then, I've learned the importance of listening, learning, and taking charge of my thinking.[4]

Listen

For the next seven days, you'll turn your attention to the *inner voices* or internal dialogues that continually chatter inside your mind. You may already be aware of the inner conversations that battle within you, or you may be oblivious to the role of internal dialogues in your life. But the things you tell yourself—about yourself, others, your circumstances, the world, and God—play an enormous role in your mental, emotional, and spiritual health. Surprisingly, you can believe two conflicting things at the same time. Abuse victims commonly believe the Word of God but can't believe that his truth applies to them.

Shelly Beach, author of *The Silent Seduction of Self-Talk*, states that we speak to ourselves at a rate of approximately 1,300 words a minute, while we speak to others at an average rate of 150 words a minute.[5] Every day 45,000 thoughts race through our minds, and many of these thoughts are judgmental, critical, and harsh.

Therefore, it is critical that we pay attention to what we're saying to ourselves and ask the following questions:

- What story am I telling myself about who I am?
- How am I speaking to myself about myself?
- Do I need to change the narrative I tell myself about my circumstances, others, who God is, and life?
- Where have Satan's lies infiltrated my thoughts? Does what I think align with what God says? What effect do these lies have on the way I act and react in the world?
- What negative and toxic thoughts do I tell myself about myself that do not align with who God says I am?

Learn

Holding on to toxic thinking about the world or ourselves is a form of extreme pride—the lies we believe typically oppose what God says about who we are and how we should act. Examining negative self-talk is an act of submission and says to God, "Yes, I admit I've believed lies about who I am. I want to believe the truth, God. I commit to study my thoughts and to substitute my lies with your truth about who I am and how I should treat myself. I no longer want to be deceived. I agree with you because you're God."

So we will examine our inner dialogues together and expose the cords of deceptive self-talk that bind us to negativity and defeat. Our goal is to reveal, renounce, and destroy the lies we believe by overpowering them with the Word of God. This will not be an easy process. Many of us have clung to lies as part of our identity for most of our lives, but we will *choose to believe* what God says, recognizing that our emotions are feelings and not truth. We will also learn how to take our thoughts captive and to tear down prideful thinking that has controlled our minds.

Prepare to Act

This week be ultra-aware of your inner dialogues. Listen intently to the things you say to yourself. Pay attention to the conversations, thoughts, judgments, and criticisms that come into your thought life throughout the day. Consider writing them down so you can evaluate your words and motives, meditate upon them, and pray about them.

Are your thoughts uplifting, affirming, and positive? Or is your self-talk discouraging, fearful, negative, and ungodly? You will probably notice a mix of both positive and negative thoughts, but do you focus largely on the negative? Be especially attentive to the way you speak to yourself and about yourself. Look for correlations between what you're thinking and how you're feeling—and what you're saying to others and how you're behaving toward them. Chances are, you'll see a direct connection.

When I began to practice this discipline, I immediately noticed a pattern of self-condemnation, and I committed to making changes. I determined to say the things to myself that God would say to me—positive, affirming, loving, life-building words.

As we uncover false inner narratives that are unbiblical and destructive, we also often discover that their sources are demonic. As these lies become more deeply rooted within us, they lead us into bondage. Each time we speak or act upon a lie, we tie the knot tighter. In this study, however, we will train ourselves to break the bondage and untie the cords as we replace lies with God's truth.

Prepare yourself to retrain your mind this week by choosing truth and telling yourself a hope-filled story of purpose. You are loved. You are infinitely valuable. You were created with eternal purpose. God loves you more than you could ever comprehend.

Several years ago, millions of people began wearing bracelets with the letters WWJD on them: "What would Jesus do?" The bracelet reminded wearers to ask that simple question to guide them in their daily decisions. When they did, their fleshly, selfish behavior changed to reflect a more Christlike attitude. Similarly, I want you to envision wearing a bracelet that says WWJS, or "What would Jesus say?" What would he say about who you are? What would he say about your value to him? What would he say about your purpose in life and for each day?

Your Freedom Challenge for week 2 is to appropriate the truth of Scripture to your thinking, attitude, and actions each day. Renounce negative self-talk. Refuse to allow it to erode your thinking, and instead, embrace God's Word about who you are. Complete your daily confessions and prayers. As you do, believe and declare that you are free from the bondage of deceptive self-talk. As you speak and believe the truth, your mind will be transformed.

Your daily journal continues.

Week 2

Day 8

Today's Truth: I Am Free from the Voice of the Inner Critic

Finally, brothers and sisters, whatever is true,
whatever is noble, whatever is right, whatever is pure,
whatever is lovely, whatever is admirable—
if anything is excellent or praiseworthy—
think about such things.
Philippians 4:8 NIV

Sometimes we are our own worst critic. Who knows our flaws better than our souls within us? We may feel disqualified from love, success, blessings, and God's best. We do what we can to cover up our imperfections by being a good person and doing good things, but our internal critic will raise a condemning voice and whisper in our ears, "If people only knew the real you, you'd be ruined." Our secret, shaming thoughts convince us that we are frauds, especially when we attempt to do things we feel God is calling us to do. We believe we can never be worthy. We can never be enough.

Unfortunately, cycles of self-doubt like this can block our confidence to follow God's call on our lives. For a time, Satan's deception worked on me. It was easier to give in to lying voices than to trust God to set me free from the constant condemning narratives in my head. I didn't realize I could have victory over my inner critic.

The internal critic is the negative, scolding, criticizing voice that speaks to us and even harasses us about who we are and how we perform. It's often Satan's demonic voice launched into our thoughts like fiery darts intended to discourage and discredit us. When we accept these satanic lies as truth and incorporate them into our thoughts, we crowd out the truth of God's Word and ultimately end up bound by lies.

The good news is that when we learn that God gives us the power to expose and dismantle lies through the power of his Word, we find freedom from intimidation, shame, and the chains of our past. We begin to recognize that the voice of the one who condemns us speaks deceit. Our heavenly Father speaks affirmation and love. Today we learn to lean into truth, regardless of how we feel, and to trust God's Word.

This week we will release spirit-deadening self-doubt that holds us back from spiritual growth and from becoming the men God has called us to be.

Declare

I listen to the voice of God. His words to me are loving, calming, uplifting, and affirming, even when he brings correction. I will not succumb to negative self-talk or thoughts that are contrary to God's truth. Instead, I take captive every thought and place them under God's control. I tell my thoughts to line up with the truth. I fill my mind with God's thoughts. I am free from the voice of the inner critic. I declare this in Jesus's name.

Meditate, Believe, Accept

I think thoughts that are true and right. I do not criticize myself.

> Finally, brothers and sisters, whatever is true, whatever is noble, whatever is right, whatever is pure, whatever is lovely, whatever is admirable—if anything is excellent or praiseworthy—think about such things. (Philippians 4:8 NIV)

I arrest negative thoughts and demolish them. I do not believe them.

> We demolish arguments and every pretension that sets itself up against the knowledge of God, and we take

81

captive every thought to make it obedient to Christ. (2 Corinthians 10:5 NIV)

I have the mind of Christ. I agree with his thoughts.

For who hath known the mind of the Lord, that he may instruct him? but we have the mind of Christ. (1 Corinthians 2:16 KJV)

Your attitude should be the same as that of Christ Jesus. (Philippians 2:5 NIV)

I choose a new attitude, for I have put off old ways of thinking.

You were taught, with regard to your former way of life, to put off your old self, which is being corrupted by its deceitful desires; to be made new in the attitude of your minds; and to put on the new self, created to be like God in true righteousness and holiness. (Ephesians 4:22–24 NIV)

I do not dwell on or fellowship with false or demonic narratives. I listen to the Lord's voice.

Do not be yoked together with unbelievers. For what do righteousness and wickedness have in common? Or what fellowship can light have with darkness? (2 Corinthians 6:14 NIV)

My thoughts are good company and do not corrupt my heart and mind.

Do not be misled: "Bad company corrupts good character." (1 Corinthians 15:33 NIV)

My mind is renewed as I think good thoughts. Therefore, I am filled with good things.

For as he thinketh in his heart, so is he. (Proverbs 23:7 KJV)

Confess

Lord, my thoughts have not always conformed with your Word or your will. I have allowed the internal critic to speak to me and through me. I've allowed random thought patterns to take control of my mind and drag me into bondage. Today I renounce my old ways of thinking, including flawed, negative narratives and the lies of Satan. In Jesus's name, I cast down every fiery dart released against my mind.

Affirm

I have the mind of Christ. My mind is sound, and my thoughts are pure, noble, right, and true. Truth fills my soul's narrative. I renounce Satan's lies, stories, and interpretations. My mind is guarded and strong, and light fills my thoughts. I am free from the voice of the inner critic.

Repeat "I have the mind of Christ" three times. Each time you read it, add special emphasis to the bolded word or words.

I have the mind of Christ.

I **have** the mind of Christ.

I have the **mind of Christ**.

Extra Memory Challenge

We demolish arguments and every pretension that sets itself up against the knowledge of God, and we take captive every thought to make it obedient to Christ. (2 Corinthians 10:5 NIV)

Explore

1. Have you been listening to your inner dialogue this week? What do you hear yourself saying? How true is it?
2. Would Jesus say the same thing? What do you think he would say to you?
3. What does it mean to think on "things above"?

4. How do your feelings and emotions change when you center your thoughts on "things above"?

Journal

Week 2

Day 9

TODAY'S TRUTH: I AM FREE FROM THE VOICE OF NEGATIVE LABELS

Whoever would love life and see good days
must keep their tongue from evil
and their lips from deceitful speech.
1 Peter 3:10 NIV

In March of 1862, a periodical called *The Christian Recorder* printed the following: "Remember the old adage, 'Sticks and stones will break my bones, but words will never harm me'? True courage consists in doing what is right, despite the jeers and sneers of our companions."[6]

We may think this adage sounds clever or even courageous, but the truth is, words *can* break us—they can break our hearts, cut our souls, and crush our spirits.

Words hold power.

God's Word teaches that we possess the power of life or death in our tongue (Proverbs 18:21). When God created the world, he spoke it into existence. He also made us in his image, giving us incredible power to create through the words we speak. The thoughts we speak give life or bring death—the death of hope, dreams, dignity, and vision for a future.

Words are seeds.

When we release words, they become planted in people's lives and bring a harvest that will forever influence the hearer. We must wisely choose the words we speak—whether good or bad, blessings or curses—because our words carry the power to nurture hope or to destroy. Perhaps someone has spoken life-killing words over you, seeds sown in your heart that brought a crop of pain and self-doubt.

Words also become labels.

Negative words stick to us like labels on a jar. When we believe labeling words, they influence how we think, feel, and evaluate ourselves. Labels don't have to be true to hurt us. We only have to accept them as truth. Eventually, words spoken over us saturate our hearts and come to describe us. Negative words—labels—slowly shape our beliefs and attitudes. In other words, our inside essence adapts to reflect an external label. Words not only hurt us, but they also change us.

Too often we evaluate ourselves in light of the pain of our past and therefore limit our future. It's important to understand that our first labels often come from people who control our lives and who, sometimes out of cruelty and sometimes in innocence, judge us unfairly. As we journey toward healing, we must explore how and why negative labels become part of our identity, and then we must reject them because they do not reflect our true identity in Christ.

Words hold power. That is why God's Word says we must keep our thoughts from evil and deceitful speech (Psalm 34:13).

When we call ourselves stupid or an idiot or a moron, we condemningly judge who we are at our core. When we use words like these to describe ourselves, we perpetuate the idea that we are worthless individuals who cannot change.

Research reveals that when we believe that we can make positive changes, we work harder to become who we envision ourselves to be.

Jesus never insults us. He never berates us. His words to us are tender, forgiving, and merciful, and they call us to purpose and hope. Learning to speak lovingly to ourselves the way Jesus speaks to us is one of the greatest gifts we can give to ourselves and one of our most powerful tools for healing.

Declare

My words are life. I speak whatever is good, true, and life-giving, and because I do, I will reap the blessings of life. I will not agree with negative labels that others have spoken over me, nor will I release curses over my life through the words I speak. I renounce the negative labels and names that others have placed on me. I am free from negative labels. I declare this in Jesus's name.

Meditate, Believe, Accept

I am saved by the words of my mouth. No labels will destroy me.

> That if you confess with your mouth, "Jesus is Lord," and believe in your heart that God raised Him from the dead, you will be saved. For with your heart you believe and are justified, and with your mouth you confess and are saved. (Romans 10:9–10 BSB)

My words are uplifting to others and me. I benefit from hearing what I say.

> Do not let any unwholesome talk come out of your mouths, but only what is helpful for building others up according to their needs, that it may benefit those who listen. (Ephesians 4:29 NIV)

My mouth speaks words of life, not death. I thrive because I speak life.

> The tongue has the power of life and death, and those who love it will eat its fruit. (Proverbs 18:21 NIV)

I bring healing to my life and others by my words. Reckless words have no power over me.

> The words of the reckless pierce like swords, but the tongue of the wise brings healing. (Proverbs 12:18 NIV)

I will love life and see good days, for I keep my tongue from evil.

> Whoever would love life and see good days must keep their tongue from evil and their lips from deceitful speech. (1 Peter 3:10 NIV)

My faith is built strong by the words of my mouth.

> Faith comes from hearing the message, and the message is heard through the word about Christ. (Romans 10:17 NIV)

My words flow from a grateful heart, and they renew my mind.

> Out of the overflow of the heart, the mouth speaks. (Matthew 12:34 BSB)

Confess

Lord, I have not always guarded the words of my mouth. I have released words from my lips that have ensnared me, speaking curses over my body, my mind, and my circumstances. I have listened to the words of others and believed them over your Word. I renounce the negative words, labels, and curses that others have spoken over my life. I come into agreement with you and your Word. I am free from negative labels in Jesus's name.

Affirm

The words of my mouth and the meditations of my heart are pleasing and acceptable. I speak life, and therefore I reap life. My words are powerful and anointed, and I bring about God's plan for my life because I agree with him. The words of my mouth do not ensnare me. I speak life in Jesus's name.

Repeat "I speak life" three times. Each time you read it, add special emphasis to the bolded word.

I speak life.

I **speak** life.

I speak **life**.

Extra Memory Challenge

Do not let any unwholesome talk come out of your mouths, but only what is helpful for building others [and myself] up according to their [and my] needs, that it may benefit those who listen. (Ephesians 4:29 NIV)

Explore

1. Have you been listening to the words of your mouth this week? What did you find most helpful about this exercise?
2. What do you hear yourself saying? How true is it?
3. Would Jesus say the same thing?
4. Have you discovered any patterns of negative self-talk? If so, how have these cords of bondage influenced your life?
5. What words would Jesus speak to you in these areas? How could this change the way you see yourself?

Journal

Week 2

Day 10

TODAY'S TRUTH: I AM FREE FROM THE VOICE OF PAST FAILURES

The LORD makes firm the steps of the one
who delights in him;
though he may stumble, he will not fall,
for the LORD upholds him with his hand.
Psalm 37:23–24 NIV

Failure comes to each one of us. We've all missed the mark, come up short, and crashed and burned in dismal defeat. The imprint of embarrassment clings to us. The voice of condemnation whispers in our ear, "You loser."

But failure is an event and not a person, destination, or identity. You are not a failure. In fact, you can make failure work for you. The key to overcoming failure is to extract precious lessons from your experience, pick yourself up in the power of the Holy Spirit, and keep on going. Your victory is around the corner! Refuse to use failure to define yourself. You are God's son, and you are a winner.

Listen to what Pastor Nathan Jones says as he quotes Zig Ziglar on the subject of failure:

> Once we identify ourselves as a failure, this affects how we approach our lives. We take fewer chances. We give up quicker. We lack the belief in ourselves to take the actions necessary to succeed. Because we identify as a failure, we fail again. When we fail again, this just confirms the failure identity. This process of failure to identity to reinforcing failure becomes a powerful cycle that reinforces itself time and time again.[7]

The question is not whether we will fail but how we will respond when we do. How will we react when we miss the mark and come up short? Will we beat ourselves up because we lack ability, knowledge, or skill? Will we emotionally shut down and give up, choosing to assume the role of a victim instead? Those responses are often part of our unconscious default system. We fail, so we fear trying again. If we do try, we lack confidence in our ability to succeed. We fail again and believe we're worthless. We vow never to try again.

Instead of opting for the "I can never do anything right" mentality, we can recognize that failure most often works for our good, teaching us valuable lessons. We can boldly say, "I am smarter today than I was yesterday because I have learned what won't work!"

Today you will untie the cords of past failures. This is your opportunity to forgive yourself for mistakes you've made and release yourself from the lie that tells you you're no good. Remember, failure is an event—not a person. Accept the truth of God's Word, and remember your identity and who he says you are—a capable, gifted, loveable, and accepted son of the Most High King. Today you can find release from the pain of past failures.

Declare

I do not listen to the voice of past failure. It does not define me. I use failure as a stepping-stone to learn and grow. I am a winner.

Meditate, Believe, Accept

I am righteous, and I will always rise again after failure.

> Though the righteous fall seven times, they rise again.
> (Proverbs 24:16 NIV)

My steps are firm. Though I may fail, I will not fall, for the Lord upholds me.

> The Lord makes firm the steps of the one who delights in him; though he may stumble, he will not fall, for the Lord upholds him with his hand. (Psalm 37:23–24 NIV)

I start fresh each and every morning. Past failures are over.

> The faithful love of the **LORD** never ends! His mercies never cease. Great is his faithfulness; his mercies begin afresh each morning. (Lamentations 3:22–23)

Confess

Lord, I confess I have failed many times. I have failed you, others, and myself. But I thank you that my past failures do not define me. I choose to rise in your grace and mercy and walk in my fresh new beginning.

AffirmI am an overcomer. Whenever I stumble, I cling to God's hand, and he lifts me up. I treat failure as an opportunity for learning how to grow more like Christ. I am not defeated because I fail. I am wiser, more compassionate, and stronger in character. I do not listen to the voices of past failures.

Repeat "I am an overcomer" three times. Each time you read it, add special emphasis to the bolded word.

I am an overcomer.

I **am** an overcomer.

I am an **overcomer**.

Extra Memory Challenge

> Though the righteous fall seven times, they rise again. (Proverbs 24:16 NIV)

Explore

1. How have you viewed your past failures?
2. Has your view been healthy or unhealthy? In what ways?
3. How can you reframe each failure and view it as a positive experience God can use?

Journal

Week 2

Day 11

TODAY'S TRUTH: I AM FREE FROM THE VOICE OF RATIONALIZATION

If we say we have no sin, we deceive ourselves,
and the truth is not in us. If we confess our sins,
He is faithful and just to forgive us our sins and
to cleanse us from all unrighteousness.
1 John 1:8–9 BSB

When the truth is too difficult to face, too painful to imagine, or it strikes a blow to our pride and self-worth, we often choose to employ a defense mechanism called *rationalization*. We often develop these thinking patterns in childhood to protect us from anxiety or feelings of helplessness in a world that feels unsafe or even hostile.

When we move into an adult world, rationalization becomes a replacement for healthy, balanced thinking. Listening to whispers of rationalization can falsely convince us that we're okay when we aren't, we're not at fault when we are, and unacceptable behavior (ours or someone else's) is acceptable. Rationalization gives us ways to justify irrational thinking.

Our finely constructed excuses can feel logical—even plausible. But in the end, rationalization leads to false security, poor relationships, and stunted growth in our character. At its core, rationalization is an attempt to dodge facing the truth and accepting responsibility. When we use rationalization as a coping skill to get along in life, we thwart God's plan to lead us to maturity and to increase our faith.

Rationalization is an attempt to justify unhealthy or sinful behavior. We may often use it as a defense mechanism, rationalizing behavior that is too embarrassing or painful to face. Rationalizing negative actions or thoughts can lead to destructive behavior and always leads to twisted thinking. Rationalization can be an attempt to protect ourselves from emotions that frighten us or motives that we do not want to expose. It can also become an obstacle to healthy, balanced thinking.

Of course, we're not always to blame when, for example, relationships go wrong, or our job becomes overwhelming. But rather than blame (spelled *b-lame*), we can choose to take responsibility for our lives, refuse to be victims, and experience freedom.

Laying down rationalization means we're willing to change and make difficult lifestyle changes, even when those changes may feel scary or threatening.

Today we learn to detect the voice of rationalization, which gives us a false and sinful feeling of permission to blame others, make excuses, and shirk responsibility. Instead, we choose empowerment and truth. We choose truth and are thankful for the opportunity to grow and become rooted and secure in who we are. We will explore the motives and fears behind our rationalization and recognize Jesus as our source of identity and safety.

Declare

I humble myself and accept the truth about myself. I am strong and mature in my faith. I need positive feedback to grow and develop. I will positively and genuinely receive feedback about my character, attitudes, and conduct as tools for my growth and benefit—tools I can use to glorify God.

Meditate, Believe, Accept

I don't have to fear the truth. Jesus will advocate for me.

> My children, I am writing this so that you won't sin. But if you do sin, Jesus Christ always does the right thing, and he will speak to the father for us. Christ is the sacrifice that

takes away our sins and the sins of all the world's people. (1 John 2:1–2 CEV)

I will not avoid personal growth by listening to the voice of rationalization.

If we say we have no sin, we deceive ourselves, and the truth is not in us. If we confess our sins, he is faithful and just to forgive us our sins and to cleanse us from all unrighteousness. (1 John 1:8–9 ESV)

I don't make excuses. I trust Jesus to meet my needs and help me overcome.

One of the men lying there had been sick for thirty-eight years. When Jesus saw him and knew he had been ill for a long time, he asked him, "Would you like to get well?"

"I can't sir," the sick man said, "for I have no one to put me into the pool when the water bubbles up. Someone else always gets there ahead of me."

Jesus told him, "Stand up, pick up your mat, and walk!"

Instantly, the man was healed! He rolled up his sleeping mat and began walking! (John 5:6–9)

Confess

Lord, I confess that I've shifted blame, made excuses, and relied on rationalization. Today I renounce the voice of rationalization, and I'm set free from the cords and habits that bound me.

Affirm

I am bold and courageous enough to face God's truth about me, my behavior, and my situation. When I accept this truth, I am set free. I don't need to blame or make excuses. I am free from the lame use of rationalization. I own my responsibility and trust God to change me.

Repeat "I renounce rationalization and accept responsibility" three times. Each time you read it, add special emphasis to the bolded word or words.

I renounce rationalization and accept responsibility.

I renounce **rationalization** and accept responsibility.

I renounce rationalization and **accept responsibility**.

Extra Memory Challenge

> My little children, I am writing this to you so that you may not sin; but if any one does sin, we have an advocate with the Father, Jesus Christ the righteous; and he is the expiation for our sins, and not for ours only but also for the sins of the whole world. (1 John 2:1–2 RSV)

Explore

1. How have you overcome using rationalization to excuse your poor behavior?
2. Do you see excuse-making and blame-shifting encroaching on your integrity? Do you think others do? Why or why not?
3. If you do, what will you do about it?
4. How have you seen rationalization and blame-shifting at work in the lives of others?

Journal

Week 2

Day 12

TODAY'S TRUTH: I AM FREE FROM THE VOICE OF SHAME

"Come now, and let us reason together," says the LORD.
"Though your sins are like scarlet,
they shall be as white as snow;
though they are red like crimson,
they shall be as wool."
Isaiah 1:18 NKJV

As we continue to untie the cords of false voices, we now recognize the most common deceptive voice: shame. Shame,
unlike guilt, is rooted in how we believe we appear to others. While
we may carry both guilt (a feeling of responsibility or remorse) and
shame for an action, the two emotions are different. *Guilt is how
we feel about doing something we shouldn't have done or not doing
something we should have done. Shame is how we feel about ourselves.*

Many men battle with shame, although they may not realize it:

- Men who carry embarrassment from past affairs, addictions, incarcerations, or sexual or violent behaviors carry
  shame.
- Men who feel embarrassed or humiliated by body image
  carry shame.
- Men who carry embarrassment from their perceived economic status carry shame.
- Men who carry humiliation because they believe they're
  not smart enough or educated enough carry shame.
- Men who experience insecurity because they think they're
  not good enough carry shame.

Satan is called the accuser of Christians, and he accuses us before God night and day (Revelation 12:10). His words are worthless, though, because Jesus's sacrifice declares us perfect. Despite this reality, we ignore Jesus's death and persist in carrying shame, regret, and worthlessness. We wrap ourselves in these false emotions like a security blanket and claim Satan's perverted identity: ruined, unwanted, unforgiven, and irreparably flawed.

Sadly the truth about shame is simple. We long to be valued, and God placed inestimable value on us when his Son, Jesus, died for us. He has given us what we desire most, *yet we refuse the gift.*

The verse at the beginning of this devotion stresses the importance of reasoning. Shame is an emotion—it is not the truth. Because the Bible, God's love letter to us, contains the truth about who we are and how God sees us, it's important to dig into Scripture and daily affirm the truth about who we are in Christ.

No one can earn God's favor by doing good works. We don't come into the family of God because we impress him or live a "good enough" life. God has chosen to honor us as his children. Imagine the insult of returning his precious gift by rejecting our identity and wrapping ourselves in rags of shame.

The answer to shame is accepting God's abundant love for us: "For God so loved the world that he gave his one and only Son, that whoever believes in him shall not perish but have eternal life" (John 3:16 NIV).

Today we shut the mouth of shame.

Declare

I am free from shame and condemnation. I do not listen to voices that tell me I'm worthless, not good enough, or unforgiveable. I claim a fulfilled, joyful, and prosperous life.

Meditate, Believe, Accept

Jesus removes my shame, and now I have a double portion of joy and prosperity.

> Instead of shame and dishonor, you shall have a double portion of prosperity and everlasting joy. (Isaiah 61:7 TLB)

My face is radiant, and I shine forth God's love. I do not walk in shame.

> Those who look to him are radiant; their faces are never covered with shame. (Psalm 34:5 NIV)

I trust in God, and he keeps me from shame.

> Everyone who believes in him will not be put to shame. (Romans 10:11 ESV)

My life is new in Christ, and I am not condemned.

> There is therefore now no condemnation for those who are in Christ Jesus. (Romans 8:1 ESV)

Confess

Lord, I confess that I've been oppressed at times by voices of shame and condemnation. But you paid the price for my sin, and I am free from the shame and guilt that my sin created. I receive your grace.

Affirm

I am not ashamed. I am God's son, and I do not listen to voices that make me feel shame or condemnation. I know who I am in Christ. I walk in joy and radiance, and I am free from shame.

Repeat "I release shame" three times. Each time you read it, add special emphasis to the bolded word.

I release shame.

I **release** shame.

I release **shame**.

Extra Memory Challenge

> There is therefore now no condemnation for those who are in Christ Jesus. (Romans 8:1 ESV)

Explore

1. Name a time when the Enemy tried to shame you. How did you feel and act?
2. What happened to your confidence?
3. How can you respond the next time you hear the whispers of the Enemy trying to make you feel small, shameful, or unworthy?

Journal

Week 2

Day 13

Today's Truth: I Am Free from the Voice of Doom

I have told you these things,
so that in me you may have peace.
In this world you will have trouble.
But take heart! I have overcome the world.
John 16:33 NIV

A mysterious voice whispers to me in quiet moments. It ominously speaks to me of frightening things to come, sending shivers of fear rushing through me as I envision possibilities of bad news. My spirit feels heavy as I wait—sometimes for hours, sometimes for days. I do not know what word will come, but I'm expecting tragedy—a death, an accident, a diagnosis.

Days pass.

Nothing.

I have wasted my emotions, my time, and my vision listening to the voice of doom.

Like me, you have probably experienced strong feelings of fear and anxiety or a sense of foreboding about the future. Most of us have. Anxiety often builds to a sense of impending doom as we wait for something horrible to happen and envision possible scenarios.

At other times, the voice of doom comes suddenly and for no apparent reason. It attacks from out of nowhere and drags us into a mental wrestling match for hope, faith, and vision. It often defeats us with lies that we cannot trust God, others, or life—that once again we will be hurt and crushed.

Fear and anxiety can drag us into a downward spiral of despair and doom. *Panic disorder* is medically defined as a "fear of impending doom," but many people experience this feeling on a scale considered less than a disorder. Still, panic can wash over us and can paralyze our souls in an instant.

This can be due to everyday circumstances:

- Our company is in financial trouble, and we might lose our job.
- Our child has the flu—how serious could it become?
- The car is making strange noises, and we don't have the money for another repair.
- They've found an irregularity, and the doctor suggests a biopsy.

We've all felt emotions that trigger a downward spiral in our thinking, such as:

- A sudden sensation of impending doom, destruction, despair, and gloom
- Feeling like something tragic is going to happen
- An irrational, overwhelming feeling that we or someone we love is going to die
- A strong feeling of helplessness and sadness
- A horrible feeling of doom accompanied by a panic attack
- A strong feeling of impending doom that triggers a fight-flight-freeze response

When I was a kid, I loved watching scary movies with my friends. (I honestly don't recommend watching them today.) Something was exhilarating about being afraid, yet the scenes of horror also secretly frightened me, unless I'd already seen the movie. Once I knew the ending, my fear evaporated.

Fear evaporates when we understand that, as believers, we're promised a secure and final conclusion. We know how the story ends, and we win. Instead of focusing on impending doom, why not focus on impending joy and promised protection?

Today we untie the deadly cord of the voice of doom, and we meditate instead on positive outcomes secured by God's promises. No more scenarios of negative, gloomy futures. God has promised his presence will always be with us. Therefore, we can confidently say, "I will not fear any impending doom."[1]

Declare

The assurance of a secure and certain positive outcome allows me to have peace in the present. Because I *know* who holds, directs, and owns the future, I will not fear unknown circumstances. I trust in the One who holds all things in his hands. Today I rest in the safety of the shadow of the Almighty (Psalm 91:1). Under his wings, I find my safe and strong refuge, my peaceful resting place; therefore, I declare that I am secure in Christ.

Meditate, Believe, Accept

I will not fear the voice of doom, for my trust is in God. He will keep me safe.

> This I declare about the LORD: He alone is my refuge,
> my place of safety; he is my God, and I trust him.
> (Psalm 91:2)

God rescues me when I face trouble. He surrounds me with his protection. Nothing can harm me.

> For he will rescue you from every trap and protect you
> from deadly disease. He will cover you with his feath-
> ers. He will shelter you with his wings. His faithful
> promises are your armor and protection. (Psalm 91:3–4)

---

[1] If feelings of impending doom persist or anxiety becomes uncontrollable (or if you have received a diagnosis of panic disorder or anxiety disorder), consult a medical doctor.

I have a positive and secure outcome, and everything I face will work for my good.

> And we know that God causes everything to work together for the good of those who love God and are called according to his purpose for them. (Romans 8:28)

I will not have anxiety over tomorrow. I will live in the present and give my fears to God.

> Therefore do not worry about tomorrow, for tomorrow will worry about itself. Each day has enough trouble of its own. (Matthew 6:34 NIV)

Confess

Lord, I confess that I sometimes dread the future. I hear the voice of doom predicting a negative outcome for me, and I give way to fear and anxiety. But today I claim victory over this irrational voice. Your Word tells me I am safe in you, and you have a glorious life planned for me. I place my trust in you. "We confidently and joyfully look forward to actually becoming all that God has had in mind for us to be" (Romans 5:2 TLB).

Affirm

I confidently and joyfully look forward to my future. With eager expectation I face each day with hope and confidence. I remove this deadly cord of dread and doom from my mind, and I stand free in faith and hope, believing God for great things. "And this hope will never disappoint us, because God has poured out his love to fill our hearts" (Romans 5:5 NCV).

Repeat "I release dread and doom" three times. Each time you read it, add special emphasis to the bolded word or words.

I release dread and doom.

I **release** dread and doom.

I release **dread and doom.**

Explore

1. Have there been times when you've heard the voice of impending doom? How did you respond?
2. Do you recognize that this voice comes from anxiety, fear, or depression? How can you find peace in God when this occurs?
3. When thoughts come to you, stop and identify the source of the thought or impression. Sometimes this is Satan's lying voice attempting to steal your joy. How can you tear down the lie and replace it with God's truth?

Journal

Week 2

Day 14

TODAY'S TRUTH: I AM FREE FROM THE VOICE OF VICTIMIZATION

I will walk about in freedom,
for I have sought out your precepts.
Psalm 119:45 NIV

He was a victim—not in reality, but in his mind. He saw himself as the target of mistreatment, continual unfairness, and intentional persecution.

"Everyone is out to get me," he'd say.

"It's their fault I'm like this."

"I can't help it."

"No one helps me, and everyone hates me."

His excuses went on and on. He refused to accept personal responsibility.

Victims make their unhappiness everyone else's fault. They blame everyone but themselves. They make others responsible for meeting their needs, and they become angry if other people don't respond to their expectations. Victims don't want to shed their victimhood because it's the only way they know how to respond to the world. They'd rather point a finger, shift the blame, and throw pity parties. They believe life is beyond their control, and other people are responsible for making their world fair and ensuring they get what they want.

If this sounds like the way you respond to the world, you may have acquired a victim mentality. Go ahead and consider how you respond to difficulties, how you handle criticism, and whether or not you shoulder personal responsibility for your actions. We can all learn from taking inventory—I know that I have, and I will continue to.

A victim mindset forms from self-pity mixed with manipulation and control. Victims seek out suffering and calamity to meet their psychological needs. They believe the worst about the world, and in so doing, they create a negative reality in their lives, with all the accompanying drama and chaos.

"I know nothing good is ever going to happen to me."

"If someone's gonna lose, it's gonna be me."

They think like losers, draw other losers for friends, and wallow in the identity of the "poor me" life. The victim mindset equals a victim identity. Their mindset determines who they think they are, how they show up in the world, and how they navigate their relationships, careers, and life choices.

Playing the victim card is disempowering. It may meet my need for a while with attention, care, friends, and support, but those relationships soon fall away, friends give me tough love, and opportunities for true love and success pass by me. In the long run, a victim mentality cannot support a positive future. If I believe I am a victim, I will speak like a victim, act like a victim, and receive a victim's reward—a small, meager life.

This doesn't mean we weren't victimized or wounded in life, but *we can choose how our wounds will affect us.* Will we choose pity and victimization and refuse to move forward, or will we rise from the ashes and become stronger, braver, and more determined to succeed than ever before?

To gain freedom from a victim mindset, we must discover that playing mistreated, unfortunate men who always receive the short end of the stick does not meet our needs. A victim mindset controls us when we:

- Refuse to take responsibility for our choices
- Become dependent upon the care and attention of others

- Believe we have the right to complain and be unhappy—after all, "I'm a victim"
- Create drama to remain the center of attention

To be free from a victim mentality, we must:

- Recognize our "victim moments"
- Decide what we need to create a better future—and choose it
- Take responsibility and act; own up to our mistakes and failures
- Pay attention to resistant thoughts, which tell us where we are bound to past behaviors and when we need to press on

To one degree or another, we must all resist a victim mentality and fight the desire to throw up our hands and exclaim that life is unfair. A victim mentality typically binds us in ever-tighter cords and chokes the life from us.

Today we untie the cords of victimization. We renounce playing the "poor me" victim role, and we repent of living disempowered and afraid. Instead, we shift our perspective and look through the lens of God's Word. We see ourselves strong, capable, and whole. Today we choose to embrace life, make decisions, be responsible, and shed the "poor me" mindset and identity in Jesus's name.

Declare

I am not a victim. I am redeemed by Christ Jesus and empowered by the Holy Spirit. I am in control of my happiness. I stand in his strength and choose to shed my victim mentality. I no longer listen to the voice of victimization.

Meditate, Believe, Accept

I am not a victim. I overcome. God empowers me.

> God is within [him], [he] will not fall; God will help [him] at break of day. (Psalm 46:5 NIV)

I am strong. I take ownership of my life. God is my strength.

> [He] is clothed with strength and dignity, and [he] laughs without fear of the future. (Proverbs 31:25)

I am capable, energetic, and resourceful. God is with me.

> [He] is energetic and strong, a hard worker. (Proverbs 31:17)

I have the power to choose my path. Life is not beyond my control.

> Let us choose for ourselves what is right; let us know among ourselves what is good. (Job 34:4 NASB)

I can take the risk to live a rich and full life. God will always rescue me.

> Even when I walk through the darkest valley, I will not be afraid, for you are close beside me. Your rod and your staff protect and comfort me. (Psalm 23:4)

Confess

Lord, I confess there are times when I act like a victim. I feel defeated, persecuted, and afraid to face myself. I have blamed others, pointed the finger, and refused to reject the false limitations I have placed on my life with my victim mindset. Forgive me for not living in the power of your Holy Spirit and rising out of the ashes. Today I untie the cords of victimization. I am ready to soar!

Affirm

I am not a victim. God's Holy Spirit empowers me, and I can do all things through Christ who is my strength. I am free. I am brave. I am bold.

Repeat "I am not a victim" three times. Each time you read it, add special emphasis to the bolded word.

I am not a victim.

I am **not** a victim.

I am not a **victim**.

Explore

1. In what ways do you relate to today's lesson?
2. If you play the victim card, what emotional needs might you be trying to fill?
3. What would be a better way to have your needs met?

Journal

Free Thinking

At some time or other, we've all played the victim card. Perhaps this has become your default way of interacting with others and deflecting responsibility. Spend focused time in prayer this week asking the Holy Spirit to show you when you're triggered to think like a victim rather than looking to God to meet your needs and taking responsibility for your life and decisions.

You've made it through the second week. Hopefully, you're beginning to feel a shift in your spirit and in the way you see yourself.

Remember that you have the power to choose. Life is not beyond your control. God has given you everything you need to do all he has purposed for you to do. Believing and acting on this blood-bought promise provides you with the courage to face your past and press toward the blessed life God offers.

Journal

CHAPTER 5

CORDS OF CONTROL

Never be afraid to trust an unknown future
to a known God.
—Corrie ten Boom

Challenge Week 3

Weekly Reading: Control

I have been crucified with Christ and I no longer live,
but Christ lives in me. The life I now live in the body,
I live by faith in the Son of God, who loved me
and gave himself for me.
Galatians 2:20 NIV

By now I pray you've been experiencing freedom, relief, and transformation in your Freedom Challenge. I hope we've built enough trust to move into the next section by looking at an important question: are you a control freak?

Take a moment and honestly think about that question. Be brave.

Let me ask another way. In your work life, relationships, or parenting, do you need to be in charge? Do you give more advice than people ask for? Do you try to fix or monitor the lives of those around you? Have you discovered that controlling them is not only exhausting but also an illusion? You have no control—and it's not your job.

Ouch.

Wait, what? you may be thinking. *But I'm only trying to help.*

Well, most people don't like to be controlled. Think about it: do *you* like others to control *your* life? At best, most people tolerate controlling behaviors, but more often, they resent these efforts. And to be completely honest, efforts to control others arise out of fear and not from love for others.

God loves us so much that he gives us freedom—freedom to choose, to make mistakes, and to decide our path and how we will live. Love, by its nature, releases control and gives freedom and independence.

Fear and anxiety, on the other hand, cause us to grip tightly. We clutch the things we adore close to our chest, believing that in so doing, we will keep danger at bay. Somewhere in the recesses of our minds, fear says, "If I let go, something bad will happen."

This week we will strengthen our trust in God to keep his ever-loving and watchful eye on all we love. As our trust for God increases, we surrender control and examine the motives behind our attempts at power and control as we choose a new path.

I pray this special blessing over you this week: *be blessed as you learn to let go.*

Week 3

Day 15

Today's Truth: I Surrender to God's Control

For whoever wants to save their life will lose it,
but whoever loses their life for me will save it.
Luke 9:24 NIV

This week God calls us to a fresh surrender—an abandonment of all we cling to for false and temporal support. This step of release is critical to deal with the heart of control. You see, the Bible does not ask for us to make a casual commitment to Christ or only to spend a season surrendering to him. Instead, God's Word teaches something far more radical—death to self.

Sound horrible?

It would be if that were all there was to the equation. In Christ Jesus, however, death to self means much more—a resurrection. This does not mean a resurrection of the sinful, fleshly part of us—although that part of us does try to climb off the altar. Instead, it means a resurrection of our spirit-self who is alive and in perfect harmony with God.

Dying to ourselves means we give God his rightful place on the throne of our hearts, that we release control and allow him to call the shots in our lives. We recognize that we're free from sin's power and can make choices that please God. If we walk in the Spirit and not after the flesh, remembering that we have died to sin and no longer live under its control, we will not succumb to the sinful cravings, desires, and demands of our unsubmitted, carnal nature. As a result, true freedom comes. But we do more than surrender the things we choose to God—freedom comes when we die to ourselves and live for Christ.

God created us as triune beings: body, soul, and spirit. The soul is the center of our emotions, thoughts, values, and worldviews (Matthew 12:34–35). The spirit is the eternal part of us created with the ability to communicate with God. For those who do not know Jesus personally as their Savior, the spirit is "dead" (Ephesians 2:1). When we accept Christ as Savior, our spirit comes alive to God. Alive in God, we move from the driver's seat and relinquish control of our lives to God and his flawless care. We submit to God's leading with joy, for we know his ways are always best. Surrender is an ongoing daily process that requires yielding our will and embracing the truth of God's Word for our lives.

This week you'll abandon all claims on your life to the righteous, holy God who created you. Surrendering one part of yourself requires surrendering all parts: body, soul, and spirit.

Declare

I freely and fully surrender my will and my ways to God and his control in my life. I lay down my need to control and relinquish the reins of my life to God. I place my life and all that concerns me in his hands. I am alive to Christ and dead to the snares, traps, and temptations of this world. The sins of this world cannot hold me.

Meditate, Believe, Accept

I surrender to Jesus daily. I am free and fully alive because I trust my life to him.

> Then he [Jesus] said to them all: "Whoever wants to be my disciple must deny themselves and take up their cross daily and follow me. For whoever wants to save their life will lose it, but whoever loses their life for me will save it." (Luke 9:23–24 NIV)

I abandon myself to Christ and consider myself dead to the control of the flesh (my will and my ways of doing things). I am free from sin's domination.

> We know that our old life, our old sinful self, was nailed to the cross with Christ. And so the power of sin that held us was destroyed. Sin is no longer our boss. When a man is dead, he is free from the power of sin. (Romans 6:6–7 NLV)

I am alive in Christ and dead to the old things of this world.

> And since your old sin-loving nature "died" with Christ, we know that you will share his new life. (Romans 6:8 TLB)

> So look upon your old sin nature as dead and unresponsive to sin, and instead be alive to God, alert to him, through Jesus Christ our Lord. (Romans 6:11 TLB)

> I have been put up on the cross to die with Christ. I no longer live. Christ lives in me. The life I now live in this body, I live by putting my trust in the Son of God. He was the One Who loved me and gave Himself for me. (Galatians 2:20 NLV)

I have life and peace because my mind is submitted to Christ.

> The mind governed by the flesh is death, but the mind governed by the Spirit is life and peace. The mind governed by the flesh is hostile to God; it does not submit to God's law, nor can it do so. (Romans 8:6–7 NIV)

I live by the Spirit of God, and I don't gratify the sinful nature.

> So I say, live by the Spirit, and you will not gratify the desires of the sinful nature. For the sinful nature desires what is contrary to the Spirit, and the Spirit what is contrary to the sinful nature. They are in conflict with each

other, so that you do not do what you want. (Galatians 5:16–17 NIV)

I daily offer myself to God. I am a living sacrifice and belong to Christ.

Therefore, I urge you, brothers and sisters, in view of God's mercy, to offer your bodies as a living sacrifice, holy and pleasing to God. (Romans 12:1 NIV)

You were bought at a price. Therefore honor God with your bodies. (1 Corinthians 6:20 NIV)

Confess

Lord, I confess that I often compete with you for the throne of my life. I've taken the reins of my own destiny and have chosen my own path. But today I relinquish control. I die to my selfish desires and live as a new creation. I am free from sin's control and am alive in Christ.

Affirm

I'm alive because I am dead—dead to the old things of this world. The sins, struggles, and bondage that worked against me in the past have no hold on me today. I am free from them. I fully surrender the control of my life to Christ, and as a result, I have peace of mind. I trust you to lead me, bless me, and fill my life. I surrender to you, God, and I find my life in you—my purpose, my destiny, and my fulfillment.

Repeat "I surrender to God" three times. Each time you read it, add special emphasis to the bolded word.

I surrender to God.

I **surrender** to God.

I surrender to **God**.

Extra Memory Challenge

> I have been put up on the cross to die with Christ. I no longer live. Christ lives in me. The life I now live in this body, I live by putting my trust in the Son of God. He was the One Who loved me and gave Himself for me. (Galatians 2:20 NLV)

Explore

1. What does it mean to die to my will and my ways?
2. Jesus said it's when I lose my life that I truly save it. What do you think he meant?
3. Our flesh—our old selfish mindset, stubborn will, and prideful ways—doesn't submit to God. We must consider it dead. How have you done that?
4. How does being alive in Christ change your life? Your peace of mind? The way you take control?

Journal

Week 3

Day 16

TODAY'S TRUTH: I TRUST GOD

Those who know your name trust in you,
for you, LORD, have never forsaken those who seek you.
Psalm 9:10 NIV

Many of us men were told to "stay in control, don't show fear, be careful not to express emotions." We learned that the measure of a man was equal to his ability to control his world and the people in it. When we went through painful experiences, we believed we were losing control, so we gripped even tighter. We may have told ourselves, "I could lose everything if I don't maintain control of my life," or "It's my job," or perhaps, "I can't trust anyone anymore." We might think humanity has let us down. Our expectations weren't met, and our hearts have hardened with the hurt. Even God seems to have failed us.

We unconsciously believe that to secure our well-being, we must stay in control, or perhaps we think, "I need to help God out." God, however, calls us to surrender our lives fully to him—to relinquish control.

That creates a dilemma: How can we release the reins of control to someone unless we trust him? How can we trust him unless we know him?

This week is an invitation to know God better—to learn that he is faithful and worthy of our trust. No matter what the circumstances in our lives have been, God has never failed, never let us down, and never made a mistake. He is altogether trustworthy.

Because he knows what is best for us, God wants us to relinquish control of our lives to him. He loves us and is working in our lives to do more than we can hope, think, or imagine.

God never expects us to figure life out on our own. He has already orchestrated the details of our future to work for our good, no matter what lies ahead. He does not promise Christians an easy, trouble-free life. But he *does* promise that our trials are not without purpose and that he is with us in our pain, working evil for our good.

Proverbs 3:5–6 (ESV) tells us to "Trust in the LORD with all your heart, and do not lean on your own understanding." Trusting with all our heart means that we align our emotions, minds, souls, and wills with God's Word. We make the conscious choice not to "lean on" or focus on our own understanding.

We find power when we place our trust in God and take our eyes off our circumstances. We can stop striving, manipulating, planning, strategizing, and worrying. No matter our circumstances, we can be sure that God has walked the pathway before us, working for our best in ways we cannot discern and that influence the course of history. Hold on to the truth of who God is, his love for you, and his plans for your future. "In all your ways acknowledge Him, and He will make your paths straight" (Proverbs 3:6 BSB).

Declare

I place my trust in God. Because I know him, I trust his decisions for my life. God leads me in straight paths; the places he guides me are good and pleasant places. I let go of the things I try to control, and instead, I put my trust in him. He is trustworthy and will never fail me. I am confident, peaceful, and victorious when I place my trust in God.

Meditate, Believe, Accept

I stand firm because I trust in the Lord. I will not fall.

> Some trust in chariots and some in horses, but we trust in the name of the LORD our God. They are brought

to their knees and fall, but we rise up and stand firm.
(Psalm 20:7–8 NIV)

I am filled with joy, peace, and hope because I trust in the Lord.

> May the God of hope fill you with all joy and peace as
> you trust in him, so that you may overflow with hope
> by the power of the Holy Spirit. (Romans 15:13 NIV)

I trust in God, and therefore I am free from control. My times are in his hands.

> I trust in you, LORD; I say, "You are my God." My
> times are in your hands. (Psalm 31:14–15 NIV)

I am delivered from fear of the future and fear of man because I trust in God.

> I trust in God I will not be afraid. What can people do
> to me? (Psalm 56:11 NCV)

> Look! God is my Savior. I am confident and unafraid,
> because the LORD is my strength and my song. He is my
> Savior. (Isaiah 12:2 GW)

I take refuge in God; my heart is not troubled. God hears my heart's cry.

> Trust in him at all times, O people; pour out your heart
> before him; God is a refuge for us. (Psalm 62:8 ESV)
> Don't let your hearts be troubled. Trust in God,
> and trust also in me [Jesus]. (John 14:1)

> The LORD is good, a refuge in times of trouble. He cares
> for those who trust in him. (Nahum 1:7 NIV)

The paths I walk are firm and straight. I lean on God and trust him in all I do.

Trust in the LORD with all your heart, and do not lean on your own understanding. In all your ways acknowledge him, and he will make straight your paths. (Proverbs 3:5–6 ESV)

I'm at rest because I trust in God and not in man; he alone never fails me.

Stop trusting in mere humans, who have but a breath in their nostrils. Why hold them in esteem? (Isaiah 2:22 NIV)

Be still before the LORD and wait patiently for him; do not fret when people succeed in their ways, when they carry out their wicked schemes. (Psalm 37:7 NIV)

It is better to take refuge in the LORD than to trust in people. (Psalm 118:8)

Confess

Lord, trusting you is sometimes difficult. I often take the reins of control and behave as if I can do a better job than you at managing my world. I fail to lean on you and fully trust you in all I do, and then I find myself frustrated and exhausted. Today I renounce self-trust and reliance, and I choose to trust in you.

Affirm

I trust in the Lord with all my heart. I do not lean on my strength, might, or ability. Because I know God by name, I trust in him, and he delivers me from all harm. He guides my life and satisfies me with every good thing. I am free from the fear of man. I am free from fear. I trust in God.

Repeat "I trust God" three times. Each time you read it, add special emphasis to the bolded word.

I trust God.

I **trust** God.

I trust **God**.

Extra Memory Challenge

> Those who know your name trust in you, for you, LORD, have never forsaken those who seek you. (Psalm 9:10 NIV)

Explore

1. What does it mean to trust the Lord fully?
2. How does surrendering to and trusting in God change the way you live?
3. God's Word tells us not to trust in man but to trust in him. Why do you suppose he says that?
4. Have you surrendered your life to Christ? If so, does that mean you trust him with everything? With what areas do you still struggle?

Journal

Week 3

Day 17

TODAY'S TRUTH: I CAN RELEASE MY BURDENS TO GOD

And who of you by being worried
can add a single hour to his [or her] life?
Matthew 6:27 NASB

When we tightly clutch the reins of control in life, we discover that control comes with worry and anxiety. Too often we try to control other people, their decisions, and their happiness as if we're the happiness police. We take on the responsibility of trying to fix their problems and make everything right. Even when we know we can't be successful in a role that doesn't belong to us, we carry the burden of trying.

Sometimes we attempt to control our circumstances, as well as the outcome of our problems and heartaches. We worry and fret when circumstances seem out of our control, assuming our decisions can provide the solutions to life's pain and hurt.

But we are mistaken.

In reality, we have no control over any of these things. If we're foolish enough to believe we are in control, we soon become weighed down by burdens never meant to be ours. Trying to control people, events, and circumstances makes everyone miserable. This means us, brother. As the above Bible verse states, we can't add a single day to our lives by exerting controlling behavior (but it may shorten our lives!).

Instead of struggling with a load we were never meant to carry, God gives us an amazing invitation: we can open our hands and give him our cares, burdens, and worries, and in return, he allows us to place our hand in his and walk with him. Of course, this is easier said than done. Thankfully, the book of Psalms shows us how to do it.

The Psalms show how to pray honestly. God wants you to share your feelings, anxieties, heartaches, and dreams. Pray with your heart, not with a list. Talk to God conversationally. Claim this verse as your own: "Those who know your name trust in you, for you, LORD, have never forsaken those who seek you" (Psalm 9:10 NIV).

Ask the Holy Spirit to reveal any sin you may be resisting, hiding, or that is influencing your life. You're probably already aware of what this may be, but confess it, repent immediately, and receive God's grace for you to overcome. Then name your burden specifically, and tell God you're choosing to trust him for it. The burden may return, and if it does, don't take it back. Reject it, and immediately give it back to Jesus. Finally, read through the Bible looking for verses on trust and speak them out loud to yourself throughout the day. This helps create new neural pathways in the brain. More importantly, it feeds your soul with the truth of God's Word.

Today we untie the cords of heavy burdens. We turn them over to God and claim his promise that he will lift our burdens and bear them for us.

Declare

I am free from false burdens and cares. I trust in God to carry any load that concerns me. When cares, worries, and troubles overtake me, I bring them to Jesus in prayer, and he is faithful to lift those burdens off my shoulders. I do not need to control my circumstances, and I cannot improve my life by trying to carry worry, cares, and burdens. I live by faith and trust in God. He alone can carry my problems.

Meditate, Believe, Accept

I cast my cares on the Lord, and I am carried and sustained. He will not let me fall.

Cast your cares on the LORD and he will sustain you; he will never let the righteous be shaken. (Psalm 55:22 NIV)

Cast all your anxiety on him because he cares for you. (1 Peter 5:7 NIV)

My mind has true peace because I depend on and trust in God.

You, LORD, give true peace to those who depend on you, because they trust in you. So, trust the LORD always, because he is our Rock forever. (Isaiah 26:3–4 NCV)

I come to Jesus and find rest for my soul. Instead of anxiety, I have joy.

When anxiety was great within me, your consolation brought me joy. (Psalm 94:19 NIV)

Are you having a real struggle? Come to me! Are you carrying a big load on your back? Come to me—I'll give you a rest! Pick up my yoke and put it on; take lessons from me! My heart is gentle, not arrogant. You'll find the rest you deeply need. My yoke is easy to wear, my load is easy to bear. (Matthew 11:28–30 NTE)

I live in miraculous peace, and I am anxious for nothing. God guards my heart and mind in a way the world can't understand.

The Lord is near. Never worry about anything. But in every situation let God know what you need in prayers and requests while giving thanks. Then God's peace, which goes beyond anything we can imagine, will guard your thoughts and emotions through Christ Jesus (Philippians 4:5–7 GW).

God strengthens my heart daily. Every morning I receive fresh compassion.

The Lord deserves praise! Day after day he carries our burden, the God who delivers us (Psalm 68:19 NET).

Because of the LORD's great love we are not consumed, for his compassions never fail. They are new
every morning; great is your faithfulness (Lamentations
3:22–23 NIV).

Confess

Lord, I confess that cares and worries sometime control my
mind. Rather than give them to you, I often carry them. When I
hold on to these burdens, I lose peace of mind and revert to trying
to control these things myself. Today I surrender my cares, worries,
and false burdens to you. I am free from those unnecessary troubles
in Jesus's name.

Affirm

God, you are the God of all comfort and peace. You have invited me to surrender my burdens and earthly cares to you and
receive your supernatural peace instead. Today I give you my burdens. I release my worry. I can't change one thing by holding on
to my troubles. You are faithful to carry all my concerns, and I am
free—my soul is at rest. My mind is confidently focused, I have
incredible joy, and I possess a peace that the world cannot explain.

Repeat "I surrender my burdens" three times. Each time you
read it, add special emphasis to the bolded word or words.

I surrender my burdens.

I **surrender** my burdens.

I surrender **my burdens**.

Extra Memory Challenge

Praise be to **the Lord, to God our Savior, who** daily
bears our burdens. (Psalm 68:19 NIV, emphasis added)

Explore

1. How have the burdens of this life weighed you down?
2. Can you identify the areas in which you have reverted to control instead of trusting in God?
3. What does it mean to you to have peace that "transcends all understanding"?
4. We often give our cares to God, only to take them back again. Can you name a time when you did that? Are you doing that now? Explain.

Journal

Week 3

Day 18

Today's Truth: I Release My Efforts to Control Others

For the Spirit God gave us does not make us timid,
but gives us power, love and self-discipline.
2 Timothy 1:7 NIV

Here's a news flash for control freaks: the ability to control people and circumstances is an illusion. We can't control our circumstances any more than we can control the weather. And as much as we try, we can't control people either, nor should we try to do so. (I can hear some of you arguing with me here.)

The truth is, we're not responsible for other people's choices or the consequences of their decisions, beliefs, political opinions, or lifestyles. We like to think we are. (After all, we're right, aren't we?)

We must release pride that says we should be the boss. Who are we trying to kid? God loves the people we love far more than we could ever imagine. He knows the past, present, and future. He is orchestrating history. He holds their future in his hands, and he can guard and guide them far better than we ever could.

Surrendering control of others is a battle. We want things our way. We can envision how life should be and how people should act, and we feel it's our job to ensure the world runs like a well-oiled machine. We want to make the rules.

Psalm 46:10 (GW) tells us, "Let go of your concerns! Then you will know that I am God. I rule the nations. I rule the earth." God wants us to release our grip on people. He wants us to focus on our spiritual walk and not kick the Holy Spirit to the curb while we take over his job.

The more people act out in ways that irritate us or conflict with our view of how the world should be, the greater our desire to control them. Pastor Rick Warren reminds us that praying the last lines of the "Serenity Prayer" provides a solution to our compulsions to control our circumstances and others:

Living one day at a time,
Enjoying one moment at a time,
Accepting hardship as a pathway to peace,
Taking, as Jesus did,
This sinful world as it is,
Not as I would have it,
Trusting that You will make all things right,
If I surrender to Your will,
So that I may be reasonably happy in this life,
And supremely happy with You forever in the next.
Amen.[8]

So sit back and relax. Let go of the reins of control. Be free from trying to manipulate others' behavior and thinking. Confess the fear and pride that lie beneath your controlling behavior, grip your heart, and choke emotional and spiritual life from you. Jesus is the Master. We are not.

Repeat these words with me: God is God, and I am not!

Declare

God is in control. I trust him. Therefore, I declare that I am free from the habit of trying to exert control over others. I no longer take responsibility for others' actions, decisions, behaviors, and attitudes. I am free to love others without controlling their lives. I release the reins of control, and I trust that God is powerfully at work in the lives of others. I will pray and trust God. Today I choose freedom from controlling others.

Meditate, Believe, Accept

I can release control because people answer to God, not to me.

> They are God's servants, not yours. They are responsible
> to him, not to you. Let him tell them whether they are
> right or wrong. And God is able to make them do as
> they should. (Romans 14:4 TLB)

I can keep my tongue from speaking bad things and hold my opinions to myself.

> If a person thinks he religious, but does not keep his
> tongue from speaking bad things, he is fooling himself.
> His religion is worth nothing. (James 1:26 NLV)

Trying to control others is carnal, fleshly behavior—a form of rebellion. It's saying, "I don't want to do things their way. I want everything my way!"

Therefore:

I submit to God, trusting that he is in control, and his power will change what needs to be changed.

> For rebellion is as the sin of divination, and presump-
> tion is as iniquity and idolatry. (1 Samuel 15:23 ESV)

I walk in the Spirit and not after the will of evil human nature.

> I advise you to obey only the Holy Spirit's instructions.
> He will tell you where to go and what to do, and then
> you won't always be doing the wrong things your evil
> nature wants you to. For we naturally love to do evil
> things that are just the opposite from the things that the
> Holy Spirit tells us to do; and the good things we want
> to do when the Spirit has his way with us are just the
> opposite of our natural desires. These two forces within

us are constantly fighting each other to win control over us, and our wishes are never free from their pressures. (Galatians 5:16–21 TLB)

Confess

Lord, I humble myself before you and take an honest look at myself. I realize that I interfere with your work in others' lives when I try to take control and responsibility for the behaviors and choices of the people I love. When I become a controller, I am choosing a false sense of security and am not entirely placing my trust in you. [Tell the Lord here what is true for you.] Forgive me, Lord. I release control to you.

Affirm

I am free from control. I no longer need to control people and circumstances around me to keep myself safe or to feel secure and empowered. I renounce all forms of control, and I release the people for whom I've tried to assume responsibility. I trust in God. I trust in his ways and judgments. I am free from the habit of controlling others.

Repeat "I am free from controlling behaviors" three times. Each time you read it, add special emphasis to the bolded word or words.

I am free from controlling behaviors.

I **am free** from controlling behaviors**.**

I am free **from controlling behaviors**.

Extra Memory Challenge

They are God's servants, not yours. They are responsible to him, not to you. Let him tell them whether they are right or wrong. And God is able to make them do as they should. (Romans 14:4 TLB)

Explore

1. In what ways does this lesson apply to you?
2. What three things can you do to change the habit of control?

Journal

Week 3

Day 19

TODAY'S TRUTH: I WILL PRACTICE SELF-CONTROL

But the fruit of the Spirit is love, joy, peace, patience,
kindness, goodness, faithfulness, gentleness, self-control.
Galatians 5:22–23 ESV

Now that we've discovered that our human efforts to control are not only useless and vain but also displease God, we may think we're off the hook for our responsibility for trying to take control.

Not so.

There is one form of control we are to use daily: self-control. Our control efforts are not meant to be used to manipulate others. Instead, the Bible teaches us that we are to practice restraint or self-governance.

God's Word calls self-control a fruit of the Spirit. In other words, we need the power of the Holy Spirit to truly produce, cultivate, and grow in self-control.

Self-control occurs when we:

- Refrain from speaking demeaning or critical words
- Control our appetites—sex, food, and other desires
- Exert patience
- Practice self-discipline over habits and negative behavior
- Refrain from angry outbursts and fits of temper
- Control our moods and emotions
- Follow through with commitments, plans, and goals
- Persevere in unpleasant tasks to achieve desired goals
- Choose obedience to God in all circumstances

This list reveals that it's not easy or quick to form the character quality of self-control. God's Spirit must help us cultivate, develop, and practice self-control.

Another way to explain self-control is by using the term *self-leadership*. God calls us to lead ourselves in a manner that is upright and demonstrates integrity. We must not require something of another that we cannot do ourselves.

However, self-control is one of the hardest aspects of character to master. We make resolutions and fail to keep them. We ask friends to hold us accountable, but our enthusiasm wanes. Deep inside, we know that desire is not enough. But God has the answer.

Self-control comes as we allow the Holy Spirit to control us. Galatians 5:22–23 (ESV) tells us that the "fruit of the Spirit is love, joy, peace, patience, kindness, goodness, faithfulness, gentleness, self-control." We do not attain self-control through our effort but instead through surrender as we submit our will to God moment by moment.

Whatever tempts us—a mood, a habit, a sinful attitude, or a bad choice—we must say no to ourselves and yes to God.

Today we choose self-control.

Declare

I am filled with the Holy Spirit and submit to his control. As a result of God's power working in me, I gain self-control—the fruit of the Holy Spirit manifested in me. I don't give in to the pull from my flesh, Satan, or others. I choose obedience to Christ and his Word. Today I will use self-control.

Meditate, Believe, Accept

I possess qualities that make me effective and productive.

> For this very reason, make every effort to add to your
> faith goodness; and to goodness, knowledge; and to

knowledge, self-control; and to self-control, perseverance; and to perseverance, godliness; and to godliness,
mutual affection; and to mutual affection, love. For if
you possess these qualities in increasing measure, they
will keep you from being ineffective and unproduc-
tive in your knowledge of our Lord Jesus Christ. (2
Peter 1:5–8 NIV)

*The fruit of self-control grows in me, and I crucify sinful passions and
desires.*

But the fruit of the Spirit is love, joy, peace, patience,
kindness, goodness, faithfulness, gentleness, self-control; against such things there is no law. And those who
belong to Christ Jesus have crucified the flesh with its
passions and desires. (Galatians 5:22–24 ESV)

*I am self-controlled and alert, standing firm in my faith. Satan has no
hold on me.*

Be alert and of sober mind. Your enemy the devil prowls
around like a roaring lion looking for someone to devour. Resist him, standing firm in the faith. (1 Peter
5:8–9 NIV)

My spirit is alive and fully awake because I possess self-control.

So then, let us not be like others, who are asleep, but let
us be awake and sober. (1 Thessalonians 5:6 NIV)

*I control my desires as I willingly submit myself to God. Therefore,
Satan has to flee.*

Submit yourselves, then, to God. Resist the devil, and
he will flee from you. Come near to God and he will
come near to you. (James 4:7–8 NIV)

I am self-controlled and live in step with the Holy Spirit.

> Since we live by the Spirit, let us keep in step with the
> Spirit. (Galatians 5:25 NIV)

Confess

Lord, it can be difficult to exercise self-control. Sometimes I become weary and frustrated, and I give in to the demands of my human nature. But you have provided a way for me to walk in the Spirit and not make excuses for my sinful nature. So today I renounce my selfish and unrestrained ways, and I choose a life of self-control fueled and filled by your Holy Spirit.

Affirm

God's Spirit lives in me. God has given me the ability to cultivate and exercise self-control, which is a fruit of his Holy Spirit. I am filled with perseverance, determination, and godly restraint. I walk in the power of God's Holy Spirit, to whom I submit. I can manage and control myself in a way that is pleasing to God and productive and effective for others and me. I am an overcomer, a victorious warrior. Satan's snares of chaotic living do not work on me because I possess self-control.

Repeat "I possess self-control" three times. Each time you read it, add special emphasis to the bolded word.

I possess self-control.

I **possess** self-control.

I possess **self-control**.

Extra Memory Challenge

> But the fruit of the Spirit is love, joy, peace, patience, kindness, goodness, faithfulness, gentleness, self-control; against such things there is no law. And those who belong to Christ Jesus have crucified the flesh with its passions and desires. (Galatians 5:22–24 ESV)

Explore

1. In what areas of your life do you need to do a better job exerting self-control?
2. In what ways can you practice more self-control?
3. As you practice self-control, do you call on the Holy Spirit to empower you? Why or why not? He is there to fill you. Describe this process.
4. In what areas of your life have you done a good job of walking in self-control?

Optional Challenge

This week give yourself a challenge. Declare an area in which you will begin a new level of self-control. Monitor your results.

Journal

Week 3

Day 20

TODAY'S TRUTH: I CAN RELEASE MY PAIN TO GOD

He has sent me [Jesus] to bind up the brokenhearted,
to proclaim freedom for the captives and release
from darkness for the prisoners.
Isaiah 61:1 NIV

Thinking we can control our world is an illusion—and trying to remain in control restricts us. It keeps us emotionally walled off and stoic and prevents people from knowing about our pain. We wishfully believe that guarding our emotions will protect us from being hurt again.

But the truth is the opposite. Only when we release our pain, naming it specifically and surrendering it to God, do we become free from control's trap. When we release control, God protects us from the deep pain and hurt we create when we flail about trying to protect ourselves.

Holding on to wounds is dangerous. Pain from relational hurts, betrayal, injustice, and trauma lingers in our soul like smoldering ashes. The fire may go out, but hot coals glow beneath the rubble, quickly reignited when stirred. In our pain, we lash out at others, ruin relationships, and sabotage our successes.

Increasing bitterness entangles our hearts and chains us like captives to a prison floor. It's time to be set free. Jesus wants to take our pain, hurt, disappointments, and wounds.

As we approach God in prayer and unburden our sorrows, sins, wounds, heartache, and grief by giving those things to him, he fills us with himself—his love, peace, healing, and comfort. We open our hearts and hands and release our sorrows, and God takes our pain and gives us comfort and assurance.

The psalmist understood this process:

> Let all that I am praise the Lord; with my whole heart,
> I will praise his holy name. Let all that I am praise the
> Lord; may I never forget the good things he does for
> me. He forgives all my sins and heals all my diseases. He
> redeems me from death and crowns me with love and
> tender mercies. He fills my life with good things. My
> youth is renewed like the eagle's! (Psalm 103:1–5)

James 4:8 tells us that when we draw near to God, he answers
and draws near to us. On days when your heart hurts, remember
that God knows your every heartache and pain. Lean into him,
and he will draw close to you. Admit it if you feel empty and alone,
and ask him to help pull you from the pit of despair. Release your
painful emotions to him and trade them for the assurance of your
true identity, his faithfulness, and the promise that he works all
things—even the difficult things in your life—for your good.

Declare

I give my pain to God. I release the wounds that have festered
in my heart. I trust God because I know he will not harm me and
is ready to heal me. I open up my hurt to him and allow his healing
power to wash over my soul. I untie the cord of control by releasing
my pain.

Meditate, Believe, Accept

I find healing from all my wounds because the Lord is close to me.

> He heals the brokenhearted and binds up their wounds.
> (Psalm 147:3 NIV)

> The Lord is close to the brokenhearted and saves those
> who are crushed in spirit. (Psalm 34:18 NIV)

I am restored. God turns the ashes of my life into beauty. His comfort heals me.

> [I will] comfort all who mourn and provide for those who grieve in Zion—to bestow on them a crown of beauty instead of ashes, the oil of joy instead of mourning, and a garment of praise instead of a spirit of despair. They will be called oaks of righteousness, a planting of the Lord for the display of his splendor. (Isaiah 61:2–3 NIV)

The Lord turns my sorrow into joy. Gladness overtakes my pain.

> Weeping may stay for the night, but rejoicing comes in the morning. (Psalm 30:5 NIV)

> Those the Lord has rescued will return. They will enter Zion with singing; everlasting joy will crown their heads. Gladness and joy will overtake them, and sorrow and sighing will flee away. (Isaiah 51:11 NIV)

I am strong because of what I have overcome. I do not lose heart.

> Therefore we do not lose heart. Though outwardly we are wasting away, yet inwardly we are being renewed day by day. For our light and momentary troubles are achieving for us an eternal glory that far outweighs them all. (2 Corinthians 4:16–17 NIV)

I am delivered from all my troubles.

> The righteous person may have many troubles, but the Lord delivers him from them all. (Psalm 34:19 NIV)

God understands all my pain; the Lord heals my wounds and restores my soul.

> The Lord God will dry tears from all faces. He will take

away the shame of His people from all the earth. For the Lord has spoken. (Isaiah 25:8 NLV)

Record my misery; list my tears on your scroll—are they not in your record? (Psalm 56:8 NIV)

I can dream again. I am healed, restored, and blessed.

When the Lord brought us back to Jerusalem, it was like a dream! How we laughed, how we sang for joy! Then the other nations said about us, "The Lord did great things for the." Indeed he did great things for us; how happy we were! (Psalm 126:1–3 GNT)

Confess

I have carried my pain for too long. I have become accustomed to holding on to the wounds of life, retaining control instead of surrendering my hurt to you. Today, Lord, I open my hands and release my pain to you. I give you the wounds, hurts, disappointments, and sorrows I have experienced. I renounce harmful coping methods, and I yield my life to you.

Affirm

I'm free from the old hurts of the past. I live healed, restored, and as an overcomer. I receive comfort from Jesus when I am hurting, and his words of life heal me and renew my soul. I trust God's control in my life, and I do not have to cling to false coping skills, such as control, to feel safe. I am free to live, to laugh, and to pursue my dreams.

Repeat "My wounds are healed" three times. Each time you read it, add special emphasis to the bolded word or words.

My wounds are healed.

My **wounds** are healed.

My wounds **are healed**.

Extra Memory Challenge

> Therefore we do not lose heart. Though outwardly we are
> wasting away, yet inwardly we are being renewed day by
> day. For our light and momentary troubles are achiev-
> ing for us an eternal glory that far outweighs them all.
> (2 Corinthians 4:16–17 NIV)

Explore

1. What hurt or wound do you need to surrender to God?
2. In what ways do you use control as a means to protect yourself from further pain?
3. Have you invited Jesus, the God of all comfort, to heal your past pain?
4. How will you dream again now that you are free from control?

Journal

Week 3

FREE THINKING

Be not angry that you cannot make others
as you wish them to be,
since you cannot make yourself as you wish to be.
—Thomas à Kempis, *The Imitation of Christ*

Today, rest and reflect on the commitments you've made this past week. What changes do you want to make for yourself? Take adequate time during this meditation. Release your emotional burdens one by one and place them in God's ever-capable hands. Let go of the people you feel responsible for, trusting them to God's care.

Exhale.

Rest.

Be at peace.

Meditate on the Prayer Below

God, give us grace to accept with serenity
the things that cannot be changed,
Courage to change the things
which should be changed,
and the wisdom to distinguish
the one from the other.
Living one day at a time,
Enjoying one moment at a time,
Accepting hardship as a pathway to peace,
Taking, as Jesus did,
This sinful world as it is,
Not as I would have it,

Trusting that You will make all things right,
If I surrender to Your will,
So that I may be reasonably happy in this life,
And supremely happy with You forever in the next.
Amen.
—Full original "Serenity Prayer" by Reinhold Niebuhr

Journal

CHAPTER 6

CORDS OF UNFORGIVENESS AND ANGER

Challenge Week 4

Weekly Reading: Unforgiveness and Anger

> *Do not judge, and you will not be judged.*
> *Do not condemn, and you will not be condemned.*
> *Forgive, and you will be forgiven.*
> Luke 6:37 NIV

As we continue the Freedom Challenge, we will take a more in-depth look at forgiveness: what it is, what it isn't, and how it works. As we do, we'll discover that when we learn to forgive, we often forget to include forgiving God and ourselves.

I hear you saying, "What? Forgive God!" Perhaps you can't imagine forgiving God. After all, "He is holy and righteous and always right," you may argue.

Of course he is. Always. But that doesn't mean that deep in your heart, somewhere in the secret recesses of your soul, you're not disappointed with God. If you're honest, you may even be angry at him.

Forgiving God means coming to the awareness that you've experienced some—or many—unmet, unfulfilled expectations and that you've held hurt feelings or offenses against God. Did you ever plead for something you desperately wanted God to do? Have you ever placed all your faith in God concerning a promise or a belief, only to have your heart shattered? Did you grow distant from God after that experience? Did your Bible reading and prayer time wane, when once there was passion and pursuit of God through Scripture? These are symptoms of disappointment with God.

Forgiveness means letting go of your anger and disappointment and trusting that God, the just judge, will always do right and that he *did right* for you—no matter the circumstances.

We will also explore the unforgiveness we hold toward ourselves. I can relate to this subject far too well. How about you?

In a particularly difficult season of life, I (Dawn) walked a journey of inner healing. I was angry and ashamed about things that had happened, and I felt disgusted with myself. Like many women who were abused as children, I turned the blame for everything in life on myself. Instead of being angry with my abuser, I was mad at myself. My thoughts centered on self-blame:

- I should have stopped it.
- It was my fault.
- I was a stupid, weak little kid, and now I'm a weakling.
- I don't deserve anything good.

On and on I scolded myself for the abuse *against* me.

Then one day the Lord spoke to my heart: "Dawn, you have to stop hating yourself; you need to forgive yourself. This is not your fault."

I suddenly realized that I had to apply God's Word to my heart. Believing the Bible was true wasn't enough. I had to believe that God's truth was true and powerful for me. I needed to act upon what I knew. God's Word tells us to "Bear with each other and forgive one another if any of you has a grievance against someone. Forgive as the Lord forgave you" (Colossians 3:13 NIV). It was time to forgive the grievances I held toward myself.

Dawn's circumstance isn't unique. Men become abuse victims, too, and experience the same thoughts of self-hatred and despair. Forgiving those who hurt us and against whom we hold grievances is a powerful way to untie cords of bondage that defeat us. Whether the individuals are innocent or guilty is irrelevant. This week and moving forward, we choose to forgive God, others, and ourselves because we choose the most excellent way.

Week 4

Day 21

TODAY'S TRUTH: I TURN FROM SIN AND I AM FORGIVEN

As far as the east is from the west,
so far has he removed our transgressions from us.
Psalm 103:12 NIV

It's time to talk about a biblical word that often gets a bad rap, one we might shy away from using because it can conjure up negative images.

The word is *repent.*

Perhaps you envision a fiery preacher pounding his fist on a rickety wooden pulpit and demanding you walk the sawdust trail of repentance to get right with God.

Okay, maybe not, but the word seems to scare some people right out of the thought of repenting. That's because we often don't understand what repentance is.

First, repentance isn't feeling bad about ourselves or the things we've done. Those feelings can, however, lead us *toward* repentance if they bring us to a sense of conviction for our sins and a deep desire to change. True repentance is a beautiful response that flows naturally from a heart touched by the Holy Spirit. Once hardened and indifferent, a repentant heart expresses deep sorrow and remorse over sin.

But repentance involves more than sorrow—and this is where our freedom begins. Authentic repentance requires change, and change is critical to our freedom. *Repentance* comes from the Greek word *metanoeo,* which means, "to change your mind; to reconsider; to think differently; to turn and go a different way."

When we repent before God, we are declaring much more than we're sorry for what we've done. We pronounce, "I change my mind and go in a different direction. I turn from my old way of thinking. I have reconsidered what I used to believe. My mind has been changed, and I have embraced a new belief."

In true repentance, we tear down old mindsets and put on a new mind—the mind of Christ Jesus. We turn away from old behaviors and attitudes that bound us in defeat, and we claim a renewed mind—pure, sound, and victorious. Our act of repentance now thwarts the tactics that Satan employed to control our minds, thoughts, and behaviors. God's Holy Spirit strengthens us and empowers us to live in the freedom God gives—for once we repent, we are also forgiven.

God's forgiveness is total and complete. According to his Word, when we repent, he removes our transgressions "as far as the east is from the west" (Psalm 103:12 NIV). Even more wonderful news is that God will never reject or deny a repentant heart.

Change your mind today. Turn to God and receive his forgiveness, and the cords of unforgiveness will drop to your feet. You are set free.

Declare

I have a new mindset—one that is strong, sound, and set on God. Because I repent from sin, my heart is purified, and I receive forgiveness. The cords of bondage that once bound and defeated me fall in shreds at my feet. By the power of the Holy Spirit, I step out of old ways and into a new day. My path is sure, my future is bright, and my mind is free. I confess my failures before the Lord. He heals me, forgives me, renews me, and delivers me. I claim this in Jesus's name.

Meditate, Believe, Accept

God loves me, and I am forgiven. He removes my sin far from me.

For as high as heaven is over the earth, so strong is his

love to those who fear him. And as far as sunrise is
from sunset, he has separated us from our sins. (Psalm
103:11–12 MSG)

Then I acknowledged my sin to you and did not cover
up my iniquity. I said, "I will confess my transgressions to the Lord." And you forgave the guilt of my sin.
(Psalm 32:5 NIV)

My sin is wiped out, and my spirit is refreshed.

Repent, then, and turn to God, so that your sins may be
wiped out, that times of refreshing may come from the
Lord. (Acts 3:19 NIV)

I am washed clean like fresh snow. Sin no longer holds me.

If we tell him our sins, he is faithful and we can depend
on Him to forgive us of our sins. He will make our lives
clean from all sin. (1 John 1:9 NIV)

"Come now, and let us reason together," says the Lord.
"Though your sins are like scarlet, they shall be as white
as snow; though they are red like crimson, they shall be
as wool." (Isaiah 1:18 NKJV)

Cleanse me with hyssop, and I will be clean; wash me,
and I will be whiter than snow. (Psalm 51:7 NIV)

I have a new heart and a new spirit.

I will sprinkle clean water on you, and you will be clean;
I will cleanse you from all your impurities and from
all your idols. I will give you a new heart and put a
new spirit in you; I will remove from you your heart of
stone and give you a heart of flesh. (Ezekiel 36:25–26
NIV)

I am accepted and forgiven. God will not reject me.

> The sacrifice God wants is a broken spirit. God, you will
> not reject a heart that is broken and sorry for sin. (Psalm
> 51:17 NCV)

God is merciful to me. He purified me and washed away all my sins.
I am free.

> Have mercy on me, O God, because of your unfailing
> love. Because of your great compassion, blot out the
> stain of my sins. Wash me clean from my guilt. Purify
> me from my sin. (Psalm 51:1–4)

> The Lord says to his people, "I will come to Jerusalem
> to defend you and to save all of you that turn from your
> sins." (Isaiah 59:20 GNT)

I am restored, and God is using my life in powerful ways.

> Because of this, the Lord said, "You must repent of such
> words and thoughts! If you do, I will restore you to the
> privilege of serving me. If you say what is worthwhile
> instead of what is worthless, I will again allow you to be
> my spokesman. They must become as you have been.
> You must not become like them." (Jeremiah 15:19 NET).

I am forgiven and at peace; my mind is free from torment. I rest in God
and he gives me strength.

> This is what the Sovereign Lord, the Holy One of Israel,
> says: "In repentance and rest is your salvation, in quiet-
> ness and trust is your strength." (Isaiah 30:15 NIV)

Confess

Father, I come to you today with a broken and contrite heart. I
humbly repent of the sin in my life. I turn away from old mindsets,

attitudes, and behaviors that are defeating me and keeping me in bondage. By the power of your Holy Spirit, I choose to shed old ways, and I put on a new mind and heart. I am forgiven and free.

Affirm

I have a new mind and a new heart. God's Holy Spirit empowers my thoughts, attitudes, and actions, and the cords of sin that used to entangle me no longer bind me. I am forgiven. I no longer live in guilt and shame, but I live in victory over Satan and overcome his demonic snares. I walk in freedom and wholeness, and I triumph in every area of my life through Jesus Christ, my Lord. God uses my life for his glory.

Repeat "I have a new mind and heart" three times. Each time you read it, add special emphasis to the bolded word or words.

I have a new mind and heart.

I **have** a new mind and heart.

I have **a new mind and heart.**

Extra Memory Challenge

> I will give you a new heart and put a new spirit in you;
> I will remove from you your heart of stone and give you
> a heart of flesh. (Ezekiel 36:26 NIV)

Explore

1. What does it mean for you to repent?
2. Have you done that before God? Describe what happened.
3. What areas in your life do you need to change your mind about?
4. When we repent, God freely and fully forgives us. Have you accepted his forgiveness?
5. Take time to thank God for his great mercy and love for you.

Journal

Week 4

Day 22

TODAY'S TRUTH: I WILL LET GO OF UNFORGIVENESS AND GRUDGES

Do not let the sun go down while you are still angry,
and do not give the devil a foothold.
Ephesians 4:26–27 NIV

In the Bible (Matthew 18:21–35), Jesus tells a crowd of eager listeners a remarkable story of a servant who owed his master an exorbitant amount of money. The amount owed was so absurd—about 100 billion dollars—that his listeners could not miss Jesus's overstated point. The debt could never be paid back, not in a hundred lifetimes. The master's incredibly gracious and generous gesture was an unprecedented act of mercy. The unfaithful servant deserved prison until the debt could be paid—which would have been a life sentence since the enormous debt was impossible to repay. But instead, his master forgave him.

Amazing.

What Jesus shared next in this story, however, was shocking. It no doubt captured his listeners' attention and left them speechless.

The forgiven servant left the gracious master and went straight to find another fellow servant who owed *him* a debt, much smaller in size—about twelve thousand dollars. The forgiven servant grabbed the indebted servant and began to choke him, screaming, "Pay me back right now!" The indebted servant begged for mercy, promising to pay him back—he just needed a bit more time. But the indignant, forgiven servant (those two words, *indignant* and *forgiven*, seem mutually exclusive) refused, and he had his fellow servant thrown into prison until he could pay back the money.

Another small group of servants saw what was happening. They knew of the master's kindness to the forgiven servant, and they were displeased and angry at his behavior. This group immediately ran to tell the master what they had observed.

> Then the master called the servant in. "You wicked servant," he said, "I canceled all that debt of yours because you begged me to. Shouldn't you have had mercy on your fellow servant just as I had on you?" In anger his master turned him over to the jailers to be tortured, until he should pay back all he owed. (Matthew 18:32–34 NIV)

I can imagine the crowd Jesus was speaking to beginning to shift their weight from side to side—this story was becoming too uncomfortable. *What's the point?* they may have wondered.

Then Jesus made the point clear: "This is how my heavenly Father will treat each of you unless you forgive your brother or sister from your heart" (Matthew 18:35 NIV).

Jesus expects us to forgive. Our freedom depends on it. Without God's forgiveness, we would be turned over to the torturers—Satan and his demonic jailers—and left cold in a prison cell of our own making.

We must deal with offenses right away before they turn to bitterness and corrupt our hearts. Unforgiveness, grudges, and bitterness grow over time. Their cords tighten around our souls, binding our attitudes, emotions, and motives more tightly each day and each hour.

The solution?

Forgive quickly. Forgive freely. Forgive fully. And repent the same way.

Today we choose forgiveness.

Declare

I declare that I am forgiven! Because I am forgiven, I open my heart and release all bitterness, anger, and unforgiveness that I had toward others. I do not let the cords of unforgiveness entangle me, but instead, I forgive others quickly, freely, and fully—from the heart. God's love fills my heart, and I am free from the bondage of unforgiveness.

Meditate, Believe, Accept

I am forgiven; therefore, I freely forgive others.

> Be kind and compassionate to one another, forgiving each other, just as in Christ God forgave you. (Ephesians 4:32 NIV)

> For if you forgive other people when they sin against you, your heavenly Father will also forgive you. But if you do not forgive others their sins, your Father will not forgive your sins. (Matthew 6:14–15 NIV)

I forgive from the heart with the Holy Spirit's help.

> Then the master called the servant in. "You wicked servant," he said, "I canceled all that debt of yours because you begged me to. Shouldn't you have had mercy on your fellow servant just as I had on you?" In anger his master turned him over to the jailers to be tortured, until he should pay back all he owed. "This is how my heavenly Father will treat each of you unless you forgive your brother or sister from your heart." (Matthew 18:32–35 NIV)

I am free from all judgments. I am forgiven and not condemned.

> Do not judge, and you will not be judged. Do not condemn, and you will not be condemned. Forgive, and you will be forgiven. (Luke 6:37 NIV)

> But when you are praying, first forgive anyone you are

holding a grudge against, so that your Father in heaven will forgive your sins, too. (Mark 11:25)

I am free from all grudges. I do not seek revenge.

Do not seek revenge or bear a grudge against anyone among your people, but love your neighbor as yourself. I am the Lord. (Leviticus 19:18 NIV)

Do not take revenge, my dear friends, but leave room for God's wrath, for it is written: "It is mine to avenge; I will repay," says the Lord. (Romans 12:19 NIV)

I show mercy; therefore, I receive mercy, and God blesses my life.

God blesses those who are merciful, for they will be shown mercy. (Matthew 5:7)

But I tell you: love your enemies! Pray for the people who persecute you! (Matthew 5:44 NTE)

I forgive freely, confident that God is working circumstances for my good.

You planned to do a bad thing to me. But God planned it for good, to make it happen that many people should be kept alive, as they are today. (Genesis 50:20 NLV)

We know that God is always at work for the good of everyone who loves him. They are the ones God has chosen for his purpose. (Romans 8:28 CEV)

Confess

I have allowed pain and hurt to seep into my soul. Indeed, the sun has gone down while I was still angry. That anger eventually turned into bitterness and unforgiveness. Today, Lord, I open my heart and repent of holding wrongs and offenses against others when you have so fully forgiven me of all my shortcomings and sins. I renounce all unforgiveness and let go of the wound, as well as the people who have wounded me.

Affirm

I am free from the cords of unforgiveness and bitterness. I forgive quickly, freely, and fully—from the heart. I am filled with God's love and empowered by his Holy Spirit. I can live in freedom, with joy and peace in my heart, because I know God is working in my life for good, and I trust him to make all things beautiful in his time. I will not let Satan bind me with cords of bitterness. I let go and I am free in Jesus's name.

Repeat "I am free" three times. Each time you read it, add special emphasis to the bolded word.

I am free.

I **am** free.

I am **free**.

Extra Memory Challenge

> Be kind and compassionate to one another, forgiving each other, just as in Christ God forgave you. (Ephesians 4:32 NIV)

Explore

1. Forgiveness is healing—and it's available. Have you asked God to forgive you? Thank him for his grace and mercy.
2. Forgiveness does not mean forgetting. It does mean, though, that you must let go of the debt owed to you by those who hurt you. Are there people in your life that you need to forgive and wounds that you need to release?
3. What does it mean to you to forgive from the heart? God will never reject a submitted and humble heart before him.

4. Take a moment and write in your journal. Remember this date as the day you let it all go.

Journal

Week 4

Day 23

TODAY'S TRUTH: I CAN FORGIVE MYSELF BECAUSE GOD HAS FORGIVEN ME

Love your neighbor as yourself.
Mark 12:31 NIV

Sometimes forgiving others is the easy part. We often struggle to extend the same compassion, grace, and mercy to ourselves that we're commanded to give others. Self-hatred and self-rejection because of things they've done or haven't done hold many people captive. They turn their anger inward and refuse to release themselves from self-condemnation.

But Jesus wants us to extend forgiveness to everyone—and that means forgiving ourselves. When God forgives us, he remembers our sin no more (Jeremiah 31:34). Jesus's blood paid for our sins. God *chooses* never to bring up our sins again. Not forgiving ourselves is a rejection of Jesus's blood atonement for our sins. God forgives everyone who comes to him in the name of Jesus.

Forgiving ourselves doesn't mean we forget about our past, but it does mean we choose not to hold those things against ourselves. We are to fix our minds on things that are true, noble, pure, lovely, and admirable (Philippians 4:8).

Every choice we make begins with a thought. Forgiving ourselves is a matter of choosing what we focus on and the truth we tell ourselves about ourselves. Every thought we think either gives life or poisons our souls. We cannot walk in our true identity in Jesus until we practice forgiving ourselves and rebuking the Enemy's accusations with the words God our Father speaks to us.

Forgiving ourselves changes the focus of our thoughts and releases us to walk in newness of life and fulfill God's purposes for us. We have nothing to gain, but have our freedom in Christ to lose, by chaining ourselves to the past through unforgiveness.

Forgiving myself involves

- loving myself,
- accepting myself, and
- being patient and merciful to myself.

It means I speak kindly to and about myself, and offer grace to myself when I haven't done things perfectly. I allow myself room to make mistakes and freedom to be the unique person God made me to be.

Forgiving myself means I permit myself to be human and re-lease myself from unreasonable expectations I've placed on myself in the past. When I don't meet my expectations of perfection, for-giving myself means I release self-rejection. I learn to accept and love myself, just as I am accepted and loved by God.

When we learn to forgive ourselves, it's helpful to think about how we forgive friends and those we love—by extending mercy and offering compassion. Because we're beloved by God, we should offer these same gifts to ourselves. We are not the exception to his grace and mercy.

Today, I choose to forgive and set someone free—myself.

Declare

I forgive myself. I release myself from unreasonable expecta-tions and harsh standards. I allow myself the freedom to express my personality, to grow into and become all that God has created me to be. I choose to accept, love, and nurture myself with God's compassion. I declare this in Jesus's name.

Meditate, Believe, Accept

I will love myself because God loves me and covers my sin.

> Above all, love each other deeply, because love covers over a multitude of sins. (1 Peter 4:8 NIV)

> My command is this: Love each other as I have loved you. (John 15:12 NIV)

I will forgive myself because God forgives me and crowns me with love and compassion.

> Praise the Lord, my soul, and forget not all his benefits—who forgives all your sins and heals all your diseases, who redeems your life from the pit and crowns you with love and compassion. (Psalm 103:2–4 NIV)

I have compassion for myself, knowing God rises with compassion to be gracious to me.

> Yet the Lord longs to be gracious to you; therefore he will rise up to show you compassion. For the Lord is a God of justice. Blessed are all who wait for him! (Isaiah 30:18 NIV)

I am patient with myself, clothed with kindness and gentleness. I forgive myself and give myself compassion.

> Therefore, as God's chosen people, holy and dearly loved, clothe yourselves with compassion, kindness, humility, gentleness and patience. Bear with each other and forgive one another if any of you has a grievance against someone. Forgive as the Lord forgave you. (Colossians 3:12–13 NIV)

> Be completely humble and gentle; be patient, bearing with one another in love. (Ephesians 4:2 NIV)

I am kind to myself. I do not punish myself for my failures.

> Make sure that nobody pays back wrong for wrong, but always try to be kind to each other and to everyone else. (1 Thessalonians 5:15 NIV1984)

> Be kind and compassionate to one another, forgiving each other, just as in Christ God forgave you. (Ephesians 4:32 NIV)

I build myself up with my words and benefit by what I say about myself to myself.

> Do not let any unwholesome talk come out of your mouths, but only what is helpful for building others up according to their needs, that it may benefit those who listen. (Ephesians 4:29 NIV)

I do not condemn myself; neither am I condemned.

> "The sinless one among you, go first: Throw the stone." Bending down again, he wrote some more in the dirt. Hearing that, they walked away, one after another, beginning with the oldest. The woman was left alone. Jesus stood up and spoke to her. "Woman, where are they? Does no one condemn you?" "No one, Master." "Neither do I," said Jesus. "Go on your way. From now on, don't sin." (John 8:7–11 MSG)

Confess

Lord, I confess that I have held anger and unforgiveness toward myself. I have withheld compassionate from myself, holding myself to a harsh and high standard of perfection. When I failed to meet these standards, I rejected myself. Today I choose to forgive and set myself free from the chains of unforgiveness in Jesus's name.

Affirm

I am forgiven, and I learn to live forgiven and free. I renounce the harsh, hard attitudes of unforgiveness and rejection I've placed on myself. I'm loved, accepted, and ready to live as such. I no longer use hurtful words or behaviors to punish myself. I receive God's compassion. I forgive myself, and I refuse thoughts, actions, or words that would place me back in bondage. I am free. I forgive myself.

Repeat "I forgive myself" three times. Each time you read it, add special emphasis to the bolded word.

I forgive myself.

I **forgive** myself.

I forgive **myself.**

Extra Memory Challenge

> Praise the Lord, my soul, and forget not all his benefits—who forgives all your sins and heals all your diseases, who redeems your life from the pit and crowns you with love and compassion. (Psalm 103:2–4 NIV)

Explore

1. Have you ever considered that you may hold unforgiveness toward yourself?
2. What harsh expectation or past failure are you still holding against yourself?
3. How does knowing that God forgives you and wants you to forgive others change the way you think about forgiving yourself?
4. Take time to name the areas you are angry at yourself about—then free yourself by forgiving *you.*

Journal

Week 4

Day 24

TODAY'S TRUTH: I MUST FORGIVE GOD

Return to your rest, my soul,
for the Lord has been good to you.
Psalm 116:7 NIV

Why must we forgive God? He is holy; his ways are just. He hasn't done anything wrong. Yet if we're honest, we must admit that we sometimes get disillusioned and frustrated with God. He doesn't always do things the way we want him to.

We experience hurtful rejection. Our prayers go unanswered. God's silence confuses us. Perhaps God allowed something painful—something horrible—to touch our lives, and we don't understand why or see any redeeming value that could come from the hurt. Or maybe someone we love was hurt or died prematurely. In situations like these, we may discover that we've harbored anger and disappointment with God, and we have closed off our hearts to trusting him.

The solution: we must forgive God.

Before you dismiss this thought, I want to acknowledge that confusion is a human response. In other words, we believe God is just and right and pure in all his ways, but we must recognize that we can't fully understand the mind or the ways of God. He does what he does; he is the potter, and we are the clay (Isaiah 64:8). There is no shadow of turning from his love for us—no hedging or exception, no betrayal.

God is not capable of expressing anything but love for us.

My point is that we *feel* like he denied us. He *seems* unfair, uncaring, or unwilling. We prayed and prayed, and he didn't respond—at least not the way we believed he would or should. As a result, our heart hardened toward God.

While we know in our heads that God is not capable of doing wrong, we might sometimes experience circumstances so painful that we feel as though we have lost all reason for living. Surely God could have prevented this, we say. He is all-powerful. How could he allow this?

But these emotions are normal and do not cause God to turn away from us, but as we question, we often assume our perceptions and knowledge supersede his omniscience. We assume our ways are better than his. We judge him because he did not rescue us from our circumstances.

But our perceptions are flawed and limited. Everything God does is motivated by love. We must allow him to be the righteous, loving, holy God revealed in the Bible and admit we do not have answers.

If this describes you, then today is an important day. Release God from blame. Forgive him, and ask for forgiveness for harboring resentment he did not deserve. Stop trying to figure out things beyond your comprehension. Humble yourself before God, and then start fresh with your Savior—growing closer to him in total trust and faith.

Declare

I humble myself before God. I accept his will and plan for my life. I understand that his ways are not my ways, but they are higher than I can comprehend. I release God from my expectations, and I let go of the anger I've held in my heart because of my disappointment. I submit my heart and mind to God and trust myself to his everlasting care.

Meditate, Believe, Accept

When I question God's decisions, I will remember that God is right, and his ways are true.

> The things You do are great and powerful. You are the all-powerful Lord God. You are always right and true in everything you do. You are King of all nations. (Revelation 15:3 NLV)

> After this vision and announcement I heard what sounded like a great many people in heaven saying: "Hallelujah! Salvation, glory, and power belong to our God, because his judgments are true and right." (Revelation 19:1–2 NCV)

When I feel like I'm overlooked, I will remember that God does not deny me any good thing.

> Our Lord and our God, you are like the sun and also like a shield. You treat us with kindness and with honor, never denying any good thing to those who live right. (Psalm 84:11 CEV)

When I feel like God has done me wrong, I will remember that all God's ways are perfect and just.

> He is the Rock, his works are perfect, and all his ways are just. A faithful God who does no wrong, upright and just is he. (Deuteronomy 32:4 NIV)

> Now I, Nebuchadnezzar, praise and glorify and honor the King of heaven. All his acts are just and true, and he is able to humble the proud. (Daniel 4:37)

When I feel betrayed, I will remember that God does not lie. He will do what he has promised me.

God is not a man, so he does not lie. He is not human, so he does not change his mind. Has he ever spoken and failed to act? Has he ever promised and not carried it through? (Numbers 23:19)

God, who called you to become his child, will do all this for you just as he promised. (1 Thessalonians 5:24 TLB)

When I don't understand God, I will remember that his ways are higher than mine.

"My thoughts," says the Lord, "are not like yours, and my ways are different from yours. As high as the heavens are above the earth, so high are my ways and thoughts above yours." (Isaiah 55:8–9 GNT)

When I feel abandoned by God, I will remember that he will not forget me.

Yes, all his lovers who bow before him, trust in the Lord. For he is our only true hero, God-wrapped-around-us as our shield. The Lord will never forget us in our need; he will bless us indeed! (Psalm 115:11–12 TPT)

God has said, "Never will I leave you; never will I forsake you." (Hebrews 13:5 NIV)

But Zion said, "The Lord has abandoned me. My Lord has forgotten me." Can a woman forget her nursing child? Will she have no compassion on the child from her womb? Although mothers may forget, I will not forget you. I have engraved you on the palms of my hands. Your walls are always in my presence. (Isaiah 49:14–16 GW)

When I doubt God's care and love for me, I will remember that he is always good.

The Lord is good, a refuge in times of trouble. He cares for those who trust in him. (Nahum 1:7 NIV)

The Lord is good and right; he points sinners to the right way. He shows those who are humble how to do right, and he teaches them his ways. All the Lord's ways are loving and true for those who follow the demands of his agreement. (Psalm 25:8–10 NCV)

The Lord is gracious and righteous; our God is full of compassion. The Lord protects the unwary; when I was brought low, he saved me. Return to your rest, my soul, for the Lord has been good to you. (Psalm 116:5–7 NIV)

Confess

I don't always understand you, God. Though I say with my mouth, *I trust you*, I find that sometimes I question in the dark what I know is true when I'm in the light. Forgive me, Father, for doubting your wisdom and questioning your goodness. Today I choose to release my disappointment and anger with you, and I ask you to restore me in Jesus's name.

Affirm

I am at peace with God. I trust his ways; he is righteous and true, and all his ways are good and for my good. I will trust his decisions, for his judgments are just and wise. God will only do those things that are for my benefit. He loves me and will not fail me. He will not withhold any good thing from me. My heart is open to God; I am free from unforgiveness and resentment toward him. I am restored to my faith, and I'm confident in his plan for my life.

Repeat "I trust God's unfailing goodness" three times. Each time you read it, add special emphasis to the bolded word or words.

I trust God's unfailing goodness.

I **trust** God's unfailing goodness.

I trust God's **unfailing goodness.**

Extra Memory Challenge

Return to your rest, my soul, for the Lord has been good to you. (Psalm 116:7 NIV)

Explore

1. Have you ever considered forgiving God before? Why or why not? In what ways have you held a grudge against him?
2. How have you expressed your feelings when you felt disappointed in the way God seemed to respond or not respond to a painful situation?
3. How will you express your feelings to God now?

Journal

Week 4

Day 25

Today's Truth: Because Unforgiveness Turns to Bitterness and Anger, I Must Explore My Anger

Do not be quickly provoked in your spirit,
for anger resides in the lap of fools.
Ecclesiastes 7:9 NIV

After doing the work of forgiving, some people receive instant freedom and healing. However, others continue to experience anger and bitterness. If you've held negative emotions for months or even years, you may not know how to release anger.

You may have learned a faulty coping mechanism for handling life—you become angry and protect yourself. Unfortunately, this defense system will eventually destroy you and the people around you.

Anger isn't necessarily good or bad, and it can be a righteous response to sin. For instance, if a predator molested your four-year-old daughter, it would be unthinkable for you *not* to be angry. However, it's important to understand where anger comes from and how to direct it.

For instance, Ephesians 4:26–27 (NIV) says, "'In your anger do not sin': Do not let the sun go down while you are still angry, and do not give the devil a foothold." Verse 31 goes on to say, "Get rid of all bitterness, rage and anger, brawling and slander, along with every form of malice." These verses tell us that (1) anger is not always sinful; (2) we are not to harbor anger; and (3) anger can turn into bitterness, rage, and malice, which are sinful. James 1:19–20 tells us we are to be slow to become angry because our anger doesn't produce the righteousness that God desires in us.

It's appropriate to feel angry about abuse, and we need to explore both our motives and responses to anger. Anger is an essential first step in the grief process as we inventory what we've lost through painful, wounding experiences. This step is especially true for abuse survivors.

Over the next few days, we will explore anger. Is anger always bad? What does God's Word have to say about how to handle anger? We will see, if we look closely, that the book of Mark gives us insight.

Mark 11:11 says, "So Jesus came to Jerusalem and went into the Temple. After *looking around carefully at everything*, he left" (emphasis added). Jesus took his time and examined what was going on. He gave consideration to what he heard and observed. *Then he left*.

Four verses later, which happened to be the next day, Jesus returned and carried out a weighted response. He didn't unleash his initial blast of anger but left and returned later. Mark 11:15–16 tells us, "When they arrived back in Jerusalem, Jesus entered the Temple and began to drive out the people buying and selling animals for sacrifices. He knocked over the tables of the money changers and the chairs of those selling doves, and he stopped everyone from using the Temple as a marketplace."

It's important to note that Jesus *did* get angry. Anger itself is not sinful. We must explore the motivation behind and also the timing and purpose of our anger—and learn to use it positively.

Positive anger is directed toward positive goals:

- Getting to the root of a problem
- Helping us see our faults
- Helping us frame a problem
- Helping to advance the cause of social justice

Negative anger comes at the cost of others:

- Venting feelings
- Intimidating, inciting fear, or promoting guilt, shame, and other negative emotions
- Rationalizing our actions
- Expressing power

The time has come to examine how and why we express anger and how we use it. Do we use it as a positive tool that aids the spiritual growth of others and ourselves, or do we use it as a club to batter people?

Declare

I'm ready to deal with my unrighteous anger. I no longer want to use anger to avoid pain or manipulate others. Today I release the faulty coping skill of anger.

Meditate, Believe, Accept

I have the power to slow down, listen, and be slow to anger.

> Be quick to listen, slow to speak and slow to become angry, because human anger does not produce the righteousness that God desires. Therefore, get rid of all moral filth and the evil that is so prevalent and humbly accept the word planted in you, which can save you. (James 1:19–21 NIV)

I can remain calm and not be quickly agitated or provoked to anger.

> Do not be quickly provoked in your spirit, for anger resides in the lap of fools. (Ecclesiastes 7:9 NIV)

I am patient—not hotheaded or quarrelsome.

> A hot-tempered person stirs up conflict, but the one who is patient calms a quarrel. (Proverbs 15:18 NIV)

My hope is in God; therefore, I can refrain from anger, and I inherit God's best.

> Stop your anger! Turn off your wrath. Don't fret and worry—it only leads to harm. For the wicked shall be destroyed, but those who trust the Lord shall be given every blessing. (Psalm 37:8–9 TLB)

Confess

Lord, I confess I've been bound by anger, and I have used it to protect myself. Today I ask you to loose me from the chains of my anger and teach me how to renounce and walk away from the anger trap in Jesus's name.

Affirm

I am free from ungodly anger. I have self-control and a calm spirit. I can be deliberate about what I do with anger and how it will operate in my life. Its false comfort will not deceive me. Instead, I will listen, pray, and remain peaceful in my spirit.

Repeat "I am free from anger" three times. Each time you read it, add special emphasis to the bolded word or words.

I am free from anger.

I **am free** from anger.

I am free **from anger**.

Extra Memory Challenge

> Refrain from anger and turn from wrath; do not fret—it leads only to evil. For those who are evil will be destroyed, but those who hope in the Lord will inherit the land. (Psalm 37:8–9 NIV)

Explore

1. Have there been times when you became angry to protect yourself against hurt?

2. What would happen if you slowed down your responses and chose to listen instead?
3. In what ways do you struggle with anger?

Journal

Week 4

Day 26

TODAY'S TRUTH: I HAVE POWER OVER ANGER
AND CHOOSE A POSITIVE RESPONSE

But now you must also rid yourselves
of all such things as these:
anger, rage, malice, slander,
and filthy language from your lips.
Colossians 3:8 NIV

Recently, a story in our Grand Rapids news made national headlines. A woman at a drive-through restaurant didn't receive her correct order. Frustrated, she drove around and reordered again at the window. When they mixed up her order a second time, her anger boiled over. She reached into her purse, drew out a pistol, and opened fire into the drive-through window. Fortunately, she didn't injure anyone, but her uncontrollable rage manifested a display of outrageous and mentally imbalanced behavior.

God created our emotions, including anger. Anger can be a helpful and healthy warning that something is out of order in the world. We experience anger when we see injustice, violence, perversion, humiliation, and abuse. We can also experience anger as a response to a lack of control or an abuse of power. Our sources of anger can be internal, such as anger at ourselves, or external, like someone driving too slowly for our taste.

But when anger controls our thoughts, turns to bitterness, and becomes destructive, we must repent and seek a solution at the root of the problem. Our natural response to anger is to become aggressive, fight, and defend ourselves. Protecting ourselves and our loved ones when we're threatened can be a valuable response, but it's not the appropriate response to every situation.

Can people or things compel us to lash out in rage, or do we have the ability to choose how we respond?

God designed the human brain so that the center of reason is stronger than emotions—we thus have a choice about how to respond when we feel a flash of anger: we can either engage reasoning skills or let emotions take control.

Important questions to ask ourselves include:

- Why am I angry?
- What response does God ask of me in this situation?
- Is my heart hurting for the other person involved in this situation?
- What can I do to bring glory to God through my response?

God instructs us not to carry anger. We are to lay it aside at the end of every day (Ephesians 4:26). If the person who angered us is a Christian, God has already forgiven their offense. God makes it clear in Romans 12 that he will exact vengeance on our behalf—it's not our job. This truth is critical for us to remember as men.

Ask yourself:

- Is my anger motivated by selfishness?
- Is my anger dishonoring to God's name?
- Does my anger give Satan a foothold by growing bitterness or victimization in my heart?
- Is my anger volatile, and does it hurt others emotionally or physically?
- Am I holding a grudge that feeds pride?
- Do I wish pain, vengeance, or suffering for the other person?
- Am I unwilling to forgive and willing to be consumed by thoughts of revenge?

God created our emotions, and he also created our reasoning ability to control our emotions.

Of course, we can choose.

We become angry at many things, including God, our spouses, other people, our circumstances, or ourselves. We become angry because of our failures, unmet expectations, life's difficulties and tragedies, injustices, violations, unfairness—and anything else that doesn't go our way or measure up to our expectations.

We manifest our anger in hostile attitudes and behaviors, demeaning words, criticism, cynicism, unreasonable standards, depression, loss of enjoyment, and a pessimistic, negative outlook on life and people.

But we must take responsibility for God's gift of volition. *We have the power to choose* how to respond to anger and how to appropriately release it.

Declare

Because I am filled with the Holy Spirit, I have the power to choose how I will deal with anger. I will neither deny anger nor give it full vent, but I will resolve it God's way instead.

Meditate, Believe, Accept

I am empowered to rid myself of ungodly anger.

> But now you must also rid yourselves of all such things as these: anger, rage, malice, slander, and filthy language from your lips. (Colossians 3:8 NIV)

I'm empowered to patiently examine my feelings and the feelings of others without becoming angry. As a result, I have great understanding.

> Whoever is patient has great understanding, but one who is quick-tempered displays folly. (Proverbs 14:29 NIV)

In my anger, I'm empowered to not sin. I choose to release anger before the end of the day.

> "In your anger do not sin": Do not let the sun go down while you are still angry, and do not give the devil a foothold. (Ephesians 4:26–27 NIV)

Satan will *not* gain a foothold in my life.

> Do not give the devil a foothold. (Ephesians 4:27 NIV)

Confess

Lord, I haven't always made the right decisions when it comes to my anger and hurt. I've hurt others and myself. Please forgive me. Today I choose to release my so-called rights and choose the role of a servant and a peacemaker.

Affirm

I am free from anger. Although I may feel angry at times, I am empowered to process and resolve it in ways that please God and bless my life. I am a man with great patience and understanding.

Repeat "I will resolve anger God's way" three times. Each time you read it, add special emphasis to the bolded word or words.

I will resolve anger God's way.

I **will resolve anger** God's way.

I will resolve anger **God's way**.

Extra Memory Challenge

> "In your anger do not sin": Do not let the sun go down while you are still angry, and do not give the devil a foothold. (Ephesians 4:26–27 NIV)

Explore

1. What does it mean to rid yourself of anger? What does that imply?
2. Have you ever given Satan a foothold because of your anger? What was the result?
3. How will you choose a different path?
4. How will you need to change your thinking to release anger from your life? What anger from your past have you been holding on to?

Journal

Week 4

Day 27

TODAY'S TRUTH: I CHOOSE A HEALTHY RELATIONSHIP WITH ANGER

Create in me a pure heart, O God,
and renew a steadfast spirit within me.
Psalm 51:10 NIV

W hile mopping up after an unprecedented winter storm, a custodian received the task of assessing the damage of the melting snow. As he explored the basement and foundation of the building where he worked, the extensive damage resulting from the melting snow became more and more apparent. In frustration, the custodian exclaimed, "This water is unmanageable. It goes wherever it darn well wants!"

Unresolved anger that soaks into our spirits is much like melting snow. Anger finds a path that seeps into every area of our lives, causing debilitating damage in places we seldom look. This kind of anger erodes our ability to discern God's heart and glorify him.

However, biblical anger—righteous indignation—is an appropriate expression. We reflect the heart of God when we feel angry over injustice and sin. I was angry over the sin committed against my wife when she was a child, and rightfully so. But God doesn't want anger to take root and grow in our spirits. In other words, we can use anger rightly, as long as anger does not use us and bring us into sin and bondage.

Consider God's Word:

> Go ahead and be angry. You do well to be angry—but
> don't use your anger as fuel for revenge. And don't stay
> angry. Don't go to bed angry. Don't give the Devil that
> kind of foothold in your life. (Ephesians 4:26–27 MSG)

How do we know if our anger is righteous? One way to discern the motive behind anger is to look at the behavior anger fuels. Does our anger prod us to act in a proud, self-protective, defensive manner? Are we reluctant to examine our actions, attitudes, motives, and shared responsibility for the conflict? Do our actions, words, and attitudes stir continued hostility? Does our anger deflect glory from God? If so, the emotion we feel is not righteous and is not rooted in godly motives.

Godly anger:

- Is motivated by a desire to glorify God
- Desires God's best, according to his will and plan
- Does not diminish the ability to evaluate motives, words, actions, and responsibility for sinning or hurting others
- Seeks godly action

Unchecked anger can turn into binding strongholds such as bitterness, resentment, a critical spirit, hatred, and more.

We all experience anger. The emotion is not a sin, but it's what we do with that feeling that can turn into sin. If we harbor or nurture anger, it undoubtedly grows and causes trouble.

Depression is anger turned inward, and depression turned inward on ourselves can create such harmful effects as self-hatred, apathy, ambivalence, and low self-esteem.

Anger turned outward takes on many damaging forms, as well, such as intolerance, impatience, temper, rage, volatility, wrath or fury, mean-spiritedness, frustration, irritation, criticism, sarcasm and cruel joking, a judgmental spirit, cynicism, and passive-aggressiveness.

Instead of falling into one of these extremes, we can choose a better plan: we can first acknowledge our anger. We must recognize that our depression, anxiety, or agitation might be rooted in anger, which ultimately finds its source in a hidden wound.

Today we will take an honest look at our hearts and search for buried anger that may require resolution.

Declare

I am a seeker of truth. I no longer hide or deny anger in my life. Instead, I ask God to shine a light on every wounded, hidden, or broken place in my soul as he shows me my heart.

Meditate, Believe, Accept

God wants me to know the truth about my heart.

> Behold, You desire truth in the inward parts, and in the hidden part You will make me to know wisdom. (Psalm 51:6 NKJV)

I need God's revelation to see within my own heart.

> Search me, O God, and know my heart; try me, and know my anxieties; and see if there is any wicked way in me, and lead me in the way everlasting. (Psalm 139:23–24 NKJV)

My heart is wicked; only God can truly know it and cure it.

> The heart is deceitful above all things, and desperately wicked; who can know it? I, the Lord, search the heart, I test the mind, even to give every man according to his ways, according to the fruit of his doings. (Jeremiah 17:9–10 NKJV)

God will purify and cleanse my heart.

> Create in me a pure heart, O God, and renew a steadfast spirit within me. (Psalm 51:10 NIV)

The Lord will reveal my heart, good or bad, if I seek him.

The Lord searches every heart and understands every desire and every thought. If you seek him, he will be found by you. (1 Chronicles 28:9 NIV)

Confess

Lord, I confess there are times when my anger does not please you, nor does it bring about the righteous behavior you desire from me. I've used anger in unhealthy ways, and I confess that I no longer desire anger and its hurtful power to overcome me. Set me free and teach me how to use anger in positive ways.

Affirm

I can have a healthy relationship with anger and use it to move me into my destiny. When anger comes, I will discern if it is righteous and appropriate or if it is destructive to others and me. In Jesus's name, I will walk in freedom from the unrighteous effects of anger.

Repeat "I have a healthy relationship with anger" three times. Each time you read it, add special emphasis to the bolded word or words.

I have a healthy relationship with anger.

I **have** a healthy relationship with anger.

I have **a healthy relationship with anger**.

Extra Memory Challenge

Search me, O God, and know my heart; try me, and know my anxieties; and see if there is any wicked way in me, and lead me in the way everlasting. (Psalm 139:23–24 NKJV)

Explore

1. Identify a time you experienced righteous anger. What actions did you take as a result?

2. Identify a time when you were angry, but it wasn't godly. What happened as a result?

3. Can you see the difference between God's righteous anger—which we still must process correctly—and man's anger? Explain.

4. Identify a time when you felt angry, but your root emotions were hurt and sorrow.

Free Thinking

You have probably experienced interactions where anger escalated bad situations into terrible situations. I'm sure we can all share stories of unfortunate events like these. Typically, deep hurt or loss ignites our anger. Anger that lashes out for revenge or to hurt someone creates a downward spiral of defensive responses.

God calls Christians to live a life motivated by love. We don't get passes for moments when we feel angry, wounded, or (fill in your negative emotion here).

You can have a healthy relationship with anger. Ask the Holy Spirit to help you discern between righteous anger that reflects God's heart and self-centered anger that pushes others aside to achieve your agenda.

You've completed week 4! Congratulate yourself for your hard work. The Spirit of God is working through his Word to change you from the inside out, and your life will never be the same.

Journal

CHAPTER 7

CORDS OF FEAR

The brave man is not he who does not feel afraid,
but he who conquers that fear.
—Nelson Mandela

Challenge Week 5
Weekly Reading: Fear

He brought me out into a spacious place;
he rescued me because he delighted in me.
Psalm 18:19 NIV

How many opportunities have you missed in life because you were too afraid to take a risk?

Let me state the question another way: What might you have accomplished in life if fear had not influenced your decisions? Are there adventures, opportunities, and pathways you didn't experience because fear kept you from moving forward?

I can list several things I've missed out on in my life because of fear. The nature of fear is to keep us chained to less—to the mundane, the average, and the ordinary. When fear tethers our lives, we live smaller than we should. We play it safe, avoid risk, and perhaps encourage those we love to do the same.

The story of a life filled with fear can lead to missed opportunities and rewards.

- A spirit of cowardice taps you on your shoulder, so you do not take a leap of faith.
- Timidity pulls you back, and you do not speak up—missing yet another opportunity.
- Shyness chokes a simple "hi" from your voice, and fear again prevents you from meeting new friends when you long to be known.

Most of us are familiar with this everyday brand of fear, but taking nibbles from our freedom does not satisfy fear. Left unchallenged, fear grows and consumes more and more of us.

- Worrisome thoughts turn to torment.
- Timidity becomes anxiety, forcing us to flee social encounters and meaningful relationships.
- Fear of people's expectations prohibits us from discovering who we are and how God has designed us.

Our unique contributions to the world lie dormant. Stifled by fear's cohorts, we do not live out our full potential or truly love what we do or who we are. Whether our fear is rational or irrational does not matter. Fear's goal is to keep us from living an abundant life. Fear is an ugly, deceptive tax collector that takes more than we owe.

Fear keeps us from investing in life—in our own lives. It steals our God-given purpose and creates atrophy in our creative spirit. Instead of feeling the satisfaction of facing down fear, we are left with regret, wishing we had it to do all over.

Fear is a robber, a thief of all we desire. It's the essence of Satan's presence. Just as we step forward in faith, the fiery dart of fear plunges into our minds, and we shrink back, losing the rewards of trusting God.

This week we look at how to conquer fear. We trace its origin, face it down, and stand nose-to-nose with it. We will remember who we are and how God has delivered us from the spirit of fear. We will claim the spacious land that God has promised us as we take courage like Joshua of old to possess what is ours.

This week we will step into our true position—freedom in Christ. We untie the cords of fear and command them to fall powerless at our feet. We boldly step out of the ties that bind and discover that a new life is waiting.

Your Freedom Time is *now*.

Week 5

Day 28

TODAY'S TRUTH: THROUGH JESUS, I OVERCOME FEAR

Behold, I have given you authority to tread
on serpents and scorpions,
and over all the power of the enemy,
and nothing shall hurt you.
Luke 10:19 ESV

Who of us can say we've never experienced some level of fear? No one I've ever met. Without exception, we've all felt fear lurking somewhere in the shadows. That's because fear is a basic human response.

In natural and physical terms, fear is an *emotional* response to a real or perceived danger. Fear is also an *instinctive* response that comes to us in moments of perceived of present danger.

In a world filled with scary realities, we continually face fear-inducing challenges. That's why it's important to understand how fear works in both natural and spiritual realms and to know that we have authority over fear.

Fear and accompanying startle responses have a biological impact on our brains, causing changes in our biochemistry. Immediate activation occurs in both the amygdala and the hypothalamus. Chemicals such as adrenaline and the stress hormone known as cortisol *flood into our bloodstream*, causing our first physical response to fear. This rush of chemicals controls our bodies and behaviors. Physical reactions may follow, such as:

- Increased heart rate
- Blood pressure changes
- Acutely focused senses

- Triggered sweat glands
- Dilated pupils, allowing more light into the eyes to sharpen vision
- Tensed and tightened muscles
- Triggered flight, fight, or freeze response
- Activated response to hide

These are God-given and instinctive responses to fear designed to increase our chances of survival when we face life-threatening situations. In appropriate degrees and situations, this fear response can be helpful.

But what about when our fear is out of proportion? People often battle with *perceived* fears—fears that grow out of balance. These perceived fears may appear illogical to others but feel palpable to the person experiencing them. Perceived fears often hold people captive with worrisome thoughts and fearful patterns of thinking, stalling individuals in emotional, physical, and spiritual paralysis. For many people, fear can become debilitating.

Synonyms for *fear* include:

- dread
- worry
- angst
- anxiety
- terror
- alarm
- panic
- trepidation
- distress
- apprehension
- nervousness
- foreboding

Can you relate to any of these feelings? I know I can. Fear often arrives uninvited at our emotional door and threatens certain danger, taunting us to cower and hide.

We may fear harm coming to our families or to us, which can keep us from moving forward. We may fear that Satan will attack us, so we're afraid to do God's will. We're afraid to make changes and take leaps of faith. We fear failure, inadequacy, responsibilities, and work. We fear financial ruin, rejection, risk, and danger. These are just some of the reasons we don't pursue our dreams when we're bound by fear. We remain spiritually frozen—caught in catatonic immobility.

Understandably, fear is a powerful tool the Enemy uses to hinder our freedom, growth, and the fulfillment of our destiny. God has so much for his people, yet fear keeps far too many from reaching their full potential.

You have power and authority over fear, whether the fear is real or perceived. You can reject fear through the power of choice. Interrupt your thinking patterns and physiology, change your confession, apply God's Word, and you'll send fear packing.

Decide today to *take authority over fear*!

Declare

I am free from fear. I have received authority over the spirit of fear, and it may not operate in my life. I have a sound mind and am free from frightening thoughts and limiting beliefs in Jesus's name.

Meditate, Believe, Accept

I have authority over fear.

> I have given you authority to trample on snakes and scorpions and to overcome all the power of the enemy; nothing will harm you. (Luke 10:19 NIV)

You, dear children, are from God and have overcome them, because the one who is in you is greater than the one who is in the world. (1 John 4:4 NIV)

I have divine weapons against fear.

The weapons we fight with are not the weapons of the world. On the contrary, they have divine power to demolish strongholds (2 Corinthians 10:4 NIV).

They won the victory over him because of the blood of the lamb and the word of their testimony. (Revelation 12:11 GW)

By using the name of Jesus, I shut the door on fear and do not give Satan a foothold.

Do not give the devil a foothold. (Ephesians 4:27 NIV)

Submit yourselves, then, to God. Resist the devil, and he will flee from you. (James 4:7 NIV)

Confess

Lord, I confess I've not always used the authority you've given me. I've allowed the Enemy to torment my mind with thoughts that are not from you. Wash my mind and cover me with your blood, Lord Jesus. Set me free from fear as I claim your Word.

Affirm

I am free from fear. Greater is he that is in me than the spirit of fear. I come in the name of Jesus, covered by his blood, and my mouth filled with his Word. I overcome the satanic assault against me and my mind in Jesus's name.

Repeat "I have authority over fear" three times. Each time you read it, add special emphasis to the bolded word or words.

I have authority over fear.
I **have authority** over fear.
I have authority **over fear**.

Extra Memory Challenge

Submit yourselves, then, to God. Resist the devil, and
he will flee from you. (James 4:7 NIV)

Explore

1. Are you aware that you have authority over fear? What does this mean?
2. How and when have you stood against fear in your life?
3. What roles have prayer and Scripture played in your struggles with fear?

Journal

Week 5

Day 29

Today's Truth: God Has Not Given Me a Spirit of Fear, but of Power, Love, and Self-Discipline

For God has not given us a spirit of fear and timidity,
but of power, love, and self-discipline.
2 Timothy 1:7

Sometimes fear is more than an emotion. Sometimes it's a presence, a persona.

When fear rises to this level, we may be struggling with more than an emotional response to circumstances or forces at work in nature. This kind of fear is what the Bible refers to as "a spirit of fear." A spirit of fear is a demonic force directed at a person to bring bondage and torment. A spirit of fear attacks the mind and soul. It may also take the form of an emotional habit that escalates and establishes a stronghold of control in a person's life.

When a spirit of fear is at work, people often fear the past, the present, and the future. Some people fear exposure, and some fear isolation and rejection. Others are pulled into fear's icy grip and thrown into a black hole of despair.

God's Word is clear—this type of fear is not from him: "For God has not given us a spirit of fear, but of power and of love and of a sound mind" (2 Timothy 1:7 NKJV). God does not give us a spirit of fear, so who instills fear in us? The archenemy of God, of course, whose name is Satan.

Satan is a bully. He assigns his emissaries to sit on our shoulders and fill our thoughts with fright. These emissaries come to us with whispers and taunts. They induce more than the *emotion* of fear; when we listen, a *spirit* of fear controls us.

But we are not hopeless. The good news is that we have authority over the Enemy and the spirit of fear.

Because fear cannot coexist with faith, we must activate our faith and our voice as spiritual warfare and stake our claim. When fear tells us, "I'm not going to be okay," faith tells us, "God promises me that no matter my circumstances, I'm okay—because he is with me and works for my good in all things."

Romans 8:15 (ESV) tells us, "For you did not receive the spirit of slavery to fall back into fear." God's presence is with us. The Creator of the universe promises that he will never leave us or forsake us. The Lord is our helper—we do not have to fear. Nothing can happen to us outside of his loving care (Hebrews 13:5–6).

This week, with the Holy Spirit's help, you'll explore and expose the areas in your life where fear has crept in and held you hostage. God is with you. Meditate on that truth. You have nothing to fear.

Declare

God has not given me a spirit of fear. Therefore, fear, anxiety, worry, and distress have no place in my life. I declare that fear will not hold me back, nor will its cohorts torment me. All fear must be banished and put under my feet according to God's Word, in Jesus's name.

Meditate, Believe, Accept

I have a spirit of power, love, and self-discipline.

> For God has not given us a spirit of fear and timidity, but of power, love, and self-discipline. (2 Timothy 1:7)

I am not a coward. I am a man of power, love, and wise discretion.

> For God has not given us a spirit of cowardice, but of power, and of love, and of wise discretion. (2 Timothy 1:7 DBY)

God loves me and I have nothing to fear.

> There is no fear in love, but perfect love casts out fear; for fear has torment, and he that fears has not been made perfect in love. (1 John 4:18 DBY)

I reject a spirit of slavery, and I will not fall back into fear.

> For you did not receive the spirit of slavery to fall back into fear, but you have received the Spirit of adoption as sons, by whom we cry, "Abba! Father!" (Romans 8:15 ESV)

Confess

Lord, I confess there are times when I fear. I fear the present, the future, and all the "what ifs" of life. Today I renounce fear in my life, and I lean on you and your perfect and trustworthy character. Amen.

Affirm

I will not entertain a spirit of fear. When fear rises in my heart, I will declare God's perfect love over me. I possess a bold and courageous spirit filled with love, power, wisdom, and discretion.

Repeat "I am free from a spirit of fear" three times. Each time you read it, add special emphasis to the bolded word or words.

I am free from a spirit of fear.

I **am free** from a spirit of fear**.**

I am free from **a spirit of fear**.

Extra Memory Challenge

> For you did not receive the spirit of slavery to fall back into fear, but you have received the Spirit of adoption as sons, by whom we cry, "Abba! Father!" (Romans 8:15 ESV)

Explore

1. In what ways have you experienced fear?
2. What have you done to overcome fear?
3. In what ways is fear much more than just an emotion? What fears have had the greatest power in your life?

Journal

Week 5

Day 30

TODAY'S TRUTH: I WILL FACE MY FEARS

He will fulfill the desire of those who fear Him;
He will also hear their cry and will save them.
Psalm 145:19 NASB

I've been known to be brave. And although I don't like to admit it, I've also been known to shake in my boots with fear. But I've decided that I don't want to lose out on life's opportunities because I'm afraid. I don't want to live paralyzed by fear. Instead, I want to be an overcomer—living boldly and courageously. I want to face my fears and experience the thrill of being triumphant, not trumped.

Do you feel that way too?

God has important goals for us, but like Joshua, we must be strong and courageous and take hold of God's purpose for our lives. Conquering fear is not optional but critical to complete our God-given assignment.

Conquering fear is possible. Although overcoming fear is not a comfortable process, we can confront the things we're afraid of and stand as champions over them. No more fear. No more intimidation. No more holding back.

But how do we take steps to conquer our fear?

1. Name your fear.

Acknowledge that you're afraid. Ask yourself, "What, specifically, am I afraid of?" Define the fear you struggle with. Naming and examining fear will reveal that the things you dread have limits and are not insurmountable. As Mark

Twain stated, "It's not the size of the dog in the fight, it's the size of the fight in the dog."[9]

2. Act, even when you're afraid.

"Go back?" he thought. "No good at all! Go sideways? Impossible! Go forward? Only thing to do! On we go!" So up he got, and trotted along with his little sword held in front of him and one hand feeling the wall, and his heart all of a patter and a pitter (J. R. R. Tolkien, *The Hobbit*).[10]

No one is ever totally free from the emotion of fear. It circles our heads like a bird in flight, but only we can choose to let fear build a nest in our hair and peck away at our skulls.

3. Focus on the win.

French author André Gide wrote, "Man cannot discover new oceans unless he has the courage to lose sight of the shore."[11]

How would the quality of your life improve if you faced each day with courage? What great things would you accomplish? What is your desired goal? What do you want to achieve? Define the win and focus on what you will gain, not lose.

4. Show up.

Courage comes as we make right choices, and small steps compound over time and result in success. Sometimes all we can do is show up. Don't think about it—do it. We often overthink a problem, and it elevates our uneasiness. Instead, take one step forward—show up, and the rest will unfold.

"Courage doesn't always roar. Sometimes courage is the

little voice at the end of the day that says I'll try again to-morrow" (Mary Anne Radmacher).[12] Remember, courage determines the parameters of your life. How big do you want to live?

Declare

I am bold and courageous. I face my fears, and I overcome. As I take steps toward my goals, fear cannot stop me. I press through fear, facing it with faith and courage. I am brave.

Meditate, Believe, Accept

God is with me. He delivers me from all fear.

> I sought the Lord, and he answered me; he delivered me from all my fears. (Psalm 34:4 NIV)

I am not intimidated. God is for me.

> Don't be afraid, because I am with you. Don't be intimidated; I am your God. I will strengthen you. I will help you. I will support you with my victorious right hand. (Isaiah 41:10 GW)

I put my trust in God. I am not afraid.

> When I am afraid, I put my trust in you. In God, whose word I praise—in God I trust and am not afraid. What can mere mortals do to me? (Psalm 56:3–4 NIV)

I am brave and courageous.

> Have I not commanded you? Be strong and courageous. Do not be afraid; do not be discouraged, for the Lord your God will be with you wherever you go. (Joshua 1:9 NIV)

Confess

Lord, I choose to be brave and courageous. Empower me by your Word as I take steps to conquer fear.

Affirm

I can face the future without fear. I can live my life with boldness and confidence and dwell in the land of the living because God is with me. I am not afraid. I am brave. I am courageous.

Repeat "I face the future fearlessly" three times. Each time you read it, add special emphasis to the bolded word or words.

I face the future fearlessly.

I **face the future** fearlessly.

I face the future **fearlessly**.

Extra Memory Challenge

> Have I not commanded you? Be strong and courageous. Do not be afraid; do not be discouraged, for the Lord your God will be with you wherever you go. (Joshua 1:9 NIV)

Explore

1. What changes will you make today to face fear? What will be your first small step?
2. Create a series of small steps for moving toward your goal. Include a reasonable timeline for implementing those small steps.
3. How will your life be different when you have demolished your fear? What, specifically, will be different? In what ways will you find freedom?

Journal

Week 5

Day 31

Today's Truth: I Fear the Lord

Fear of the Lord is the foundation of true wisdom.
All who obey his commandments will grow in wisdom.
Praise him forever.
Psalm 111:10

This week we've looked at fear and our response to it. But what if our fear isn't about bad things, such as illness, accidents, natural disasters, war, crime, things that can hurt us or those we love, or circumstances beyond our understanding or control? This kind of fear typically causes us to hide, panic, or freeze.

What if our fear is about pleasing people, letting people down, or not being or doing what they expect of us? What if we fear losing our image or saying no because we will disappoint others? This kind of fear can make us jump through hoops of expectation, expend our energies, and focus on everyone's agenda but our own—and more importantly, God's. Because of these kinds of fears, we may inadvertently disobey God in an attempt to please others.

The solution? Fear the Lord.

When Scripture says to fear the Lord, it means not to panic or be afraid. To fear the Lord means maintaining awe and respect for who he is—his power, character, nature, and Word. Fearing the Lord is a positive attitude. Since we already know that God's perfect love casts out all fear (1 John 4:18), fearing God has more to do with loving and respecting him than being afraid of approaching him. God longs for us to come to him without fear or shame (Hebrews 4:16).

Robert B. Strimple, president emeritus of systematic theology at Westminster Seminary California, says the fear of the Lord includes "the convergence of awe, reverence, adoration, honor, worship, confidence, thankfulness, love, and, yes, fear."[13]

Another resource describes the fear of God this way: "The fear of God is an attitude of respect, a response of reverence and wonder. It is the only appropriate response to our Creator and Redeemer. . . . [It is] a healthy dread of displeasing him."[14]

So if I sin, I don't fear what God will do to me. Instead, I fear what I have done against him. When we fear the Lord, we care more about what God thinks and commands than what the world thinks about us or tries to pressure us into. Honoring him is our highest priority. A healthy reverence for God will save us from many of life's problems—including people-pleasing because we will make choices that please him.

Fearing God holds another benefit: wisdom. David spelled out the reason in Psalm 111:10 (NKJV): "The fear of the LORD is the beginning of wisdom; a good understanding have all those who do His commandments. His praise endures forever."

Fearing the Lord is truly the beginning of wisdom because we are motivated to please God out of the overflow of our love for him. We stand in awe of him as our sovereign Creator and Redeemer, yet we understand that in his great love, he desires a relationship with us.

Today we untie the cords that bind us to expectations of others. They drop powerless around our feet as we step out in faith to please God.

Declare

I stand in awe of you, God. You are deserving of all my admiration and respect. As I reverence you, I become wise and filled with knowledge.

Meditate, Believe, Accept

I will live and be blessed.

> The fear of the LORD prolongs life, but the years of the wicked will be shortened. (Proverbs 10:27 NASB)

> Blessings on all who reverence and trust the Lord—on all who obey him! Their reward shall be prosperity and happiness. (Psalm 128:1–2 TLB)

I am filled with God's wisdom and understanding.

> The fear of the Lord is the beginning of wisdom; a good understanding have all those who do His commandments. His praise endures forever. (Psalm 111:10 NKJV)

God has goodness in store for me.

> How great is the goodness you have stored up for those who fear you. You lavish it on those who come to you for protection, blessing them before the watching world. (Psalm 31:19)

I fear the Lord, and he watches over me.

> But look, the Lord keeps his eye on those who fear him—those who depend on his faithful love to rescue them from death and to keep them alive in famine. (Psalm 33:18–19 CSB)

God will fulfill my desires.

> He will fulfill the desire of those who fear Him; He also will hear their cry and save them. (Psalm 145:19 NKJV)

Confess

Lord, sometimes I fear man more than I fear you. Please for-

think about these things. . . . *Practice these things*, and the God of peace will be with you" (emphasis added).

God's Word never says Christians will experience anxiety-free lives. Psalm 56:3 (NIV) says, "When I am afraid, I put my trust in you." David wrote this psalm during the time when the Philistines in Gath had captured him, held him prisoner, and beat him daily. Do you ever feel as if life is holding you prisoner and beating you up? Do the struggles of life trigger anxiety for you? When you feel this way, do you put your trust in God, as David did?

In Psalm 56, David repeatedly declared his trust in God and then described God recording his every tear and heartache. Turn to God and give him your sorrow. He is listening and waiting to take your burdens.

Today we continue our journey toward freedom by declaring victory over anxiety.

Declare

I will not accept anxiety in my life. I go to God with my fears, worries, and anxieties, and he gives me supernatural peace.

Meditate, Believe, Accept

I am not anxious. I seek God first, and he knows what I need. I have nothing to fear.

> Therefore do not be anxious, saying, "What shall we eat?" or "What shall we drink?" or "What shall we wear?" For the Gentiles seek after all these things, and your heavenly Father knows that you need them all. But seek first the kingdom of God and his righteousness, and all these things will be added to you. (Matthew 6:31–33 ESV)

I cast my anxieties upon God because he takes care of me.

> Humble yourselves, therefore, under the mighty hand of God so that at the proper time he may exalt you, casting all your anxieties on him, because he cares for you. (1 Peter 5:6–7 ESV)

> If you will humble yourselves under the mighty hand of God, in his good time he will lift you up. Let him have all your worries and cares, for he is always thinking about you and watching everything that concerns you. (1 Peter 5:6–7 TLB)

I'm not anxious about anything. I talk to God about everything I'm concerned about, and he gives me peace.

> Do not be anxious about anything, but in everything by prayer and supplication with thanksgiving let your requests be made known to God. And the peace of God, which surpasses all understanding, will guard your hearts and your minds in Christ Jesus. (Philippians 4:6–7 ESV)

God comforts me, and I am encouraged as I overcome anxiety.

> When my anxious inner thoughts become overwhelming, your comfort encourages me. (Psalm 94:19 ISV)

Confess

Lord, I confess that sometimes worry and anxiety overcome me. I fail to remember to seek you first and receive your consolation and encouragement. Today I claim victory over anxiety. I will not fear.

Affirm

Anxiety has no place in my life. Faith and hope fill me, and I receive instant empowerment from God when I turn to him. When I call out to my holy God, all my fears melt like wax in his presence.

Repeat "I am filled with faith and hope" three times. Each time you read it, add special emphasis to the bolded word or words.

I am filled with faith and hope.

I **am filled** with faith and hope.

I am filled **with faith and hope**.

Extra Memory Challenge

> When my anxious inner thoughts become overwhelming, your comfort encourages me. (Psalm 94:19 isv)

Explore

1. Name the ways you've overcome anxiety in the past.
2. Do you see how your mindset plays a role in how you feel?
3. When you seek God first, how is your experience different than when you face anxiety on your own?

Journal

Week 5

Day 33

TODAY'S TRUTH: I AM FREE FROM THE HABIT OF WORRY

Who of you by worrying can add a single hour
to your life?
Since you cannot do this very little thing,
why do you worry about the rest?
Luke 12:25–26 NIV

Most of us have habits of which we're unaware. Some habits are beneficial and bring us strength and health. Regularly brushing our teeth and exercising are good habits that improve our overall health and state of mind. But we also practice destructive habits like smoking, overspending, and looking at porn. Perhaps we have a habit of interrupting people or criticizing others. One habit that often goes undiagnosed is the habit of worry. That's right—worry is a habit.

Marci G. Fox, PhD, says:

> Worry is made up of nagging, persistent thoughts that circle around in your head. It is "what if" statements, worst-case scenarios, and awful predictions. The act of worrying is an obsessive, habitual behavior—and one that you can give up. But before you can give it up, you must accept that the act of worrying serves no purpose. Worrying is stealing your energy, fatiguing your muscles and body, exacerbating your aches and pains, increasing your vulnerability to stress and infection, distracting you from the present, interfering with your sleep, inappropriately increasing or decreasing your appetite, and keeping you from more pleasurable or important tasks.

It is time to recognize the act of worry serves no purpose and has become a bad habit.[15]

Many of us know that worry is a bad habit, but we don't know how to stop. Most of us have no power to control the things we worry about. The first step to controlling worry is to recognize that it can't help us, and it harms us. It causes high blood pressure and insomnia, and it suppresses our immune system, as well as discouraging faith in God and wasting our time and energy.

It's important to distinguish between concern, which is healthy, and worry, which is unhealthy. Concern motivates us to solve a problem, but worry causes us to ruminate on a problem and doesn't lead to a solution.

When we recognize the things that trigger worry for us, we can bring them to God and evaluate the root of our anxiety, whether it is powerlessness, vulnerability, abandonment, or some other emotion.

We can't prevent bad things from happening or keep people from making their own choices, but we can choose to trust God to work in situations we don't understand. Evaluate your thoughts in the light of biblical truth, and replace lies with truth. Then look beyond present circumstances, and take your worries to God in prayer.

Today we explore the negative habit of worry. We tear it down and dismantle its operation in our lives.

Are you ready?

Declare

I am free from the habit of worry. I trust that God is working all things together for my good, and I am an overcomer. I use my energy to pray, praise, and declare God's faithfulness. I do not worry.

Meditate, Believe, Accept

I do not worry; I lean on God, and he makes my paths straight.

> Trust in the Lord with all your heart and lean not on your own understanding; in all your ways submit to him, and he will make your paths straight. (Proverbs 3:5–6 NIV)

I can't change anything by worrying. I can change things by trusting in God.

> Who of you by worrying can add a single hour to your life? Since you cannot do this very little thing, why do you worry about the rest? (Luke 12:25–26 NIV)

When I am stressed and worried, I go to Jesus. He carries my load.

> Come to me, all you who are struggling hard and carrying heavy loads, and I will give you rest. (Matthew 11:28 CEB)

God gives me peace and I am not afraid.

> Peace I leave with you; my peace I give you. I do not give to you as the world gives. Do not let your hearts be troubled and do not be afraid. (John 14:27 NIV)

God always sustains me and I am not shaken.

> Cast your cares on the Lord and he will sustain you; he will never let the righteous be shaken. (Psalm 55:22 NIV)

Confess

Lord, I confess that I've held on to the habit of worry. I've not come to you in prayer as readily or as often as I should. Today I thank you for a new revelation that sets me free from worry. I run to you from now on, and I am saved.

Affirm

I do not worry. I trust in God with my whole being, and I lean on him. When worry tries to assail me, I choose instead to pray and recommit my concerns and circumstances to God. I praise him out loud for taking care of me.

Repeat "I give my worries to God" three times. Each time you read it, add special emphasis to the bolded word or words.

I give my worries to God.

I **give my worries** to God.

I give my worries **to God**.

Extra Memory Challenge

> Cast your cares on the Lord and he will sustain you;
> he will never let the righteous be shaken. (Psalm 55:22
> NIV)

Explore

1. When the habit of worry is at work, how will you change your thoughts and words?
2. How will you change your physical posture?

Journal

Week 5

Day 34

TODAY'S TRUTH: I AM FREE FROM INSECURITY
AND FEAR OF INADEQUACY

And you did not receive the "spirit of religious duty,"
leading you back into the fear of never being good enough.
But you have received the "Spirit of full acceptance,"
enfolding you into the family of God. And you will never
feel orphaned, for as he rises up within us our spirits join
him in saying the words of tender affection,
"Beloved Father!"
Romans 8:15 TPT

U ncertainty.
Self-doubt.
Lack of confidence.
Inadequacy.

These words all describe feelings of insecurity that are familiar to most men. They're certainly familiar to me. Insecurity about life is normal. We all feel occasional anxiety about our place in the world, our relationships, or what the future holds.

However, feelings of insecurity and inadequacy about our identity are different. Questioning what we do or how we measure up in our careers or relationships is part of self-reflection and personal growth. However, insecurities about our identity challenge our purpose, unique contribution, and our intrinsic value. Fear of inadequacy in our identity is rooted in fear that says:

- I don't have value: "I'm not good enough."
- I can never do enough: "I'm inadequate."
- I won't be liked: "They won't accept me."

- I'll be seen as a fraud: "I don't have the capability or talent."
- I'll be rejected and unloved: "I'm not worth loving."
- I don't fulfill the measure of a man: "I'm less when compared to others."

Our negative self-criticism can go on and on. Insecurity and feelings of inadequacy about who we are reveal the cracks in the foundation of our identity.

Our culture feeds these feelings with messages about what a "real man" is supposed to be like. Negative traditional stereotypes contribute to the lies that say men must be dominant, strong, and never show weakness or emotion. This narrative can lead to harmful and confusing male identities and something known as Toxic Masculinity: the socialization of boys and men to become forceful, sexual, dominant, and even misogynistic.

Have you been paralyzed by feelings of insecurity and debilitated by fear of inadequacy? Do you shrink back in diffidence and hide your true self? Are you a people-pleaser? Perhaps you're overcompensating for feelings of insecurity.

Overcompensation may look like this:

- We brag about our accomplishments to increase the likelihood that others will like and affirm us.
- We're defensive and refuse to accept the evaluation and feedback we need because we fear we're not good enough.
- We're uncertain about our performance, consequently, we measure our value by our performance.
- We're standoffish and appear conceited to others because we're fearful of being hurt.
- We appear aloof to protect ourselves from hurt because we fear disapproval.
- We're unsure if people are safe and trustworthy.
- We overpower to cover our fear.

- We inflate our importance to convince ourselves and others that we're valuable.
- We fear we have no worth.

Unfortunately, none of these tactics work to satiate the hunger in our hearts, nor do they persuade others to feel more positive about us. On the contrary, insecurity is like cellophane: others can see right through it. It wraps us up in a false sense of protection. It is a worthless self-protective coping skill. This is because we must *acknowledge* our insecurity, then bring it before the light of God's Word.

We all experience moments of insecurity. In fact, God designed us to feel vulnerable and unsure at times. Insecurity can be a helpful tool that helps us perceive danger, stop what we're doing, apply wisdom, and seek God for direction.

Insecurity can also be an invitation that draws us to God. Shame causes us to withdraw, hide our true selves, and avoid exposure and the fear of embarrassment. However, insecurity can beckon us to a positive response, and if we respond, we can bring our emotions and false thinking to the Lord and surrender our fears to him. As we surrender our insecurities to him in faith, our trust grows.

Today we untie the cords of insecurity and inadequacy as we remember that our identity is found in God. Our value and worth are derived from him alone.

Declare

I am secure in Christ. My identity is rooted and established in his love. I am assured of his power as the solid foundation beneath my feet. Therefore, I can stand in total confidence, knowing I am made perfect and complete in him.

Meditate, Believe, Accept

When I feel weak and unsure, I rejoice. God's strength shows up best when I am weak.

> But he replied, "My kindness is all you need. My power is strongest when you are weak." So if Christ keeps giving me his power, I will gladly brag about how weak I am. (2 Corinthians 12:9 CEV)

When I feel inadequate, I remind myself that God has chosen me, and he gives me what I need.

> Now remember what you were, my friends, when God called you. From the human point of view few of you were wise or powerful or of high social standing. God purposely chose what the world considers nonsense in order to shame the wise, and he chose what the world considers weak in order to shame the powerful. He chose what the world looks down on and despises and thinks is nothing, in order to destroy what the world thinks is important. (1 Corinthians 1:26–28 GNT)

When I feel insignificant, I remember who I am—chosen and loved by God.

> You didn't choose me. I chose you. I appointed you to go and produce lasting fruit, so that the Father will give you whatever you ask for, using my name. (John 15:16)

When insecurity tries to rise up and overwhelm me, I reject it. I embrace my God-given identity and remain confident.

> So we say with confidence, "The Lord is my helper; I will not be afraid. What can mere mortals do to me?" (Hebrews 13:6 NIV)

Confess

Lord, I confess that I often have feelings of insecurity. I fear I'm not enough. I'm timid, and I don't always stand in confidence or in the authority you've given me. Forgive me for doubting myself—and doubting you. Set me free as I choose to live brave, bold, and secure.

Affirm

I am secure in Christ. I trust in him and the work of transformation he is doing in me. I boldly affirm that I am confident, chosen of God, and complete in every way. I do not fear lack. I have all I need to live this life. I am secure.

Repeat "I am secure in Christ" three times. Each time you read it, add special emphasis to the bolded word or words.

I am secure in Christ.

I **am secure** in Christ.

I am secure **in Christ**.

Extra Memory Challenge

> So we say with confidence, "The Lord is my helper; I will not be afraid. What can mere mortals do to me?" (Hebrews 13:6 NIV)

Explore

1. Are there times when you feel insecure? When?
2. What are you doing when insecurity rises within you?
3. What might this insecurity be telling you?
4. What new skill can you apply when you feel insecure?

Free Thinking

Perhaps you've struggled with inner voices that tell you you're not enough, not capable, not worthy, not as good as, not . . .

The good news is that Jesus came to free us from condemnation and shame. Our security does not rest in anything we can achieve or any amount of good we can do. In Christ, *we are enough*.

In Jesus, *you are enough*. Living in fear and insecurity is a rejection of your true identity.

Keep moving forward. I'm for you and am cheering you on, but more importantly, God is for you. Through the power of his Holy Spirit, you are unstoppable.

Journal

CHAPTER 8

CORDS OF DEPRESSION

*I have depression. But I prefer to say "I battle" depression
instead of "I suffer" with it. Because depression hits,
but I hit back.
Battle on.*
—Author unknown

Challenge Week 6

Weekly Reading: Untying the Cords of Depression

*The Lord himself goes before you and will be with you;
he will never leave you nor forsake you.
Do not be afraid; do not be discouraged.*
Deuteronomy 31:8 NIV

This week we look at the emotion of depression, or probably more accurately, the result of numbing your emotions. Sadness, grief, disappointment, shame, rejection, and anger are often the manifestation of underlying feelings of depression, and often they are feelings we are afraid to experience. Instead of allowing our emotions to surface, we avoid them and stuff them. But as a wise friend once told me, "You can't stuff stuff."

I want to be clear, however, that I am not talking about clinical depression, which is a medical condition that requires treatment. I'll reiterate this many times this week. If you're struggling with depression that you cannot overcome, you need to seek a doctor's counsel immediately.

But how do you know if you're struggling with sadness and feelings of depression or with clinical depression?

Guy Winch, PhD, writes in his article "The Important Difference Between Sadness and Depression":

> Depression is an abnormal emotional state, a mental illness that affects our thinking, emotions, perceptions, and behaviors in pervasive and chronic ways. When we're depressed we feel sad about everything. Depression does not necessarily require a difficult event or situation, a loss, or a change of circumstance as a trigger. In fact, it often occurs in the absence of any such triggers. People's lives on paper might be totally fine—they would even admit this is true—and yet they still feel horrible.[16]

The emotion of sadness, which is our focus this week, usually occurs when we experience hurt or disappointment. We experience an unmet expectation, and we feel hurt and sad. Life is difficult and harder than we ever dreamed. We're drained of energy, and we feel a pervasive sadness. In other words, sadness is the result of some trigger: a painful experience, a hurtful encounter, or an event. When things change in our favor, the sadness often goes away almost immediately.

Sadness can also be a learned response to life's difficulties. If, in our developing years, we never witnessed a healthy way to recover from disappointments, or if our role models never taught us how to find hope in bleak situations but instead modeled how to nurse sadness and keep a grudge, then depression and sadness may become our emotional habit. The good news is, we can be free from controlling emotions, including depression and sadness.

For the last several weeks, you've been learning skills that empower you to feel emotions, to understand the impact of pain and hurt, and to move through those emotions in positive, healthy ways. You no longer need to remain stuck or numb. This week you will acknowledge your feelings, continue gaining strength, and find joy as you overcome the stranglehold of sadness and depression.

Week 6

Day 35

TODAY'S TRUTH: I AM NOT BOUND BY DISCOURAGEMENT, FOR GOD IS THE LIFTER OF MY HEAD

But you, Lord, are a shield around me,
my glory, the One who lifts my head high.
Psalm 3:3 NIV

Depression and discouragement are part of the human experience. Because you live in this broken world, you've encountered moments of this kind of despair. It's part of our time here on earth, and it's important to remember that depression seldom occurs only once. It often follows trauma and tragedy.

The Bible shows us the primary reasons why people sink into depression. People may let us down, abandon us, shame us, blame us, or betray us. These experiences hurt, and we can become stuck in anger, bitterness, and hurt.

The disciples became discouraged about circumstances. They were frustrated that Jesus didn't fight for an earthly kingdom and that he left them. We, too, become frustrated, even angry at our circumstances and feel like God has abandoned us.

Peter was disappointed and ashamed of himself. He realized he wasn't quite the man he tried to make people believe he was. We also can become depressed when we feel we've failed or don't measure up.

Yes, the heroes of our faith went through bouts of depression. Still, God used them in incredible ways. In other words, depression does not disqualify us from God's plan, nor does it jeopardize our relationship with Christ. He understands. Depression—and I'm not speaking about the medical and physical disease of clinical depression[2]*—can, however, paralyze us from achieving and reaching for God's best for our lives.

But the good news is that we can renew our minds and become freed from the bondage of depression and discouragement. At every point of despair we can say, "I am poor and needy; may the Lord think of me. You are my help and my deliverer" (Psalm 40:17 NIV).

How do we make sure negative emotions don't get the best of us?

- Acknowledge negative emotions. Everyone has them. Learning how to process them biblically is the key.
- Honor your body. Your emotions work in collaboration with your body. If your body isn't well, your emotions follow suit.
- Focus your thoughts. Pay attention to your self-talk. You are not your emotions. Tell yourself the truth according to the Word of God. Take every thought captive and examine it. Is it life-giving or life-taking?

Declare

I will not be depressed or discouraged about my life, my accomplishments, or my relationships. I will trust God. I shake off despair and depression and choose to renew my mind with God's Word. I will rejoice and overcome.

Meditate, Believe, Accept

Our negative self-criticism goes on and on. Insecurity about who we are reveals the cracks in the foundation of our identity.

The Lord hears my cry, and he lifts me out of depression.

[2] Clinical depression needs immediate medical attention. It is treatable and should not be minimized.

> I waited patiently for the Lord: he turned to me and heard my cry. He lifted me out of the slimy pit, out of the mud and mire; he set my feet on a rock and gave me a firm place to stand. He put a new song in my mouth, a hymn of praise to our God. Many will see and fear the Lord and put their trust in him. (Psalm 40:1–3 NIV)

I am not depressed, for my head is lifted high, and God's shield surrounds me.

> But you, Lord, are a shield around me, my glory, the One who lifts my head high. (Psalm 3:3 NIV)

My soul is neither downcast nor disturbed, for I hope in God. He always comes through.

> Why, my soul, are you downcast? Why so disturbed within me? Put your hope in God, for I will yet praise him, my Savior and my God. (Psalm 42:11 NIV)

Although troubles fill this world, I will not lose heart. God surrounds me with total peace.

> I have told you these things, so that in me you may have peace. In this world you will have trouble. But take heart! I have overcome the world. (John 16:33 NIV)

Confess

Lord, I confess that life's circumstances tempt me to feel discouraged. Today I renounce the cords of depression, and instead, I choose your peace and comfort to fill me.

Affirm

The Lord lifts my head high, and I overcome through his peace. I am not dismayed, nor am I depressed by circumstances; instead,

I praise God with all my heart, knowing he gives me strength and comfort.

Repeat "God lifts my head" three times. Each time you read it, add special emphasis to the bolded word or word.

God lifts my head.

God **lifts** my head.

God lifts **my head**.

Extra Memory Challenge

> But you, Lord, are a shield around me, my glory, the One who lifts my head high. (Psalm 3:3 NIV)

Explore

1. How has depression tried to overtake you?
2. What have you done to overcome it?
3. What can you do differently?

Journal

Week 6

Day 36

Today's Truth: When Depression and Heaviness Come, I Praise the Lord and He Lifts Me Up

God is our refuge and strength,
an ever-present help in trouble.
Psalm 46:1 NIV

Dawn writes about her experience with depression:

> I experienced clinical depression—a result of post-traumatic stress disorder. It hit me suddenly, knocking me off my feet emotionally and physically.
>
> I had never before experienced depression or the anxiety that accompanied it. My former will to "just be okay" and "look on the bright side" had vanished. I could do nothing to change my condition. I needed medical help and treatment.
>
> What I could do, however, was fortify my spirit. Instead of crying—which I also freely did—I went to the Psalms and read and said the words of David to the Lord.
>
> This simple discipline radically changed my mental state. I was still depressed, but I was not discouraged. I believed the Word, and I knew God would rescue me. I placed sticky notes with Scriptures in key places throughout my house. I meditated on his Word day and night, and this meditation literally began to heal my brain. New neuro pathways formed in my brain as I focused on new thoughts—God's truth.[17]

John 20:11–13 shows us Mary Magdalene weeping at Jesus's

tomb after his death. Mary had experienced a profound life change because Jesus had rescued her. She'd lived under the influence of seven demons until he came to her and cast them out. I don't believe it's possible for us to imagine Mary's torment before Jesus rescued her. His death must have brought her profound grief. We know she loved him deeply, but rather than remain at home wallowing in despair, Mary went to look for Jesus—or to be as near to him as she could.

Are you discouraged? Draw near to Jesus and unleash your heart. Write out your prayers. Read God's Word and ask for encouragement, direction, and comfort. Offer praise and worship despite your feelings. God lifts our heads and our hearts as we come to him in worship. Don't rely on feelings. Our heart typically follows our head if we offer God gratitude and praise. Refuse to isolate. The Word of God, the Spirit of God, and the people of God strengthen us. He created us for community, and when we feel discouraged, we need the hope, wisdom, and encouragement of God's people the most.

Today we will sing the psalms and feel the cords break as we draw near to Jesus, face our discouragement, and worship and praise the Lord.

Declare

I will praise the Lord at all times, and he will lift me up. My soul and my spirit will soar with the strength God gives me, and he will lift me out of the pit and set me upon a rock. Depression will not hold me captive. I am set free as I praise the Lord.

Meditate, Believe, Accept

The Lord is close to me, and I am saved.

> The Lord is close to the brokenhearted and saves those who are crushed in spirit. (Psalm 34:18 NIV)

The Lord walks with me and comforts me, even in dark places.

> Lord, even when your path takes me through the valley of deepest darkness, fear will never conquer me, for you already have! You remain close to me and lead me through it all the way. Your authority is my strength and my peace. The comfort of your love takes away my fear. I'll never be lonely, for you are near. (Psalm 23:4 TPT)

I am protected from trouble and am hidden in a safe place.

> You are my hiding place; you will protect me from trouble and surround me with songs of deliverance. (Psalm 32:7 NIV)

God is always with me, and he gives me refuge from all harm.

> God is our refuge and strength, an ever-present help in trouble. (Psalm 46:1 NIV)

I will not be shaken; the Lord is my rock!

> The LORD is my rock, my protection, my Savior. My God is my rock. I can run to him for safety. He is my shield and my saving strength, my defender. (Psalm 18:2 NCV)

Confess

Lord, I confess that when I'm suffering with depression, I don't feel like praising you. But I find my deliverance in worshiping you. In finding my song, I find healing. So forgive me, wash me, and put a new song in my heart—a song of freedom and deliverance.

Affirm

I praise the Lord, and he hears my voice. He lifts me up and sets me high upon a rock. I am a worshiper of God, and as a result,

I stand on a firm foundation, saved from all harm. God is my refuge and my strength.

Repeat "God is my refuge and strength" three times. Each time you read it, add special emphasis to the bolded word or words.

God is my refuge and strength.

God **is my refuge** and strength.

God **is my** refuge and **strength**.

Extra Memory Challenge

> God is our refuge and strength, an ever-present help in trouble. (Psalm 46:1 NIV)

Explore

1. How can praising God change your circumstances?
2. What does this focus do for your soul?

Journal

Week 6

Day 37

TODAY'S TRUTH: I HAVE GLADNESS AND JOY, NOT HOPELESSNESS AND DESPAIR

To those who have sorrow in Zion
I will give them a crown of beauty instead of ashes.
I will give them the oil of joy instead of sorrow,
and a spirit of praise instead of a spirit of no hope.
Then they will be called oaks that are right with God,
planted by the Lord, that He may be honored.
Isaiah 61:3 NLV

Have you ever felt shrouded by the spirit of *No Hope*? You may not completely understand the meaning of the above verse, but you do recognize the feeling it describes:

Despair.

Hopelessness.

Futility.

Powerlessness.

Discouragement.

Whichever word you choose, each describes a facet of how you may feel when you're battling a spirit of No Hope. This No Hope feeling of despair creeps into our souls in subtle ways. Perhaps we're dealing with a hurtful situation that never seems to find a resolution. Maybe a chronic illness steals our vitality and ability to remain active. Wayward children sever ties, or a business can't get traction and drains us. Despair doesn't always knock on our heart and announce itself before it moves in. But one bleak morning we awaken to discover No Hope has moved in lock, stock, and barrel.

What we may miss, however, is that Despair, a No Hope spirit, takes over as a result of what we believe about our situation and our endurance. Like a bread-crumb trail, our hopeless thoughts draw Despair to our door.

The psalmist said, "I would have despaired *unless I had believed that I would see the goodness of the Lord* in the land of the living" (Psalm 27:13 NASB, emphasis added). Despair is a direct result of believing that our case is hopeless, that something in our life will never change. Despair is the manifestation of how we interpret our circumstances and the thoughts we focus on. We feel trapped, like miserable failures who can never change. We listen to voices of doom and despair and then wonder why hopelessness fills our hearts.

Someone once said, "People can live weeks without food, days without water, minutes without oxygen, but not a moment without hope." Since a connection exists between despair, how we think, and what we believe, what do we need to believe instead to rise above despair? What do *you* need to believe instead to rise above despair?

Today we will focus on the hope and truth of God's Word to change what we believe and to claim victory over despair and hopelessness.

Declare

The joy of the Lord makes me strong. I am free from cords of depression. Sadness cannot overwhelm me. God's Holy Spirit fills me with joy, and therefore, sorrow must go.

Meditate, Believe, Accept

The Holy Spirit fills me, and I possess the fruit that comes from him.

> But the fruit that comes from having the Holy Spirit in our lives is: love, joy, peace, not giving up, being kind, being good, having faith, being gentle, and being the boss over our own desires. (Galatians 5:22–23 NLV)

I am strong and filled with joy, peace, and power.

> Our hope comes from God. May He fill you with joy and peace because of your trust in Him. May your hope grow stronger by the power of the Holy Spirit. (Romans 15:13 NLV)

I am not sad or dismayed but strengthened with joy.

> Do not be sad for the joy of the Lord is your strength. (Nehemiah 8:10 NLV)

God has set me free, and sorrow and sadness flee from me.

> Those whom the Lord has paid for and set free will return. They will come to Zion with singing. Joy that lasts forever will crown their heads. They will be glad and full of joy. Sorrow and sad voices will be gone. (Isaiah 35:10 NLV)

Confess

Lord, I confess there are times I feel despair and am overcome with sadness. May your joy fill my heart instead, giving me gladness and freedom.

Affirm

I am a man filled with contentment and power. God makes me strong and fills me with a peace that passes all understanding. I am not overwhelmed by despair. Instead, I give my emotions, concerns, and fears to God, and he lifts me up and crowns me with everlasting joy.

Repeat "I am filled with joy and peace" three times. Each time you read it, add special emphasis to the bolded word or words.

I am filled with joy and peace.

I **am filled** with joy and peace.

I am filled **with joy and peace**.

Extra Memory Challenge

Our hope comes from God. May He fill you with joy and peace because of your trust in Him. May your hope grow stronger by the power of the Holy Spirit. (Romans 15:13 NLV)

Explore

1. What things in your life are you sad about? What do you think is the source of your sadness?
2. Ask the Holy Spirit to help you identify areas where you are mourning or filled with sorrow.
3. Remember, we often cover our grief or turn our pain inward. Have you done that?

Journal

Week 6

Day 38

Today's Truth: I Return to Hope,
for God Is the Source of Hope

Hope deferred makes the heart sick,
but a dream fulfilled is a tree of life.
Proverbs 13:12

Yesterday we looked at the spirits of No Hope and Despair. I desire that you realized you have every reason in God to be filled with expectancy, joy, and hope. God has promised you a prosperous and fulfilling future. His plan for you is amazing, and it is good. God is, by his essence, good, and every interaction he has with you flows from his pure goodness.

This means that even in difficult times, God is good and is working for your good. You can be assured you'll be better because of your trials and hardships. When you truly believe this, you'll easily be able to return to your hope in God. You can boldly say, "I will never be embarrassed by hoping in God."

Placing your hope in people may end in futility, but God will never fail you. As the above verse says, "Hope deferred makes the heart sick, but a dream fulfilled"—a dream realized—"is a tree of life." God wants to fulfill your dreams. More specifically, God wants to fulfill *his* dream for your life, which is more than you could ever dream.

As I'm writing this to you, I'm thinking about all of the things God has done for me, the prayers he's answered for me, and the opportunities he's given to me. As I reflect, I see that his dreams for me were much bigger than I could ever have imagined. Honestly, I'm glad he answered some of my prayers with a no. It's as if God were saying to me, "You're dreaming too small. I want to do so much more for you."

But even when we know God's goodness, we need to understand that receiving things from God should not be our ultimate hope. Knowing God and seeing him one day face to face is the greatest dream we can have.

May this be the hope you return to—drawing close to God because he is the God of hope.

Declare

No matter how I feel, I have great hope because the God of all hope is with me. He is faithful, and my hope will not be in vain. The hope I possess destroys all despair, and the spirit of No Hope cannot live in my heart or mind. Today I boldly declare that I am free from hopelessness, and faith and expectancy fill me.

Meditate, Believe, Accept

God has given me a future filled with hope.

> "For I know what I have planned for you," says the Lord. "I have plans to prosper you, not to harm you. I have plans to give you a future filled with hope." (Jeremiah 29:11 NET)

God is good to me. I wait for him.

> "The Lord is my portion; therefore I will wait for him." The Lord is good to those whose hope is in him, to the one who seeks him. (Lamentations 3:24–25 NIV)

I believe in God's faithfulness, and I overflow with confident hope.

> I pray that God, the source of hope, will fill you completely with joy and peace because you trust in him. Then you will overflow with confident hope through the power of the Holy Spirit. (Romans 15:13)

I will stay in faith, filled with hope, trusting that God will do what he promised.

> Abraham believed anyway, deciding to live not on the basis of what he saw he couldn't do but on what God said he would do. (Romans 4:18 MSG)

I am not afraid to have hope because hope in God will not disappoint me. I believe this.

> We can rejoice, too, when we run into problems and trials, for we know that they help us develop endurance. And endurance develops strength of character, and character strengthens our confident hope of salvation. And this hope will not lead to disappointment. For we know how dearly God loves us, because he has given us the Holy Spirit to fill our hearts with his love. (Romans 5:3–5)

Confess

Lord, I confess there are times when hopelessness overwhelms me. It's in those times I'm reminded to meditate on you and your Word and align my thoughts with what you say is true. As I do, my mind becomes transformed, and your hope fills my heart and strengthens me. Today I remember your great love for me, and it fills me with hope.

Affirm

God has a future for me filled with hope. My joy overflows, and I am at peace knowing my hope is not in vain.

Repeat "My future is filled with hope" three times. Each time you read it, add special emphasis to the bolded word or words.

My future is filled with hope.

My future **is filled** with hope.

My future is filled **with hope**.

Extra Memory Challenge

> May the God of hope fill you with all joy and peace in believing, so that by the power of the Holy Spirit you may abound in hope. (Romans 15:13 ESV)

Explore

1. Do you ever feel hopeless? When? Why?
2. Hopelessness comes when we fail to trust in God. How can you overcome when hope is deferred? What blocks you from trusting God?
3. One way of increasing faith is by readjusting our focus. This means taking our eyes off our circumstances (a difficult discipline that requires practice) and concentrating (meditating) on spiritual truth. We can do this by spending time in Scripture, listening to biblical music, seeking encouragement from the people of God, or listening to or reading Christian resources. What steps can you take to help you refocus?

Journal

Week 6

Day 39

TODAY'S TRUTH: REJECTION HAS NO POWER OVER ME BECAUSE GOD ACCEPTS ME

See how much the Father has loved us!
His love is so great that we are called God's children—
and so, in fact, we are.
This is why the world does not know us:
it has not known God.
1 John 3:1 GNT

Today you are exactly two-thirds of the way through the Freedom Challenge. Congratulations! By now you are deeply into transformation, and I trust that you have noticed a difference in your mind (the way you think) and heart (the way you feel)—a difference that will change your life forever.

On day 1 of the Freedom Challenge, you accepted and claimed your rightful place in this world when you declared, "I am a child of God!" Today will remind you of that truth again: you *are* God's child, and he will never ever reject you.

At some point in our lives, however, most of us have experienced the sting of rejection. Perhaps you were rejected for a date by someone you liked. Maybe your girlfriend broke up with you and started dating your best friend. Perhaps you lost out on a job opportunity because you weren't what the headhunters were looking for, or you weren't invited to a gathering of your friends. Rejection happens to all of us, and it hurts.

Sadly, the humiliating pain of *continual* rejection plagues many people. Perhaps their mothers or fathers rejected them, or maybe their siblings mocked them and turned away. As a result, these injured souls may not make friends and may feel isolated and alone.

A spirit of rejection may slip in and build a stronghold in their lives. Maybe these examples remind you of a friend or a loved one with a life shaped by rejection.

Maybe that person is you.

Rejection comes to us in numerous ways:

- Generational curses
- Bullying
- Parental disappointment
- Adoption
- Death of a parent (while a child)
- Divorced parents
- A divorce
- Siblings favored over us
- The absence or neglect of a parent, especially a father
- Abuse
- Trauma

Unfortunately, sin produces rejection and feelings of insecurity. The moment we sin (miss the mark), we sense guilt and failure. God created us with an inner sense of morality. Because we know we've done wrong, we feel that others judge us for our failings— real or imagined—and as Pastor Rick Warren says, "The starting point for all happiness is shifting the focus away from yourself. . . . It's something you have to learn to do."[18]

Psalm 94:14 tells us, "The Lord will not reject his people; he will not abandon his special possession." You are God's special possession—his child. He will not and cannot abandon you because he cannot act apart from love, and he loves you. The God of the universe accepts you—not because you're good enough, but because Jesus lived a sinless life and paid for your sins. Refuse to devalue Jesus's death by living under the power of rejection. Untie those old rotted cords and let them go. When the God of the universe loves you, how can earthly rejection matter? God determines your value, and people can only reject his true assessment. Their words are empty and worthless. Remember, you are God's chosen child.

Declare

God chooses me. He loves me and accepts me. He created me and designed me to be wonderfully unique. Rejection will not choke the life out of me. I break these cords in Jesus's name.

Meditate, Believe, Accept

God always wants me, even when others reject me.

> *My father and mother may abandon me, but the Lord will take care of me. (Psalm 27:10 GNT)*

God deeply loves me, and I am his child.

> *See* how much the Father has loved us! His love is so great that we are called God's children—and so, in fact, we are. This is why the world does *not know us: it has not* known God. (1 John 3:1 GNT)

Nothing can remove me from God's love.

> *For I am certain that nothing can separate us from his love: neither death nor life, neither angels nor other heavenly rulers or powers, neither the present nor the future, neither the world above nor the world below—there is nothing in all creation that will ever be able to separate us from the love of God which is ours through Christ Jesus our Lord.* (Romans 8:38–39 GNT)

I have power to understand the depth and fullness of God's love for me.

> *So that* you, together with all God's people, may have the power to understand how broad and long, how high

and deep, is Christ's *love. Yes, may you come to know his love—although it can never be fully known—and so be completely filled with the very nature of* God. (Ephesians 3:18–19 GNT)

Confess

Lord, I confess there are times when the spirit of rejection rises up and steals my confidence and sense of value. I feel unloved, unwanted, and unqualified in these moments. Set me free from the cords of rejection and fill me with your love.

Affirm

I am accepted. I do not listen to the voice of rejection that tries to persuade me that I'm unloved or unwanted. God is for me. He loves me and has chosen me. I am worthy and valuable, and God has great plans for me. The cords of rejection will not hold me back from experiencing love and life to the fullest.

Repeat "I am accepted and chosen by God" three times. Each time you read it, add special emphasis to the bolded word or words.

I am accepted and chosen by God.

I **am accepted and chosen** by God.

I am accepted and chosen **by God**.

Extra Memory Challenge

See how much the Father has loved us! His love is so great that we are called God's children—and so, in fact, we are. This is why the world does not know us: it has not known God. (1 John 3:1 GNT)

Explore

1. Have you experienced rejection in your past?
2. How did you handle it then?
3. How will you handle rejection now?

Journal

Week 6

Day 40

Today's Truth: When I Feel Depressed, I Reach Out and Do Not Isolate

Two people are better off than one,
for they can help each other succeed.
If one person falls, the other can reach out and help.
But someone who falls alone is in real trouble.
Ecclesiastes 4:9–10

Another aspect of depression is choosing to isolate and withdraw from our community of friends and family. I sometimes need respite and enjoy going off alone to regroup and refuel. This is solitude. Jesus himself withdrew to lonely places so he could speak with the Father and draw strength from spending time with him. I hope you practice this discipline, as well, for solitude can replenish our dry souls.

But isolation is different from solitude. It's lonely. It's antisocial. It's unhealthy.

As I write this chapter, we are in the middle of the COVID-19 pandemic. Our president has declared a state of emergency and mandated a "Stay in Place" order. That means we've been in lockdown for over thirty days. Social distancing and physical isolation have created another global concern: depression. More than ever before, we recognize the importance of social contact and support—with no church services, sporting events, family gatherings, or daily work routines, isolation is taking a significant toll.

God created us for community. Often when we're feeling blue or sad and depressed, our human instinct is to pull away from everyone and withdraw even deeper into isolation. If this describes you, then I'm here as a friend to raise a warning flag: isolation can be dangerous.

In nature, animals often travel in packs. God created them that way, providing them with an innate safety mechanism. Traveling in a group offers protection from predators who lie in wait for a single sheep or foal or cow to wander off alone. The moment an animal wanders off by itself, a wolf or coyote or lion comes in to devour. The result can be fatal.

God also created humans to journey through life in "packs"—in community with one another. God wants us to come together and rely upon and draw strength from one another.

When we wander off alone, we become the Enemy's prey. Satan twists our thoughts, throws discouragement our way, and lies to us as we sit in the shadowy corners of isolation.

"No one loves you."

"You're just in the way."

"No one will even miss you."

"Go ahead, end it all. Everyone will be better off without you."

Have you ever heard any of these intoxicating whispers drift through your thoughts?

"Well, I'm a loner," you may say. "I'm introverted, and I like my alone time."

As I said before, alone time is okay, and is even good and healthy—but not for long periods and not as a coping mechanism for life's challenges. For most people, the escapism of isolation breeds further depression.

To break a pattern of isolation and lack of accountability, you must choose to involve yourself with others. Serve at your church, a hospital, or a school when you're feeling alone. Volunteer at a nonprofit ministry or invite someone out for tea. Don't wait for someone to reach out to you. Take the first step in courage, faith, and a commitment to your well-being. Decide to take one step today to end isolation.

Declare

I believe in the family of God. I renounce isolation to cope with life's discouragement. When I am depressed, I will reach out. I will serve. I will draw strength from the community of believers. I am part of God's beautiful world, and I am free from isolation.

Meditate, Believe, Accept

I will not let the Enemy devour me, for I do not stand alone.

> A person standing alone can be attacked and defeated, but two can stand back-to-back and conquer. Three are even better, for a triple-braided cord is not easily broken. (Ecclesiastes 4:12)

> Be sober-minded; be watchful. Your adversary the devil prowls around like a roaring lion, seeking someone to devour. (1 Peter 5:8 ESV)

> If you do what is right, will you not be accepted? But if you do not do what is right, sin is crouching at your door; it desires to have you, but you must rule over it. (Genesis 4:7 NIV).

I am better when I do not isolate. I grow and succeed when I connect with others.

> Two people are better off than one, for they can help each other succeed. If one person falls, the other can reach out and help. But someone who falls alone is in real trouble. (Ecclesiastes 4:9–10)

I am encouraged and spurred on by others when I do not isolate. I will not give up meeting together with others.

> And let us consider how we may spur one another on toward love and good deeds, not giving up meeting together, as some are in the habit of doing, but encourag-

ing one another—and all the more as you see the Day approaching. (Hebrews 10:24–25 NIV)

I am strengthened by solitary places of prayer.

Very early in the morning, while it was still dark, Jesus got up, left the house and went off to a solitary place, where he prayed. (Mark 1:35 NIV)

Confess

Lord, I confess that sometimes I pull away from others and from life itself. I want to isolate and escape. But today I renounce isolation as a way to handle sadness and depression. I untie the cords of isolation, in Jesus's name.

Affirm

I am free from the habit of isolation, and I reach out when I am depressed.

Repeat "I need others" three times. Each time you read it, add special emphasis to the bolded word.

I need others.

I **need** others.

I need **others**.

Extra Memory Challenge

Be sober-minded; be watchful. Your adversary the devil prowls around like a roaring lion, seeking someone to devour. (1 Peter 5:8 ESV)

Explore

1. Is isolation a habit for you? If so, when and why do you feel like isolating?
2. What can you choose to do instead of isolating when you feel depressed?

3. How can solitude help you instead of isolation? What would this look like?

Journal

Week 6

Day 41

SELF-EVALUATION ON DEPRESSION

After meditating this week on depression, rejection, and isolation, what did you learn about yourself? Read the symptoms below. If you have had most of these for more than six months, you should consult your physician.

Symptoms of Depression:

- Loss of pleasure from things usually enjoyed
- Depressed, sad mood
- Fatigue or loss of energy
- Feelings of worthlessness
- Inability to concentrate or focus
- Inability to make decisions or a feeling of being overwhelmed
- Weight loss or weight gain
- Insomnia
- Anorexia
- Agitation or restlessness
- Recurrent thoughts of death or suicide or an attempt at suicide

General Questions:

- Have you struggled with depression in the past?
- Do other members of your family (parents or siblings) have a history of depression?
- Do you associate depression with spiritual weakness or a lack of inner strength?

A Word of Encouragement

Unfortunately, many people—especially Christians—associate depression with spiritual weakness or a lack of inner strength. This could not be further from the truth. Research in neuroscience indicates that many factors contribute to depression.[19] Consider these facts:

- In one functional magnetic resonance imaging study published in *The Journal of Neuroscience*, investigators studied twenty-four people who had a history of depression. On average, the hippocampus was 9 to 13 percent smaller in depressed people as compared with the hippocampus of those who were not depressed.
- Researchers are exploring possible links between low moods and the sluggish production of new neurons in the hippocampus.
- Neurotransmitters are chemicals that relay messages from neuron to neuron. An antidepressant medication tends to increase the concentration of these substances in the spaces between neurons (the synapses). In many cases, this shift appears to give the system enough of a nudge so the brain can do its job better.

Your body is fearfully and wonderfully made (Psalm 139:14). The same chemical processes that regulate organ function in the rest of our body must receive respect in our understanding of the brain. Biological anatomy beyond our control, as well as traumatic events, can contribute to depression and change the chemistry of the brain.

Just as you should not feel shame for taking insulin for diabetes, you should not feel shame in seeking needed medication for depression. If you are struggling with symptoms, consult your doctor.

Journal

CHAPTER 9

CORDS OF NEGATIVE EMOTIONS

*Negative emotions like loneliness, envy, guilt, have an
important role to play in a happy life; they're big flashing
signs that something needs to change.*
—Gretchen Rubin

Challenge Week 7

Weekly Reading: Negative Emotions

*When pride comes, then comes shame;
but with the humble is wisdom.*
Proverbs 11:2 NKJV

*It's okay to have emotions,
as long as emotions don't have you.*
—Dawn Damon

E motions—are they good or are they bad?
When emotions work in cooperation with our temperament
and mood, they can be helpful and fervent, but sometimes they can
also be painful and disruptive. Negative emotions can become debilitating. Persistent negative emotions can overpower us and leave
us feeling overwhelmed, powerless, and bound.

Expressing negative emotions is important. Emotions—even negative emotions—can give you valuable insight and help you move forward. You get to choose the role your emotions play and what you want to gain from them. Hopefully by now, week 7, you realize you don't have to let ugly, negative feelings take you hostage, disempower you, and beat you down. It doesn't serve you well to allow negative emotions to find an uncontested resting place in your heart and mind. Instead, interact with negative emotions. Ask what purpose they serve you in the short term and the long run. Will they move you closer to your goals? Investigate the messages that uncomfortable emotions try to speak to you. For instance, anger is a secondary emotion that flows from a deeper root cause. When you're angry, ask yourself what action or circumstance has hurt you.

Negative emotions come to all of us, and most often those feelings point to a hurt, disappointment, or unmet expectation. Whether deep-seated emotions surface that have been suppressed since childhood or we experience a flash of irritation at a family member, emotions are an invitation to explore what's going on deep inside of us.

In his book *Awaken the Giant Within*, motivational speaker and author Tony Robbins writes that we need to listen to the message our emotions are trying to give us. He says that emotions are signals that we need to act on something, change something, or be aware that something is wrong. He writes:

> If you want to make your life really work, you must make your emotions work for you. You can't run from them; you can't tune them out; you can't trivialize them or delude yourself about what they mean. Nor can you just allow them to run your life. Emotions, even those that seem painful in the short term, are truly like an internal compass that points you toward the actions you must take to arrive at your goals.[20]

Emotions are an internal message crying out to you. Unwisely releasing emotions can be harmful to others, but left silenced and ignored, negative emotions will drain you of your joy, steal your enthusiasm and energy for life, and eventually spill out on others like acid.

This is why I want to empower you to lean into the process of renewing your mind. Your emotions connect to your thoughts. As you exchange your thoughts for God's truth, your emotions will follow. You won't deny what you feel as you make this exchange, but you *will* deny emotions the right to take over and control your life and harm others.

My Heart Is My Field

> *Deadly emotions, buried alive, never die.*
> —Joyce Meyer

Emotions are like seeds planted in a field. Buried alive and nurtured, they bring beauty into the world.

In the week ahead, you'll be encouraged to uncover buried emotions and examine and exchange distorted thinking for truth. Remember, our feelings are ours, but they aren't truth. You will learn to think about what you're feeling and interact with and question your feelings as you become aware of them. Weeds are always easier to pull when they are beginning to grow.

Don't wait. Begin today to uproot lies that produce negative emotions. Cultivate your soul and watch strength, wisdom, and character grow.

> Be careful how you think; your life is shaped by your thoughts. (Proverbs 4:23 GNT)

Week 7

Day 42

TODAY'S TRUTH: I WILL NOT DENY ANGER
AND WILL EXPLORE HOW I FEEL
AND RELEASE MY ANGER TO GOD

Fools give full vent to their rage,
but the wise bring calm in the end.
Proverbs 29:11 NIV

Today we revisit the emotion of anger. In week 4 we explored unforgiveness and anger and the potential for unaddressed anger to grow into grudge-bearing bitterness. We looked at the obvious manifestations of anger: hostile attitudes, negative behaviors, demeaning words, criticism, cynicism, unreasonable standards, depression, loss of enjoyment, and a pessimistic, negative outlook on life and people. This kind of anger is easy to detect.

But what if we don't recognize our anger? What if it hides below the surface?

Aristotle stated, "We praise a man who feels angry on the right grounds and against the right persons and also in the right manner at the right moment and for the right length of time."[21]

In actuality, suppressed anger is sustained anger. It lives inside us, fed by our denial, tunneling deep into our souls. We seldom recognize how dangerous and damaging hidden anger can be. Remember, anger is energy that is either bottled up or finds an avenue for expression. When anger turns inward, it often takes the form of depression.

This is why it's so critical for us to examine our emotions. Anger is a secondary emotion, meaning it follows another feeling or emotion. For this reason, we must identify the root cause of anger. We must ask ourselves what feeling triggered our anger because anger is often an emotion intended to come to our aid to protect, shield, and even hide our deepest emotion—which frequently is fear.

Because anger is a response, the good news is that we can control what we want to do with it. We can practice healthy responses to anger.

I'd like to walk you through a simple inventory that will help you see if the anger you feel is righteous or unrighteous, healthy or unhealthy, constructive or destructive.

First of all, ask God to reveal the roots of your anger. Sometimes anger is a learned response from our parents. But even if this is true, we must examine our motives.

Do you feel an injustice has been done? Perhaps the most important lesson you can learn in life is that you can't change people, and it's not your job to try. Changing people's hearts is God's responsibility. I've found that one of the best ways to resolve my anger is to pray for my offender.

Anger can also come from pride—thinking we are better than others. Anger can be fed by gossip, arguing, nagging, and backbiting, which are often fed by false self-righteousness.

Our anger can intensify when things don't go our way and we don't receive what we want or think we deserve. This can include someone not meeting our needs the way we believe they should be met.

We must be honest with God and ourselves about our anger by facing the root causes and chopping out the deadly roots. This means digging through painful experiences and examining our responses. Have we responded in the flesh to satisfy selfish desires, or have we laid our unrighteous anger at the feet of Jesus?

Romans 12:21 (NIV) gives us the cure to unrighteous anger: "Do not be overcome by evil, but overcome evil with good."

Declare

I will feel what I am feeling. I don't have to fear my feelings, bottle them up, or suppress them. I do not have to explode in anger. I can feel what I am feeling and express my emotions in a healthy way.

Meditate, Believe, Accept

I express my feelings in a healthy way, which brings me freedom and helps others.

> Fools give full vent to their rage, but the wise bring calm in the end. (Proverbs 29:11 NIV)

My gentleness turns away wrath from others and from me.

> A gentle answer turns away wrath, but a harsh word stirs up anger. (Proverbs 15:1 NIV)

I give God my cares and emotions, knowing that he cares for me. He can handle what I'm feeling.

> Cast all your anxiety on him because he cares for you. (1 Peter 5:7 NIV)

I walk by the Spirit and do not live according to feelings and emotions.

> So I say, walk by the Spirit, and you will not gratify the desires of the flesh. (Galatians 5:16 NIV)

Confess

Lord, I confess I have not always handled my emotions honestly. I have denied what I feel, think, and believe. I don't want to be filled with the pollution of unexpressed feelings fermenting in my soul. I choose to walk in the Spirit, feeling and expressing what I am experiencing and using the skills I am learning.

Affirm

The Holy Spirit fills me, and I walk and live my life connected to him. As I walk in the Spirit, I make choices that agree with God's Word and ways. I do not hide my heart and emotions from God or myself, but I process and resolve them before him in ways that heal me and set me free.

Repeat "I handle my emotions honestly" three times. Each time you read it, add special emphasis to the bolded word or words.

I handle my emotions honestly.

I **handle my emotions** honestly.

I handle my emotions **honestly**.

Extra Memory Challenge

Cast all your anxiety on him because he cares for you.
(1 Peter 5:7 NIV)

Explore

1. What has the focus on anger revealed to you? Where have you struggled with anger this week?
2. How did you respond? Where do you see areas for improvement?
3. What have you learned about yourself, God, and anger?

Journal

Week 7

Day 43

TODAY'S TRUTH: I REFUSE A BITTER SPIRIT AND ACCEPT GOD'S GRACE

Watch out that no poisonous root of bitterness grows up
to trouble you, corrupting many.
Hebrews 12:15

Emotions are part of the human experience. Feeling emotions isn't sinful, but how we respond to our emotions and how we use them can make them sinful. If negative emotions arise and overtake us or remain in our hearts, they take root and produce sinful fruit.

Bitterness is one example of a root that can burrow deep into our hearts and overtake our motives and attitudes. Notice that the above Bible verse says that bitterness "grows up." That's because unresolved anger and hurt smolder beneath the surface and then spring up like a blazing inferno, consuming everything in their path. Bitterness creates the heart of the killer, because in our bitterness, we justify hurting and destroying others. God commands us to root out bitterness quickly because of its deadly power.

Bitterness conceives when we feel hurt and allows our hurt to fester. Perhaps we feel as if we didn't get what we deserved. Maybe someone owes us something or dishonors us in some way. In these moments, we justify our anger and indifference, make our desires top priority, and ignore God's command to love our neighbors and our enemies. This requires self-sacrifice, which is the point of our faith. It costs us nothing to love people who are easy to love.

Even righteous anger can erode into bitterness over time. How can this happen? We can be rightfully hurt when someone does us wrong, then sink into a pseudo-virtuous obsession about the situation not being resolved. Or we may become preoccupied with obtaining "justice," or we might ruminate over a wound. We may be unjustly accused and asked to pay the price for an action that was not ours. No matter the situation, if we become focused on vindication or on blaming others for our place in life, or if we continually try to get the justice we think we deserve, bitterness is at work. Unless we cut out bitterness at the root, we will live as victims—not at the hands of someone else but as a result of our attitude.

God's Word says bitterness can "cause trouble and defile many" (Hebrews 12:15 NIV). Here are just a few of the troubles that can come from bitterness:

- Unnecessary mental and emotional pain
- Loss of joy and zeal for living fully in the present
- An attitude of cynicism and distrust
- A sour and pessimistic outlook on life
- A negative influence on health, depleting energy and the immune system
- Diminished purpose and achievement of goals
- A victim mindset
- A body overloaded with toxins

Wisdom from the book of Proverbs tells us that "A tranquil heart is life to the body, but passion is rottenness to the bones" (Proverbs 14:30 NASB).

The only remedy for bitterness is forgiveness. Today we untie the cords of bitterness and choose to be free from its poison.

Declare

I refuse to harbor anger, bitter envy, and resentment. Through the power of God, I choose to walk in forgiveness, and as I do, I am free from the rotten cord of bitterness.

Meditate, Believe, Accept

I live in peace with everyone, covered by God's grace.

> Strive for peace with everyone, and for the holiness without which no one will see the Lord. See to it that no one fails to obtain the grace of God; that no "root of bitterness" springs up and causes trouble, and by it many become defiled. (Hebrews 12:14–15 ESV)

I will not let bitterness trouble or defile me, for I receive God's grace.

> Look after each other so that none of you fails to receive the grace of God. Watch out that no poisonous root of bitterness grows up to trouble you, corrupting many. (Hebrews 12:15)

I put away all bitterness, anger, and wrath.

> Let all bitterness and wrath and anger and clamor and slander be put away from you, along with all malice. (Ephesians 4:31 ESV)

I wait for God to vindicate me. I do not repay evil out of bitterness.

> Don't say, "I'll pay you back for the wrong you did." Wait for the Lord, and he will make things right. (Proverbs 20:22 NCV)

I choose love and forgiveness instead of bitterness.

> Hatred stirs up strife, but love covers all offenses. (Proverbs 10:12 ESV)

Confess

Lord, I confess I have battled with the negative emotion of bitterness. I want to be free from all bitterness, disappointment, and anger. Thank you for your forgiveness and freedom.

Affirm

I am free from bitterness. I have received God's grace, and his grace is sufficient for me. I am set free from bitterness.

Repeat "I am set free from bitterness" three times. Each time you read it, add special emphasis to the bolded word or words.

I am set free from bitterness.

I **am set free** from bitterness.

I am set free **from bitterness**.

Extra Memory Challenge

> Hatred stirs up strife, but love covers all offenses. (Proverbs 10:12 ESV)

Explore

1. How has bitterness tried to wrap itself around your heart?
2. Can you recognize it in your life? In what areas? Where do you find yourself most susceptible?
3. In what way will you deal with bitterness in the future? What changes do you think you may have to make, or what steps will you have to take to become more aware of its presence?

Journal

Week 7

Day 44

TODAY'S TRUTH: I AM CONTENT,
FOR JEALOUSY AND ENVY BRING BONDAGE

Peace of mind makes the body healthy,
but jealousy is like a cancer.
Proverbs 14:30 GNT

Of all the emotions we'll talk about in the Freedom Challenge, jealousy and envy are the most difficult of which to speak. That's because these emotions are the most difficult for us to admit honestly. It's painful and embarrassing to acknowledge that we may be carnal enough to succumb to seemingly childish feelings, but let's be honest about it—a little green-eyed monster lives in each of us.

The emotions of jealousy and envy are active in our lives, even before we know how to talk and have the language to identify them. Wanting what others have is part of our human instinct. If you've ever watched babies and children (and even pets) at play, you know they immediately want the toy that another child picks up. Sounds like envy, right?

Although there is often a link between jealousy and envy, they are uniquely distinct. Envy triggers dissatisfaction and ignites greed, while jealousy fuels fear and insecurity. Envy causes us to desire something someone else possesses, and it holds hands with lust, greed, selfish ambition, and competition. Jealousy, however, includes fear—fear of losing something you already possess, or fear of losing a loved one, a friend, a position, or your influence. Jealousy has its roots in the fear of replacement. Jealousy also produces emotions such as anger, betrayal, and insecurity.

When we were children, we naturally turned to the cousins

of jealousy and envy. Sometime in our early childhood, someone scolded us for demonstrating these qualities. We learned not to want what someone else had but to find satisfaction with our own things. We may have felt ashamed and embarrassed if we were the clingy friend who felt insecure and threatened by the presence of a third friend.

However, an important question for us as adults to answer is whether we learned to handle envy and jealousy in healthy ways, or did we learn to hide them and pretend they didn't distress us?

Instead of batting down jealousy and envy like we're playing a game of whack-a-mole, when we sense jealousy and envy tugging on our sleeves, we should learn to ask ourselves questions like:

- What do I feel I'm missing out on?
- Do I believe God is withholding something from me?
- Am I less valuable or less loved if I don't have as much as they do?
- Why am I fearful of losing this friend, lover, position, or status?
- Am I enough?

God does not withhold good things from his children. We can be secure and satisfied that he has given us all that we need to glorify him. Jealousy and envy only bring us into bondage. Once we feed jealousy and envy, they sit below our dinner table, continually begging for more, like spoiled dogs.

When you feel jealousy and envy, stop and examine your feelings. Then take these steps to overcome the trap of self-centered bondage:

- Acknowledge your feelings and bring your questions before God.
- Ask him to reassure you of your value and of his love for

you. If your feelings of insecurity stem from childhood wounds, speak reassurance, love, and your true identity to that hurting part of you.

- Thank God for his blessings in your life. Make a gratitude list.
- Accept the truth that you are adequate—then lean into trust.

God longs to give you the desires of your heart, so run your race. Keep your eyes on your finish line. Today we untie the cords of jealousy and envy.

Declare

I am secure and satisfied with what God is doing in my life. I am confident he will not withhold any good thing from me. I am blessed and content.

Meditate, Believe, Accept

God will bless me with everything I need.

> For the Lord God is a sun and shield; the Lord bestows grace and favor and honor; no good thing will He withhold from those who walk uprightly. (Psalm 84:11 AMP)

I am at peace, and my body and soul are free from the decay of envy.

> A tranquil heart gives life to the flesh, but envy makes the bones rot. (Proverbs 14:30 ESV)

God's love fills my heart. I am not jealous or envious.

> Love is patient and kind. Love is not jealous, it does not brag, and it is not proud. (1 Corinthians 13:4 NCV)

I do not need to brag because of jealousy. I am satisfied, trusting God's plan for my life.

> But if you are bitterly jealous and filled with self-centered ambition, don't brag. Don't say that you are wise when it isn't true. That kind of wisdom doesn't come from above. It belongs to this world. It is self-centered and demonic. (James 3:14–15 GW)

> Never envy the wicked! Soon they fade away like grass and disappear. Trust in the Lord instead. Be kind and good to others; then you will live safely here in the land and prosper, feeding in safety. (Psalm 37:1–3 TLB)

I delight in God, and he gives me the desires of my heart.

> Be delighted with the Lord. Then he will give you all your heart's desires. (Psalm 37:4 TLB)

Confess

Lord, I confess the times I've been jealous of others and envious of others' possessions. Set me free from this destructive cord. Instead of turning to jealousy, I will be secure in you. Instead of choosing envy, I will be thankful.

Affirm

I am free from the cords of jealousy and envy, and they no longer have control in my life. I am secure and satisfied with what God is doing in my life. I trust him to fulfill the desires of my heart.

Repeat "I am free from jealousy and envy" three times. Each time you read it, add special emphasis to the bolded word or words.

I am free from jealousy and envy.

I am **free** from jealousy and envy.

I am free **from jealousy and envy**.

Extra Memory Challenge

Be delighted with the Lord. Then he will give you all your heart's desires. (Psalm 37:4 TLB)

Explore

1. What is the difference between jealousy and envy?
2. Have you experienced either one of these in your life? What things/people/circumstances seem to trigger you?
3. In what ways have jealousy or envy defeated you in the past?
4. How will you overcome these negative emotions in the future?

Journal

Week 7

Day 45

TODAY'S TRUTH: I WILL LIVE IN LOVE,
FREE FROM CONTEMPT AND DISGUST

When an evil person comes, contempt also comes,
along with dishonor and disgrace.
Proverbs 18:3 ISV

Body language can tell us a lot about people. Facial expressions easily communicate happiness, sadness, surprise, fear, anger, boredom, and disgust. One of our most subtle and often automatic body language responses is rolling our eyes. While our mouth may be communicating compliments, our eyes may be shouting disdain or contempt. This message is dangerous and destructive to relationships. A simple roll of the eyes often communicates that scorn, disrespect, or even deep contempt or hatred are brewing.

Contempt, which relates to hatred, is poison to relationships. Ignoring, dismissing, or laughing in someone's face can communicate contempt. When mocking, sneering, snarky, or disrespectful words accompany this emotion, contempt says, "You're not worth acknowledging. You're a waste of my time. I'm far superior to you, and you don't deserve to share the air I'm breathing."

Perhaps reading those words stirs a painful memory for you. Contempt can sear the soul and leave deep wounds.

In his book *True to Our Feelings*, Robert C. Solomon says that contempt comes from a place within us that says, "You are worthless, and I am superior to you."[22] This emotion of contempt underestimates it's soul-killing poison to those we pour it on.

Resentment and anger closely intertwine with contempt. Solomon writes that we usually project resentment on authority figures—for instance, a teen who resents a parent's rules—while we

273

direct anger toward individuals we see as peers. We impose contempt, on the other hand, on those we feel are of lower status and worth.

It's easy to see why disgust and contempt are relationship killers. This is why God's cure for contempt is love:

> Love is patient, love is kind. It does not envy, it does not boast, it is not proud. It does not *dishonor others*, it is not self-seeking, it is not easily angered, it keeps no record of wrong. Love does not delight in evil but rejoices with the truth. It always protects, always trusts, always hopes, always perseveres. Love never fails. (1 Corinthians 13:4–8 NIV, emphasis added)

Sometimes we don't direct our scorn and disgust toward others, but we direct it inward toward ourselves. What then? If we hold ourselves in contempt and roll our eyes in disgust at our reflections in the mirror, what can we do?

The answer is the same: love.

You must reflect God's love for you in love for yourself. This means you must believe who he says you are and speak to yourself as he would speak to you. His love in you can then flow out to others.

If contempt has crept into your heart, choose today to replace it with love.

Declare

God's love fills me, and I am free from the cords of contempt and hatred.

Meditate, Believe, Accept

I walk in the light. I choose to love others and release all resentment.

Anyone who claims to be in the light but hates a brother

or sister is still in the darkness. Anyone who loves their brother and sister lives in the light, and there is nothing in them to make them stumble. But anyone who hates a brother or sister is in the darkness and walks around in the darkness. They do not know where they are going, because the darkness has blinded them. (1 John 2:9–11 NIV)

I use wisdom and discretion to overlook offenses. I am slow to anger and do not allow contempt to build up in me.

A wise man restrains his anger and overlooks insults. This is to his credit. (Proverbs 19:11 TLB)

God's love fills me, and hate cannot remain in my heart.

Whoever claims to love God yet hates a brother or sister is a liar. For whoever does not love their brother and sister, whom they have seen, cannot love God, whom they have not seen. (1 John 4:20 NIV)

I do not hate others or keep grudges. I allow God to repay.

Do not bear a grudge against others, but settle your differences with them, so that you will not commit a sin because of them. Do not take revenge on others or continue to hate them, but love your neighbors as you love yourself. I am the Lord. (Leviticus 19:17–18 GNT)

I believe no ones better than me, and I'm not better than any one.

Don't think you are better than you really are. Be honest in your evaluation of yourselves, measuring yourselves by the faith God has given us. (Romans 12:3)

Confess

Lord, I confess to not fully loving the way I should. Resentment and feelings of hate and contempt sometimes rise up in my heart. Forgive me and fill me with your love.

Affirm

I declare that God's love washes over me and removes all resentment, hate, disgust, and contempt. No hatred can remain, and I'm set free from the cords of contempt and disgust that have bound me.

Repeat "I release contempt" three times. Each time you read it, add special emphasis to the bolded word.

I release contempt.

I **release** contempt.

I release **contempt**.

Extra Memory Challenge

Love never fails. (1 Corinthians 13:8 NIV)

Explore

1. When has resentment built up inside you? Explain.
2. In what ways is contempt a form of pride?
3. Has contempt become a habit for you and the way you communicate? How has this affected your relationships?
4. How will you keep your heart free from contempt?

Journal

Week 7

Day 46

TODAY'S TRUTH: I AM FREE FROM SELFISH
AND UNHEALTHY COMPETITION

*Do nothing out of rivalry or conceit, but in humility
consider others as more important than yourselves.*
Philippians 2:3 HCSB

Why are men so prone to compare themselves and compete with other men? Too often we longingly look at what other men have and feel inadequate. We covet and complain about what we *don't* have rather than being grateful for what we *do* and how blessed we are. Counting our blessings, however, doesn't come naturally. We instead compete and compare things such as sports, money, career success, spouses, children, families, homes, and big boy toys, as if material possessions or awards and trophies give us value and bring happiness. Competing and comparing leads to a nasty cycle of dissatisfaction; we will always find someone who has more than we do.

Are our compulsions to compete rooted in jealous comparison? Why do we envy each other? Are we fearful of being left behind or less valued? According to King Solomon in the Bible, this is useless; a chasing after the wind (see Ecclesiastes 4:4). Yet, some say it's foolish to fold our hands in satisfaction, for in this posture, we will starve to death. Maybe so, but like John Bunyan, I say, "I am content with what I have, be it little, or be it much."[23] When we cannot find contentment in our present circumstances, we will always struggle and strive for more, chasing after the wind. The writer of the book of Philippians states it this way: "I know what it is to be in need, and I know what it is to have plenty. I have learned the secret of being content in any and every situation, whether well fed or hungry, whether living in plenty or in want" (Philippians 4:12 NIV).

If you feel you must compare, I recommend a fun resource that might cure your need to look at others. A web tool called "Global Rich List" offers the opportunity to enter your income and assets, and the tool will calculate where you rank in the world in income or wealth. For example:

- If you make $50,000 per year, you are in the top 0.31 percent of the world's population in annual income. That's right, in the top one-half of 1 percent. Wow!
- If you own $10,000 of equity in your home, $10,000 in personal assets, and $10,000 of investments, you rank in the top 20 percent of *all* the people in the world. Again, wow.

Based on this data, I suggest that most of us are in the top 10 percent of the world's population in terms of wealth and income. But even this knowledge will bring few people contentment. Wise men recognize that competition leads to unhappiness, discontent, and broken relationships.

God calls us to focus on *our own* gifts and talents and the opportunities he gives us to serve him by serving his children. We should "compete" for the prize of his calling and "compare" ourselves to the vision and purpose God designed us for. Scripture is clear that we will be held accountable for what God has given us (and only us): our time, talent, and treasure.

> If anyone thinks they are something when they are not, they deceive themselves. Each one should test their own actions. Then they can take pride in themselves alone,

without comparing themselves to someone else, for each one should carry their own load. (Galatians 6: 3–5 NIV)

How do you "compete" for your God-given purpose and call?

1. Know who you are in Christ. Read his Word. Study what Scripture says you should do with your resources.
2. Learn and study who you are in terms of temperament, gifting, spiritual gifts, qualities, and personality. There are many great tools available to help with this.
3. Look around the world and see what God is doing. Ask yourself: what breaks my heart that breaks the heart of God? This is a great place to start serving and "competing."
4. Practice gratitude. Every day thank God for three things he has given you.

Declare

I declare that I am no longer a slave to comparisons and competition. I am thankful and content for all that God has blessed me with. My success comes from reaching God's goals for my life in God's timing.

Meditate, Believe, Accept

I am content with working on my own life. I do not compete with others or compare myself to them.

> Pay careful attention to your own work, for then you
> will get the satisfaction of a job well done, and you won't
> need to compare yourself to anyone else. (Galatians 6:4)

I am thankful and give no place to jealousy and envy. I trust in God's provision for my life.

But if you have bitter jealousy and selfish ambition in

your hearts, do not boast and be false to the truth. This is not the wisdom that comes down from above, but is earthly, unspiritual, demonic. For where jealousy and selfish ambition exist, there will be disorder and every vile practice. (James 3:14–15 ESV)

Be thankful in all circumstances. This is what God wants from you in your life in union with Christ Jesus. (1 Thessalonians 5:18 GNT)

I will do mighty things because God is with me. I do not need to strive or compete.

With God's help we will do mighty things, for he will trample down our foes. (Psalm 108:13)

I am motivated to reach God's goals for my life. I seek to fulfill his call and purpose for my life.

Then I observed that most people are motivated to success because they envy their neighbors. But this, too, is meaningless—like chasing the wind. (Ecclesiastes 4:4)

With all humility, I am happy when I can help someone else achieve their best.

Do nothing from rivalry or conceit, but in humility count others more significant than yourselves. (Philippians 2:3 ESV)

I am content. I lack nothing.

I know what it is to be in need, and I know what it is to have plenty. I have learned the secret of being content in any and every situation, whether well fed or hungry, whether living in plenty or in want. (Philippians 4:12 NIV)

Our LORD and our God, you are like the sun and also like a shield. You treat us with kindness and with honor, never denying any good thing to those who live right (Psalm 84:11 CEV).

Confess

Lord, I confess that I struggle with competition and comparing myself to others. Help me to bless and appreciate those who may have more than me.

Affirm

I am content in my circumstances and thankful for all God has blessed me with.

Repeat "I am thankful" three times. Each time you read it, add special emphasis to the bolded word or words.

I am thankful.

I **am** thankful.

I am **thankful.**

Extra Memory Challenge

Be thankful in all circumstances. This is what God wants from you in your life in union with Christ Jesus. (1 Thessalonians 5:18 GNT)

Explore

1. As you look around the world, what do you believe breaks God's heart?
2. As you look around the world, what breaks your heart?
3. What gifts has God given you that you can use to serve him so you can compete with the "ideal you" God created you to be?

Journal

Week 7

Day 47

Today's Truth: I Release Guilt and Walk in the Joy of Forgiveness and Freedom

So let us come near to God with a sincere heart
and a sure faith,
with hearts that have been purified
from a guilty conscience
and with bodies washed with clean water.
Hebrews 10:22 GNT

I like to travel, but one trip I don't enjoy taking is a guilt trip. Have you ever been on one? It's a slow journey to nowhere, chock-full of potholes and speed bumps.

Guilt. It's an emotion associated with manipulation and control, and because it often produces other negative emotions, it's important to listen to the voice of guilt and understand its source.

To begin exploring guilt, let's take a look at two categories of guilt: true guilt and false guilt.

Real guilt is a God-given emotion that comes when we violate God's moral code. Conviction from the Holy Spirit, as well as an inner prompting that says, "Hey, wait a minute—that was wrong!" This voice sets the direction of our moral compass, so we know how to conduct ourselves morally within society. When we listen to this inner voice and the voice of the Spirit, we know when we are wrong, when we should ask for forgiveness, and when we need to make amends.

True guilt that originates from God and speaks to our consciences serves as a guardrail. It keeps us from veering off the road of life, careening over the edge to destruction. This kind of guilt protects us. When real guilt operates correctly, it helps us mend broken relationships, make the right choices, and express sorrow when we've blown it.

As a father with young children, I was always thankful to see my children's fledgling consciences emerge. My father's heart was happy when I observed their ability to discern right and wrong and see their consciences pricked when they crossed a moral line.

However, there is a second kind of guilt called false guilt. This kind of guilt comes from an overactive conscience, but more specifically, from a place of weakness. When we struggle with our identities, wrestle with fear, strive to please people, and let others manipulate us, guilt can infiltrate our daily lives. We blame ourselves, even if we're unsure about our responsibility. False guilt begins with the words *I should*.

- I should have gone to the event last night.
- I should have been a better dad, husband, son, brother.
- I should have volunteered at church.
- I never should have trusted her.

When we listen to the voice of false guilt, we go through life with "shouldn't" all over ourselves and feeling miserable. This false guilt serves no purpose other than to fill our minds with shaming messages that dishearten our souls. Here's a lesson about guilt: just because you feel guilty doesn't necessarily mean you are guilty or that you've done anything wrong. Guilt is an emotion—a feeling. It's vital to investigate the source of the guilt. Is the source God, you, others, or Satan? Yes, Satan, the accuser of believers, launches his guilty darts at you, hoping to pierce your soul. Beware.

Today you can choose to stop taking guilt trips. If the Holy Spirit is convicting you of something that involves true guilt, repent. God, who forgives, will cleanse you. If Satan is binding you with lies to produce false guilt, reject his deception.

Declare

I am free from guilt. When I confess my sin to God, he forgives me and cleanses me. When I have wronged someone, I quickly express sorrow and repent. Therefore, I am free. False guilt is a lie and has no place in my life. Today I am free from false guilt.

Meditate, Believe, Accept

I draw near to God in full confidence. Guilt does not keep me away.

> Let us continue to come near with sincere hearts in the full assurance that faith provides, because our hearts have been sprinkled clean from a guilty conscience, and our bodies have been washed with pure water. (Hebrews 10:22 ISV)

When I fall, Jesus advocates for me. The guilt of my sin doesn't disqualify me from God's presence.

> My dear children, I'm writing this to you so that you will not sin. Yet, if anyone does sin, we have Jesus Christ, who has God's full approval. He speaks on our behalf when we come into the presence of the Father. (1 John 2:1 GW)

False guilt will not separate me from God.

> And I am convinced that nothing can ever separate us from God's love. Neither death nor life, neither angels nor demons, neither our fears for today nor our worries about tomorrow—not even the powers of hell can separate us from God's love. (Romans 8:38–39)

I will not be outsmarted by false guilt. Satan and his lies have no place in my thoughts.

> to keep Satan from getting the advantage over us; for we

are not ignorant of his wiles and intentions. (2 Corinthians 2:11 AMPC)

Confess

Lord, I confess there are times when false guilt does a number on me. I feel ashamed and become buried under a load of "I should haves." But today I claim my freedom in Christ.

Affirm

I am free from false guilt. I live to please God and do not live under condemnation. I affirm that I will not live under the shame of pleasing others. Today I am set free from false guilt.

Repeat "I acknowledge real guilt and reject false guilt" three times. Each time you read it, add special emphasis to the bolded word or words.

I acknowledge real guilt and **reject** false guilt.

I acknowledge **real guilt** and reject false guilt.

I acknowledge real guilt and reject **false guilt**.

Extra Memory Challenge

To keep Satan from getting the advantage over us; for we are not ignorant of his wiles and intentions. (2 Corinthians 2:11 AMPC)

Explore

1. Describe the difference between real guilt and false guilt.
2. If you experience real guilt, what should you do?
3. If you submit to false guilt, how are you kept in bondage? Describe how this has affected your life.

Journal

Week 7

Day 48

Today's Truth: My Spirit Is Not Defensive, but Entreatable

The Scriptures say, "God opposes proud people,
but he helps everyone who is humble."
1 Peter 5:5 CEV

Have you ever known someone who has a defensive spirit? If so, then you know this characteristic isn't attractive. Defensiveness makes us look like victims and strips us of our dignity.

But what causes people to develop a defensive spirit? A defensive spirit grows from a wound, and people who default to this emotional response are typically unaware that their behavior erodes their dignity and true identity with each display of insecurity. They are also often unaware that their response flows from hurt and fear.

We often display a defensive spirit under the following circumstances:

- When we are emotionally triggered
- When we feel inadequate
- When we fear being wrong
- When we feel threatened or unsafe
- When we feel angry, challenged, or believe someone is resisting our efforts
- When we feel competitive

We fight to preserve our worldview and do and say things to feel safe. When threatened, we choose either fight or flight, black or white, win or lose. We become so wrapped up in our defenses that we don't listen to—let alone try to understand—another person's point of view. We tend to see compromise as weakness and surrender.

Author Sharon Ellison says:

> To be defensive is to react with "a war mentality to a non-war issue." In other words, defensiveness is an impulsive and reactive mode of responding to a situation or conversation. Rather than listening with an open heart, we respond with our metaphorical shields up and weapons drawn.[24]

We become defensive when something someone says triggers an old trauma or wound—an insecurity, fear, or other emotion that makes us feel unsafe or unloved in a way that we did in the past.

A defensive spirit is an unconscious, automatic response to a perceived danger or threat, whether or not others feel or sense that threat.

If this describes you, it's time to break free and discover a better way to live.

- Acknowledge that a defensive spirit does not help you. It erodes relationships and does not feed the fruit of the Spirit: love, joy, peace, forbearance, kindness, goodness, faithfulness, gentleness, and self-control.
- Be aware that you're reacting, not responding. You *can* choose a different way to respond.
- Stop speaking and give yourself a moment to reframe the situation.
- Learn to calm yourself and adopt the posture of a listening learner.

Declare

I am secure in Christ. I do not have to defend myself and become offended. I am confident in who I am, and I rest in knowing that God will protect me and my reputation.

Meditate, Believe, Accept

I am humble and teachable. My spirit is entreatable.

> All of you young people should obey your elders. In fact, everyone should be humble toward everyone else. The Scriptures say, "God opposes proud people, but he helps everyone who is humble." (1 Peter 5:5 CEV)

I am not defensive. God is my defense, and he makes things right.

> Dear friends, don't try to get even. Let God take revenge. In the Scriptures the Lord says, "I am the one to take revenge and pay them back." (Romans 12:19 CEV)

> But Jesus told him, "Put your sword away. Anyone who lives by fighting will die by fighting." (Matthew 26:52 CEV)

I am slow to speak. I listen before I respond, and I am not defensive.

> My dear friends, you should be quick to listen and slow to speak or to get angry. If you are angry, you cannot do any of the good things God wants done (James 1:19–20 CEV).

I do not turn to self-defense. I depend on God to protect me.

> God blesses those people who depend only on him. They belong to the kingdom of heaven! (Matthew 5:3 CEV)

Confess

Lord, I confess I want to protect myself at times. My defenses go up, and I try to justify or reason away my behavior. I get offended when others point out my imperfections. Forgive me for this. Today I release a defensive spirit, and I learn to quiet myself and listen before I speak.

Affirm

I am free from a defensive attitude and desire to learn how to grow spiritually, relationally, emotionally, and in God's wisdom.

Repeat "I am approachable and teachable and reject defensiveness" three times. Each time you read it, add special emphasis to the bolded word or words.

I am approachable and teachable and reject defensiveness.

I am approachable and teachable and **reject** defensiveness.

I am approachable and teachable and reject **defensiveness**.

Extra Memory Challenge

> My dear friends, you should be quick to listen and slow to speak or to get angry. If you are angry, you cannot do any of the good things God wants done. (James 1:19–20 CEV)

Explore

1. In what ways do you resonate with today's devotion?
2. How can you practice accepting feedback and diffusing possible triggers?
3. Sometimes when people feel attacked, they are quick to react. How do you think God wants you to respond when you feel attacked?

Journal

CHAPTER 10

CORDS OF PRIDE AND SELF-SUFFICIENCY

When we begin to build walls of prejudice, hatred, pride,
and self-indulgence around ourselves, we are more surely
imprisoned than any prisoner behind concrete walls
and iron bars.
—Mother Angelica

Challenge Week 8

Weekly Reading: Cords of Pride and Self-Sufficiency

God has chosen you and made you his holy people.
He loves you.
So you should always clothe yourselves with mercy,
kindness, humility, gentleness, and patience.
Colossians 3:12 NCV

Sometimes pride is obvious. It can drip from our mouth with boastful arrogance and braggadocious speech that can be hard to miss. But sometimes it's secretly packaged beneath layers of false humility and self-deprecation. False humility and self-deprecation may be less obvious, but pride masked as virtue remains detestable to God. However it may be packaged, pride lies at the root of all evil.

Of all the seven deadly sins—pride, greed, lust, envy, gluttony, wrath, sloth—pride is the deadliest. This is because pride severs the soul from the source of grace—God himself—and it is by grace we are saved. Pride keeps us from recognizing and accepting the help we need. Simply put, a proud spirit cannot receive God's favor, divine forgiveness, and mercy because pride blinds us to our sinful plight and keeps us from crying out to God, who is waiting to rescue us from pride's haughty grip. God resists a proud, arrogant heart while giving abundant grace and power to those who willingly humble themselves before him.

It's important to understand the characteristics and nature of pride as we examine our uses of power and independence this week:

- Pride was and still is, the nature of Satan himself, puffed-up and obsessed with power when he declared, I will *make myself* like the Most High (see Isaiah 14:14 NIV). Pride says, "I will." The root of pride is self-sufficiency. *I will make myself* (or *I am*) everything I need to be.

- Pride is self-absorbed in the continual elevation and choice of self-interests, self-protection, self-promotion, and personal opinions, above all else.

- Pride is a stubborn refusal to acknowledge one's errors or selfishness. Pride exerts itself in direct defiance of God's command to walk in humility and love.

- Pride makes us unresponsive to wisdom from godly people. Pride whispers deception, telling us our opinions are right, and we don't need the counsel of others. But God has always directed his children through his Word, his Spirit, and his people.

Ultimately, pride lies at the root of all sin.

This week we untie the cords of pride and choose contrition, wisdom, and humility.

Week 8

Day 49

Today's Truth: God Resists the Proud but Gives Favor and Grace to the Humble

But he gives us more and more strength to stand
against all such evil longings.
As the Scripture says, God gives strength to the humble
but sets himself against the proud and haughty.
James 4:6 TLB

As we learn about ourselves, none of our efforts will result in lasting transformation unless we possess a humble spirit. This is because change and transformation come *through* a broken and contrite spirit. God sees meekness and teachability. When he sees our humble heart, he rejoices over us. More than that, God grants grace and favor to the humble.

But because our contemporary culture does not teach the true meaning of humility, men tend to equate humility with weakness. The media often portrays strong men as aloof, controlling, and self-sufficient. But a biblical view of humility is freedom from pride and seeing ourselves as God sees us. Humility is a character strength that allows us to better relate to, manage, and serve others.

A Stiff Neck

I played football from age eight through college. I experienced many aches, pains, and injuries. One game I was pummeled in the head and developed a concussion. This injury to my brain was the immediate problem, but the longer-term problem was a painfully sore neck that developed after my first night's sleep—I was unable to move my head side to side or up and down. This lasted for several weeks. I was unable to practice or do much other than move cautiously. A stiff neck reminds me of the sin of pride. We are unable to humble ourselves. Pride limits our ability to be open to what God is trying to do in our lives. The pain caused by our pride keeps us from relationship with our heavenly Father. We are not able to be flexible, make changes in our behavior or attitude, and we experience pain because of our pride. I gained a new perspective about why God sometimes called his people stiff-necked and proud.

Stiff-necked, prideful people accomplish nothing for God or others because they focus on themselves and their self-centered agendas. But God doesn't leave us soaking in our pride. He saves us from ourselves and orchestrates circumstances that call us to bow humbly before him and obey.

> But they and our fathers, in their pride, made their necks stiff, and gave no attention to your orders, and would not do them, and gave no thought to the wonders you had done among them; but made their necks stiff, and turning away from you, made a captain over themselves to take them back to their prison in Egypt: but you are a God of forgiveness, full of grace and pity, slow to wrath and great in mercy, and you did not give them up. (Nehemiah 9:16–17 BBE)

Israel's pride ruled her people's hearts. They refused to bow their will to God and follow his plan for their lives. Instead, they chose to go back to prison—back to the land of their slavery.

I pray you don't make the same mistake. Examine your heart and humble yourself before the Lord.

This week we untie the cords of pride and choose contrition and humility.

Declare

God's favor and grace fill me, for my spirit is humble before my God. I renounce all pride and declare that I am free from its deadly cords.

Meditate, Believe, Accept

My spirit is humble, and I have God's favor on my life.

> God opposes the proud but shows favor to the humble. (James 4:6 NIV)

My spirit is humble, and I am filled with divine wisdom.

> When pride comes, so does shame, but wisdom brings humility. (Proverbs 11:2 CEB)

My spirit is humble, and I have influence and honor.

> One's pride will bring him low, but he who is lowly in spirit will obtain honor. (Proverbs 29:23 ESV)

My spirit is humble, and God keeps me from falling.

> Pride precedes a disaster, and an arrogant attitude precedes a fall. (Proverbs 16:18 GW)

Confess

Lord, I confess that pride rises in my spirit, and my fleshly nature wants to do things my way. I repent of my pride, and I ask you to forgive me for my selfish ways. I humble myself before you and renounce self-centered thinking. Wash me, heal me, and forgive me for my pride.

Affirm

I walk before God with humility and in the power of the Holy Spirit. I renounce pride in my life and declare that I will continue in the path of righteousness. As a result, I have God's favor, honor, wisdom, and grace, which is his supernatural power to overcome.

Repeat "I walk in humility and the power of the Holy Spirit" three times. Each time you read it, add special emphasis to the bolded word or words.

I walk in humility and the power of the Holy Spirit.

I **walk** in humility and the power of the Holy Spirit.

I walk in **humility and the power of the Holy Spirit**.

Extra Memory Challenge

> God opposes the proud but shows favor to the humble.
> (James 4:6 NIV)

Explore

1. How has pride crept into your heart? What effect has it had?
2. What have you done to rid yourself of a prideful heart?
3. What will you do differently to cultivate humility?

Journal

Week 8

Day 50

TODAY'S TRUTH: GOD IS IN CONTROL; THE ONLY POWER I NEED IS HIS POWER IN ME

For this very reason, make every effort to add to your faith
goodness; and to goodness, knowledge, and to knowledge, self-control;
and to self-control, perseverance; and to perseverance, godliness;
and to godliness, mutual affection; and to mutual affection, love.
2 Peter 1:5–7 NIV

In week 3 of the Challenge, we explored the cords of control. What positive steps have you taken to give God control since that week of study? You may have learned that the reins of control are hard to release, and you grip them tighter than you like to admit. You may often feel compelled to control other people to try to coerce them to do what *you* want; yet, how ironic that people can't even control themselves. In reality, your attempts to control your spouse/significant other, family members, coworkers, friends, and neighbors are futile. At best, you may influence others. If you're like me, you struggle to accept this reality.

Maybe if I apply more pressure or find another angle I can get people to do what I want, we reason.

I have two questions: Is your urge to control others motivated by the Spirit of God? Or is it motivated by selfishness and fear?

Control is a challenging issue for many men, but why? God created men with unique qualities, characteristics, temperaments, and attributes. Both nature and nurture influences our control issues. If we've suffered from abuse, we may struggle with control. Abused people were stripped of control and often vow never to be vulnerable again. They may feel the need to gain and maintain the control that someone took from them.

At the heart of control is a need to feel powerful, typically more powerful than others. However, the feeling of power is a false replacement for safety and significance. Power can become like an addictive drug. The more power we have, the more we want. The feeling also masks fears and insecurities and conceals our longings for love and acceptance. Misuse of power and control can lead us to abusive behavior that must be accounted for and surrendered to Jesus. These behaviors may include:

- Intimidation
- Coercion or threats
- Emotional or verbal abuse or put-downs
- Minimizing, denying or blaming, refusing to take responsibility
- Withholding money, love, sex, affection
- Using passive-aggressive behavior, failing to support
- Using children as pawns
- Using male privilege
- Isolating

The Cure: Repentance and Humility

Jesus often spoke about the blessing of humility. Greatness and power in God's kingdom are the opposite of the "greatness and power" defined by our world today. To be great in God's kingdom, we must be humble and serve others. Yet, the Enemy spoon-feeds us the lie that "to succeed, be respected, find happiness, and be safe in today's world, we must have power and exert control." However, if we eat that poisonous fruit, we will certainly discover the opposite: heartbreak, loss, and damaged relationships.

Today we surrender our power and controlling behaviors to Jesus. We lay the misuse of these habits at the foot of the cross and ask God to set us free.

Declare

I declare that I am no longer a slave to power or control. I am free to allow God to be in control, and I will live under the power of his Holy Spirit.

Meditate, Believe, Accept

I can do nothing without the power of God.

> But he said to me, "My grace is sufficient for you, for my power is made perfect in weakness." Therefore, I will boast all the more gladly about my weaknesses, so that Christ's power may rest on me. (2 Corinthians 12:9 NIV)

I focus on controlling my own thoughts and actions. My actions align with the Word of God.

> For the Spirit God gave us does not make us timid, but gives us power, love and self-discipline. (2 Timothy 1:7 NIV)

The only power I have is what the Holy Spirit gives me.

> Now to him who is able to do immeasurably more than all we ask or imagine, according to his power that is at work within us. (Ephesians 3:20 NIV)

I overcome the Enemy and stay grounded in the Lord.

> For our struggle is not against flesh and blood, but against the rulers, against the authorities, against the powers of this dark world and against the spiritual forces of evil in the heavenly realms. (Ephesians 6:12 NIV)

To gain real power, I surrender to God, opposite of what the world tells me to do.

> But you will receive power when the Holy Spirit comes

on you; and you will be my witnesses in Jerusalem, and in all Judea and Samaria, and to the ends of the earth. (Acts 1:8 NIV)

Confess

Lord, I confess that I feel like I need to be in control. My desire to have power and to control others is sinful and not what you designed me to be. I ask for your power in me to control myself and love others.

Affirm

I do not exert power and control over others. I live a surrendered life to God, and he gives me the power and self-control I need to live a victorious life.

Repeat "My true power is in humility" three times. Each time you read it, add special emphasis to the bolded word.

My true power is in humility.

My **true power** is in humility.

My true power is in **humility.**

Extra Memory Challenge

God's Spirit makes us loving, happy, peaceful, patient, kind, good, faithful, gentle, and self-controlled. There is no law against behaving in any of these ways. (Galatians 5:22–23 CEV)

Explore

1. What stood out to you in today's reading?
2. Do you now or have you ever battled with controlling behaviors or attempts to "power up" on someone? Explain.
3. How did you or will you take steps to shed these behaviors and walk in freedom?

Journal

Week 8

Day 51

TODAY'S TRUTH: I'M RESPONSIBLE TO STEWARD MONEY AS GOD'S RESOURCE

*Command those who are rich in this present world not
to be arrogant nor to put their hope in wealth, which is
so uncertain, but to put their hope in God, who richly
provides us with everything for our enjoyment. Command
them to do good, to be rich in good deeds, and to be
generous and willing to share. In this way they will lay up
for themselves as a firm foundation for the coming age, so
that they may take hold of the life that is truly life.*
1 Timothy 6:17–19 NIV

Money—the topic certainly evokes reactions.
Wisely used, money can be a powerful tool for humanity and the advancement of God's kingdom. Poorly used, it can be a snare and a stumbling block.

Money serves many purposes. It's the basis of economies and provides a means of exchange for goods and services. It's also a representation of work and value. For some people, money is a way to control others or a way to buy influence and power. But in another sense, money is also a way people keep score. Supposedly the person who has the most money wins the "success" game in life—at least in Western culture. For others, money is a way to bless people. People can accumulate money to boost their self-esteem or sense of security, spend it to impress others, or give it away as a sacrifice.

One thing is for certain: the pursuit of money apart from an underlying sense of morality and values results in a shallow, self-centered life. How do we know if our relationship with money is unhealthy? The following factors help us recognize that our priorities may be out of balance.

1. **Keeping score**. Keeping score is closely related to competitiveness, power-seeking, and striving for influence. Keeping score is one way we compete with others. The Forbes 400 lists the top 400 wealthiest people in the world. Some people passionately desire to be and stay on this elite list. Several years ago, a true story emerged that a current placeholder on the Forbes list was dropping in rank and was predicted to fall from the top 400. The news so devastated him that he committed suicide. Another man on the list stopped giving to charities because he too was afraid of being dropped. This kind of striving is a trap for men who must know that they're more successful than others and that people around them know it too. This is just one of many ways we keep score.

2. **Accumulating material things**. This is another way we compete with others. Our collections and possessions provide us with an image of success. But all too often people buy things they don't need with money they don't have to impress people they don't even like. Buying things also gives us an "emotional high." Sadly, this, too, is a chasing after the wind, for the feeling lasts only a short time and evaporates.

3. **Control**. Money when misused is one way to control others. I've seen parents and grandparents threaten to withhold funds from their children or grandchildren or cut them off from inheritances as a way to control them. Unfortunately, people also use their money to control churches, institutions, businesses, and communities, wielding power by giving or withholding their funds.

4. **Influence and impress others**. People often admire and respect those who have wealth, even if their personality and treatment of others don't warrant it. While generosity is a virtuous quality, giving to be admired and recognized can be a sign of pride and haughtiness. Giving to gain influence and recognition is giving with dual motives. True givers give to invest in God's kingdom and desire to steward their wealth to God's glory.

5. **Loving things more than loving people.** Money and investment should never take precedent over loving people. Business shouldn't come at the cost of stewarding our family, friends, and the family of God. True wealth is measured in our spiritual relationship with Jesus, commitment to his purpose for our life, and wisdom needed to steward what he's entrusted to us. We must love God with our heart, soul, and mind and love people the way we want to be loved by them.

6. **Bless others**. When we use money wisely, it becomes a wonderful resource. Stewardship that aligns with God's Word overflows as a blessing to many. Biblical stewardship instills generosity, which in turn, blesses us as givers. How amazing is that? Many stewards would gratefully state that the blessing in giving is better than the blessing experienced by those who receive.

Decide today that your relationship with material things won't be based on emotions, needs, or cultural pressure. You will be a good steward of all God's given you to steward: time, talent, treasure, and tribe (relationships, including family, friends, coworkers, and others).

Declare

I look to the Scriptures to learn how to steward money to the glory of God.

Meditate, Believe, Accept

I am content, free from the love of money because God is always with me.

> Make sure that your character is free from the love of money, being content with what you have; for He Himself has said, "*I will never desert you, nor will I ever forsake you.*" (Hebrews 13:4 NASB, emphasis added)

I am not trapped by get-rich schemes. My desires please the Lord.

> People who want to get rich keep falling into temptation. They are trapped by many stupid and harmful desires which drown them in destruction and ruin. (1 Timothy 6:9 GWT)

I have everything I need, and I am happy because God supplies all my needs.

> Those who love money will never have enough. How meaningless to think that wealth brings true happiness! (Ecclesiastes 5:10)

I know how to be content in life because God gives me what I need.

> I know what it is to be in need, and I know what it is to have plenty. I have learned the secret of being content in any and every situation, whether well fed or hungry, whether living in plenty or in want. (Philippians 4:12 NIV)

I steward my money, and God blesses me in every area as he has promised.

> For the Lord your God will bless you as he has promised, and you will lend to many nations but will borrow from none. You will rule over many nations but none will rule over you. (Deuteronomy 15:6 NIV)

I am generous and give to the needs of others.

> If anyone has material possessions and sees a brother or sister in need but has no pity on them, how can the love of God be in that person? (1 John 3:17 NIV)

Confess

Lord, I confess that at times I try to control resources as if they do not come from you. You are the owner of all, and I am the steward. At times I look to money to fulfill me and make me happy. But today I renounce the control money has on me, and I claim your freedom, in Jesus's name.

Affirm

I am a steward of all God has blessed me with. I am content and free from the love of money. I am a generous steward, and I use money as God directs me.

Repeat "I am free from the love of money" three times. Each time you read it, add special emphasis to the bolded word or words.

I am free from the love of money.

I am free **from the love** of money.

I am free from the love **of money.**

Extra Memory Challenge

> The one who loves money will never be satisfied with money, he who loves wealth will never be satisfied with his income. This also is futile. (Ecclesiastes 5:10 NET)

Explore

1. How did today's reading affect you?
2. Do you think you are a good steward of all God has blessed you with? Why or why not?
3. In what ways has a love of money tried to trap you? How do you stay free?

Journal

Week 8

Day 52

TODAY'S TRUTH: I HAVE VICTORY OVER SEXUAL DESIRES

*God's will is for you to be holy, so stay away from all
sexual sin. Then each of you will control his own body and
live in holiness and honor—not in lustful passion like the
pagans who do not know God and his ways.*
1 Thessalonians 4:3–5

I believe that most men's greatest area of temptation and potential defeat is sexual desire. You, like many other men reading this book, may be in the throes of a sexual struggle right now. You're not alone, and I have good news for you. There is *real* hope for you—for all of us. We can win the battle against sexual temptation.

Facing our sexual drive, urges, and temptations is *every* man's responsibility. We're naturally vulnerable to sexual temptation and urge. Our sex drive—the biological and psychological desire for sexual pleasure and satisfaction—is often our strongest drive (more than the drive for power, money, ambition, etc.). Therefore, we need *powerful* tools for the battle.

Consider this quote from *Every Man's Battle* by Stephen Arterburn:

> While there may not be spiritual oppression involved in
> your battle (against lust), there'll always be opposition.
> The enemy is constantly near your ear. He doesn't want
> you to win this fight, and he knows the lies that so often
> break a man's confidence and his will to win. Expect
> to hear lies and plenty of them. Satan's lie: "You're the
> only one dealing with this problem. If anyone finds out,
> you'll be the laughingstock of the church!" The Truth:
> Most men deal with this problem so no one will laugh.[25]

311

Our struggle feels constant, insurmountable, even unfair. The Enemy is always on the offense, and his weapons are destructive beyond imagination. That's why we must arm ourselves to stand against his attacks, not only for our spiritual lives but also for future generations. But we don't fight alone. This is every man's battle, and God fights with us and for us.

Here are some suggestions of weapons to reach for in your quest to find and maintain freedom:

1. **Ask for help from the Holy Spirit.** Only through the power of the Holy Spirit in us do we have power over the Enemy and his attacks. God has made provision for overcoming sexual temptation, *but we must obey the Spirit's voice, which will agree with the truth of the Bible.*
2. **You're not alone, so don't go it alone.** Bring the temptation (which is not sin) out of the dark and into the light. Refuse to accept the "shame" that keeps us silent and bound. Men who bring others into their battle find support and gain victory more often than those who try to go it alone.
3. **Stand on truth, for the truth will set you free.** Our minds must be renewed with God's Word when it comes to sexual temptation. "I have hidden your word in my heart that I might not sin against you" (Psalm 119:11). If we feel or believe there is no hope for freedom, the truth is not in our hearts; defeat is. If we believe lies of hopelessness and feed our minds with despairing narratives, then we set ourselves up for ongoing defeat. We must renew our minds with powerful, biblical affirmations about our victory. Think and speak more about the power of our God than the power of temptation.
4. **Create daily habits that position you to win.** Good habits discipline your body and mind.

5. **Read God's Word, pray, and meditate daily to help renew your mind.** Then determine to obey Scripture, which is a clear and powerful guide to life.

6. **Practice intentionally. Commit to living a sanctified and holy life.** Decide daily, sometimes many times a day, to be faithful to your spouse and/or God.

7. **Envision victory.** Picture yourself—over and over—making good choices in the face of temptation. See yourself walking away, turning the computer off, closing the magazine, or any other scenarios that may present in the future.

8. **Develop a plan for success.** How do you respond when you feel temptation? Who do you call? Do you have an accountability partner regarding your sexual desires and struggles? Who do you think would make a good accountability partner? How could accountability help you? Create a plan for success that addresses these questions.

Finally, the following truths have helped me in the area of sexual temptation and purity. I frequently remind myself that:

1. Jesus is watching me, always can see me, and I can't hide.
2. I want to make Jesus happy about how I live my life.
3. All sin leads to death and has consequences, and the consequences are never worth the fleeting pleasure of the sin.

Declare

I can have victory over sexual sin with Jesus's help.

Meditate, Believe, Accept

Jesus gives me the power to resist sexual temptation.

> Every test that you have experienced is the kind that normally comes to people. But God keeps his prom-

ise, and he will not allow you to be tested beyond your power to remain firm; at the time you are put to the test, he will give you the strength to endure it, and so provide you with a way out. (1 Corinthians 10:13 GNT)

Scripture is my armor to protect me from the Enemy.

I have hidden your word in my heart that I might not sin against you. (Psalm 119:11 NIV)

I can decide to and make plans to live a life that is pleasing to God.

Plan carefully what you do, and whatever you do will turn out right. Avoid evil and walk straight ahead. Don't go one step off the right way. (Proverbs 4:26–27 GNT)

The pain of sexual sin is greater than the temporary pleasure.

What you get by dishonesty you may enjoy like the finest food, but sooner or later it will be like a mouthful of sand. (Proverbs 20:17 GNT)

Confess

Lord, I confess that I have not handled sexuality as the gift that you have given me. I have not respected you, women, and myself. Forgive me for my human frailty and weakness.

Affirm

I am made in God's image, redeemed and forgiven. Thus, I am to be holy, as only he is holy.

Repeat "My sexuality is redeemed by God" three times. Each time you read it, add special emphasis to the bolded word or words.

My **sexuality** is redeemed by God.

My sexuality is **redeemed** by God.

My sexuality is redeemed **by God.**

Extra Memory Challenge

> I have hidden your word in my heart that I might not
> sin against you. (Psalm 119:11 NIV)

Explore

1. In what ways have you struggled with sexual temptation?
2. How does this struggle affect the way you feel about yourself?
3. Have you ever considered sharing your struggle with someone who can stand with you? Why or why not?

Journal

Week 8

Day 53

TODAY'S TRUTH: JESUS MADE ME FREE TO BE
WHO HE CREATED ME TO BE,
UNBOUND BY SOCIETAL MALE EXPECTATIONS

He who acquires wisdom loves himself;
one who safeguards understanding will find success.
Proverbs 19:8 BSB

Ever since Satan enticed Eve with the lie, "you will be like God," humans have desired to elevate their value by measuring themselves with a "better than others" yardstick. Many men think of themselves as superior and cling to a false, arrogant, and self-sufficient bravado. This hunger for superiority was not how God originally designed us; however, it's part of our fallen, insecure, and competitive nature.

On day 34 we read about a term called "toxic masculinity." This term encapsulates the expectation for men to behave in ways that society promotes and accepts but are harmful to both those they love and to themselves. The term refers to the pressure placed upon men to become self-reliant, dominant, and competitive; however, these destructive characteristics often manifest in abusive behavior toward others. Men are told to suppress their emotions, buck-up, and to refuse to cry. They often become calloused and isolated, and oh-so competitive—in political, economic, relational, recreational, and social arenas. The term *alpha male* refers to behaviors expected of men who are considered powerful, superior, aggressive, and see themselves as better than others. But as John Donne said, "No man is an island, entire of itself; every man is a piece of the continent, a part of the main."[26]

So, what does healthy male self-esteem look like?

Psychology explains the developmental stages of healthy children. It follows a familiar progression from dependent to independent and finally to interdependent. When we are born, and throughout our early years of life, we are totally dependent upon others. Over time, we grow and develop independence. We long to and become capable of taking care of ourselves. The final step in our development is interdependence. This is an exciting phase in our life where we are independent and able to provide for ourselves and others we care about, but at the same time recognize that life is better when we are connected with others in mutual interdependence. We are better—we can do more—and we are happier when we partner with others to experience the best of life. This is evidenced when our lives are intertwined with others like our spouse, friends, coworkers, and other family members.

> A person standing alone can be attacked and defeated, but two can stand back-to-back and conquer. Three are even better, for a triple-braided cord is not easily broken. (Ecclesiastes 4:12)

Scripture tells us that a three-strand cord is the strongest cord (relationship) of all. We can accomplish more in teams than as individuals, yet we are hesitant to rely on others, often believing our need for others is a weakness. On the contrary, it takes a mature and emotionally intelligent man (or woman) to move to the stage of interdependence because this stage requires compromise, adaptability, and sacrifice. Letting go of the idea that "It's all about me" or "I can do this myself" and focusing on what's best for everyone is a challenging but worthwhile achievement.

Today we surrender the lies that say, "I do not need interdependence. I should pursue my own path because that's what real men do to achieve happiness." Accepting these and other false identities about masculinity that won't satisfy is one way the Enemy keeps men bound. Today we renounce these false beliefs.

Declare

I am free from the expectation that I must be a macho man, an alpha dog, a man's man. I renounce false narratives about masculinity, and I am free to be the man God made me to be: interdependent, fulfilled, and free as I live out his vision for me.

Meditate, Believe, Accept

I am free from worldly expectations.

> When the wicked man dies, his expectation comes to nothing, and hope placed in wealth vanishes. (Proverbs 11:7 HCSB)

> And now what is my expectation? is it not the Lord? and my ground of hope is with thee. (Psalm 39:7 Brenton)

I can let others shine. I can help others excel and take great satisfaction in their success.

> There is no greater love than to lay down one's life for one's friends. (John 15:13)

> Each of you should be concerned not only about your own interests, but about the interests of others as well. (Philippians 2:4 NET)

> Do not withhold good from those to whom it is due, when it is in your power to act. (Proverbs 3:23 NIV)

I am at my best when I let others help me be my best.

> When Moses' father-in-law saw all that he was doing for the people, he said, "What is this that you are doing for

the people? Why are you sitting by yourself, and all the people stand around you from morning until evening?" (Exodus 18:14 NET)

You will surely wear out, both you and these people who are with you, for this is too heavy a burden for you; you are not able to do it by yourself. Now listen to me, I will give you advice, and may God be with you. (Exodus 18:18–19 NET)

Confess

Lord, I confess I think of myself more highly than I ought to at times. I resist interdependence and often act independently, demanding my way. I acknowledge that I am not better than others, nor am I less than others. Today, I renounce selfish independence and ask you, Lord, to teach me a more excellent way—interdependence.

Affirm

I need others. I grow and learn when I am in committed and healthy relationships. I am interdependent with others who are equal to me with differing gifts and abilities.

Repeat "I need others" three times. Each time you read it, add special emphasis to the bolded word.

I need others.

I **need** others.

I need **others.**

Extra Memory Challenge

There is no greater love than to lay down one's life for one's friends. (John 15:13)

319

Explore

1. In what ways do you act independently when you should interact more *inter*dependently?
2. Are there times when feelings of competitiveness, superiority, or independence interfere with your relationships? What do you do when this happens?
3. Think about your relationships. Are there areas in which you could offer valued help to others? Will you offer? Why or why not?

Journal

COMPLETING THE CHALLENGE:
LIVING IN FREEDOM

CHAPTER II

REBOUND: SEVEN POWER EMOTIONS GOD WANTS YOU TO HAVE

*In many areas of life, freedom is not so much the absence
of restrictions as finding the right ones, the liberating
restrictions. Those that fit with the reality of our nature
and the world produce greater power and scope for our
abilities and a deeper joy and fulfillment. . . . If we only
grow intellectually, vocationally, and physically through
judicious constraints—why would it not also be true for
spiritual and moral growth? Instead of insisting on freedom to create spiritual reality, shouldn't we be seeking to
discover it and disciplining ourselves to live
according to it?*
—Timothy J. Keller

Challenge Week 9
Weekly Reading: Rebound

*So, chosen by God for this new life of love, dress in the
wardrobe God picked out for you: compassion, kindness,
humility, quiet strength, discipline. Be even-tempered,*

content with second place, quick to forgive an offense.
Forgive as quickly and completely as the Master forgave
you. And regardless of what else you put on, wear love.
It's your basic, all-purpose garment. Never be without it.
Colossians 3:12 MSG

You've learned how to maneuver through the gauntlet of intense emotions, and you've learned a better way to express what you're feeling. You've learned that you can control your emotions, and your emotions do not have to control you.

Congratulations! You're on your way to embracing a new life.

You have powerful new tools to help you recognize, evaluate, and reroute feelings when they arise. You know the importance of asking the all-important questions: What am I feeling? What's the underlying reason I'm feeling this way? What triggered this emotion? Do I feel threatened, afraid, embarrassed, ashamed, fearful?

You've learned to look at your emotions—especially when they arise quickly—and evaluate the messages they're sending. Your emotions are trying to send you messages about deeper issues, so don't *stuff* the stuff.

Positive Thinking: Powerful or Peter Pan?

There is a connection between our emotions and our thoughts—yes, it's true. But the connection doesn't end there. The thoughts we think have a connection with the "story" we tell ourselves.

For example, say someone you love was supposed to be home thirty minutes ago. You grab your phone and call her. No answer. You text. No response. Soon you're pacing back and forth in front of the window, watching the street and worrying.

It isn't like her to be late. Something must be wrong.

Your mind begins to play out scenarios. You become more worried and anxious. You're about to call the police to inquire about reported accidents when suddenly a familiar red car turns into the driveway. Your worry instantly turns to exasperation and anger. When your loved one walks through the door, you verbally lambaste her.

"Where in the world have you been? Why didn't you call me?"

"I'm so sorry, but I had . . ."

You snap back, "Don't even talk to me. I'm so mad at you right now!"

The story you told yourself created powerful emotions. Your emotions, in turn, created corresponding actions and behaviors that created negative or positive consequences. In this scenario, you responded to circumstances with a negative story. It negatively impacted you, your relationship, and your time.

Now let's rewind the clock and replay the scenario, only this time you'll tell yourself a healthy story.

Someone you love was supposed to be home thirty minutes ago. You grab your phone and call her. No answer. You text. No response.

It isn't like her to be late. Something important must have come up, you tell yourself.

Well, good. Now I can finish that chapter in my book I've wanted to read.

You get your book, slip into your favorite chair, and begin to read. You become so caught up in the story that time flies. Soon the one you've been waiting for walks in the door.

"Hi! How was your day?"

In this version, all the same events occurred, only this time you responded in a positive, empowering way. You chose to take time for yourself to relax and unwind, and you read the chapter you'd been wanting to read. You used your time wisely, and you strengthened your relationship by your positive and warm greeting.

I don't mean to oversimplify, but this is the beauty and reward of a disciplined mind. When we learn to tell ourselves a better story—a truthful one—we replace unwanted painful thoughts with positive thoughts. Focusing on positive thoughts produces better feelings, and better feelings produce better outcomes.

Remember, emotions often come to us as a result of circumstances, but the opposite is true too; circumstances often come to us as a result of the emotions we're feeling. Our mood creates our life situations. That's why it's critical to gain mastery over our emotions and put ourselves in a positive, truthful, more powerful state—through God's Word.

Scripture tells us, "This day is holy to our Lord. Don't be sad, because the joy from the Lord is your strength!" (Nehemiah 8:10 CEB).

Put Off and Put On

This week you'll be introduced to *Seven Power Emotions that will transform your life*. For us to interrupt our patterns of negative thinking and destructive storytelling, we must not only *put off* unwanted thoughts but also *put on* wanted attitudes and mindsets.

Our study would be incomplete if you only learn how to put sad thoughts out of your mind. This is not *renewed* thinking. Putting off unwanted feelings, behaviors, and destructive reasoning is only half the equation. Putting on a new mind with new thoughts and behaviors is the crucial second part, for this is where change and victory happen.

Once again, let's look at our source of truth, the Bible:

> You were taught, with regard to your former way of life, to *put off* your old self, which is being corrupted by its deceitful desires; to be made new in the attitude of your minds; and to *put on* the new self, created to be like God in true righteousness and holiness. (Ephesians 4:22–24 NIV, emphasis added)

But now you also *put off* all these; anger, wrath, malice,

blasphemy, filthy talk out of your mouth. Lie not one to another, seeing that you have *put off* the old man with his deeds; And have *put on* the new man, that is renewed in knowledge after the image of him that created him. (Colossians 3:8–10 KJ2000, emphasis added)

Seven Power Emotions God Wants You to Have

We began our study by looking at the instruction in Romans 12:2 (GNT): "Do not conform yourselves to the standards of this world, but let God transform you inwardly by a complete change of your mind. Then you will be able to know the will of God—what is good and is pleasing to him and is perfect."

Over the last fifty-three days, that's exactly what you've been doing—transforming the way you think. Now let's look further into the book of Romans to find additional instructions for living. Hidden in these verses are what I call the Seven Power Emotions. When we equip ourselves with these seven qualities or attitudes, they lead us to an amazing life of freedom and victory.

Romans 12:9–13 in the Amplified Bible says:

Love is to be sincere and active [the real thing—without guile and hypocrisy]. Hate what is evil [detest all ungodliness, do not tolerate wickedness]; hold on tightly to what is good. Be devoted to one another with [authentic] brotherly affection [as members of one family], give preference to one another in honor; never lagging behind in diligence; aglow in the Spirit, enthusiastically serving the Lord; constantly rejoicing in hope [because of our confidence in Christ], steadfast and patient in distress, devoted to prayer [continually seeking wisdom, guidance, and strength], contributing to the needs of God's people, pursuing [the practice of] hospitality.

These verses include the seven core emotions we should cultivate. Think of these emotions as seeds. When we plant these seeds
in our minds—our spiritual gardens—we flourish and reap a harvest of healthy fruit. These attitudes root out the "deadly cords"
that, like weeds, try to choke out the fruit in our lives.

These seven core emotions are:

- Love
- Appreciation
- Enthusiasm
- Joy
- Perseverance
- Faith
- Generosity

This week, we close the sixty-day challenge by learning to cultivate the seven power emotions.

Week 9

Day 54

POWER EMOTION 1: LOVE

TODAY'S TRUTH: I AM GOD'S INSTRUMENT OF LOVE

Love is to be sincere and active
[the real thing—without guile and hypocrisy].
Romans 12:9 AMP

The most significant quality that should describe children of the King should be the love they show others. Jesus said that his followers would be known by their love—*his love* flowing through them. John 13:34–35 describes it this way: "So now I am giving you a new commandment: Love each other. Just as I have loved you, you should love each other. Your love for one another will prove to the world that you are my disciples."

God's distinguishing mark upon our lives is that love fills us. This is what sets us apart and makes us special in a me-first world.

But what is *sincere* love? How can we recognize it and cultivate it in our lives?

Merriam-Webster's Learner's Dictionary Online defines love as "a feeling of strong or constant affection for a person."[27] Other words used to describe love are intense feelings of deep affection, tenderness, warmth, devotion, compassion, and adoration.

The kind of love God wants us to demonstrate is more than a feeling; it's a choice. Yes, love is more than a noun; it's also a verb. God intends love to be active. As God's children, we must choose to "put on" love, even when we don't feel warm, tingly goose bumps. Colossians 3:14 (ISV) states it this way: "Above all, clothe yourselves with love, which ties everything together in unity."

Love is also a response that softens the hardest hearts and warms the coldest souls. Sincere love is unconditional. It is consistent. We don't hold back our love when others don't meet our expectations or let us down. Sincere love remains consistent and unconditional.

Love does not repay evil for evil but instead leaves room for God to judge. It does not hold grudges or treat others with contempt.

> Dear friends, never take revenge. Leave that to the righteous anger of God. For the Scriptures say, "I will take revenge; I will pay them back," says the Lord. Instead, "If your enemies are hungry, feed them. If they are thirsty, give them something to drink. In doing this, you will heap burning coals of shame on their heads." Don't let evil conquer you, but conquer evil by doing good. (Romans 12:17–21)

The "burning coals" in this verse refer to the heat of God's love that will melt the cold, icy heart. Dr. Martin Luther King Jr. once said, "Darkness cannot drive out darkness; only light can do that. Hate cannot drive out hate; only love can do that."[28]

Today, ask God to fill you with his love that drives out hate.

Believe that love will grow in you when you spend time with God, the One who is love. Trust that love will grow in your heart as you receive God's love for you and receive healing from the wounds of your past and present.

Finally, know that if you want love to grow in you, take action. You must express and release love.

Declare

I boldly declare that I am an instrument of God's love. His sincere love flows through me to others and to myself, ever-growing and overflowing. I am filled with God's compassion and mercy. Today I choose the way of love.

Meditate, Believe, Accept

I love others deeply with a love that covers sin.

> Above all, love each other deeply, because love covers over a multitude of sins. (1 Peter 4:8 NIV)

I can love others because God loves me, and I am filled with his love.

> My command is this: Love each other as I have loved you. Greater love has no one than this: to lay down one's life for one's friends. (John 15:12–13 NIV)

I am chosen and called by God to put on love like a garment.

> Therefore, God's chosen ones, holy and loved, put on heartfelt compassion, kindness, humility, gentleness, and patience, accepting one another and forgiving one another if anyone has a complaint against another. Just as the Lord has forgiven you, so you must also forgive. Above all, put on love—the perfect bond of unity. (Colossians 3:12–14 HCSB)

Love manifests through me with patience and kindness.

> Love is patient, love is kind. (1 Corinthians 13:4 NIV)

Confess

Lord, I confess I do not always walk in your perfect love. At times I am distracted, even selfish. But I am persuaded that your love is the most powerful force in all the world, and it is available to me. Forgive me for my short-sighted attempts at living without your love. Fill me today, in Jesus's name.

Affirm

I possess God's love, the most powerful force in the universe, and live and move with a loving spirit.

Repeat "I am an instrument of God's love" three times. Each time you read it, add special emphasis to the bolded word or words.

I am an instrument of God's love.

I am **an instrument** of God's love.

I am an instrument of **God's love**.

Extra Memory Challenge

Love is patient, love is kind. (1 Corinthians 13:4 NIV)

Explore

1. In what ways do you see God's love at work in you?
2. In what ways do you see yourself withholding God's love, both from yourself and from others?
3. Name specific ways you can grow in God's love.
4. How can you make it your habit to "put on" God's love every day?

Journal

Week 9

Day 55

POWER EMOTION 2: APPRECIATION

TODAY'S TRUTH: I APPRECIATE OTHERS AND AM GRATEFUL

FOR MY RELATIONSHIPS

Be devoted to one another with [authentic]
brotherly affection [as members of one family],
give preference to one another in honor.
Romans 12:10 AMP

As you prepare for your day, "put on" an attitude of appreciation. Perhaps you've heard it called an *attitude of gratitude*. As the circumstances of your day unfold, consider them from a mindset of appreciation. Gratitude—a perspective of appreciation for all God has blessed you with—is the antidote to negativity in our lives.

It is not possible to be grateful and bitter at the same time. We cannot harbor anger while simultaneously fostering appreciation. Cultivating sincere appreciation and heartfelt gratitude can change our lives, alter our perspective, and produce Spirit-filled joy.

Ann Voskamp, the author of *One Thousand Gifts*, says this:

> Gratitude is not only a response to God in good times—
> it's ultimately the very will of God in hard times. Gratitude isn't only a celebration when good things happen.
> It's a declaration that God is good no matter what happens.[29]

This truth is staggering. Being thankful is the will of God for our lives. God knows that when we take our eyes off ourselves and our troubles and woes, we see him in all his beauty and splendor.

As we gaze into his eyes in that sacred space, we understand his immense love and goodness. This is when we can joyfully say, "I am thankful no matter what comes my way."

You may ask, "Can I *really* put on gratitude instead of disappointment or despair?"

Yes.

As we clothe ourselves in thankfulness, life takes on new meaning. We begin to notice the lovely, the beautiful, the simple, and the spiritual. We appreciate the small things, the common, and the mundane, for the presence of God is in every detail, just as he is in the spectacular.

Alive in the Now

Thornton Wilder wrote, "We can only be said to be alive in those moments when our hearts are conscious of our treasures."[30]

When we practice gratitude, we become alive in the present. We are not stuck in the "what ifs" and "if onlys" of the past. Neither are we caught in the "someday" of the future. We live each day fully, capturing the moments as gifts from God.

So will you take this step? Will you clothe yourself with this biblical power outlook? Like putting on love, living with an attitude of appreciation is a choice. Make it your choice today.

Declare

I am grateful, appreciative of everything God has blessed me with. I am thankful, aware that God is always good, no matter what.

Meditate, Believe, Accept

I am grateful and give God thanks in every circumstance.

> In everything give thanks, for this is the will of God in Christ Jesus concerning you. (1 Thessalonians 5:18 KJV)

I fill my speech with thankful appreciation, and I bless others with my words.

> Be filled with the Spirit; speaking one to another in psalms and hymns and spiritual songs, singing and making melody with your heart to the Lord; giving thanks always for all things in the name of our Lord Jesus Christ to God, even the Father. (Ephesians 5:18–20 ASV)

> Everything you do or say should be done to obey [or as a representative of; in the name of] the Lord Jesus. And in all you do, give thanks to God the Father through Jesus. (Colossians 3:17 EXB)

I put on gratitude, and I daily walk in victory.

> Thank God that he gives us the victory through our Lord Jesus Christ. (1 Corinthians 15:57 GW)

I am grateful for and strengthened by God's love. It endures forever.

> Give thanks to the God of heaven, for His lovingkindness (graciousness, mercy, compassion) endures forever. (Psalm 136:26 AMP)

Confess

Father, every good and perfect gift comes from you. But I confess that sometimes my selfish desires blind me, and I neglect to give thanks for who you are and all you've done for me. Today I choose gratitude—true appreciation for you and for life.

Affirm

I choose gratefulness for God's love and his gifts and live with an attitude of gratitude.

Repeat "I give thanks, for this is God's will" three times. Each time you read it, add special emphasis to the bolded word or words.

I give thanks, for this is God's will.
I **give thanks,** for this is God's will.
I give thanks, for this is **God's will**.

Extra Memory Challenge

> In everything give thanks, for this is the will of God in
> Christ Jesus concerning you. (1 Thessalonians 5:18 KJV)

Explore

1. Is it your habit to give appreciation?
   - To God?
   - To others?
   - To yourself?
2. How can you cultivate your mindset of gratitude?
3. Take time today to name your blessings.

Journal

Week 9

Day 56

Never lagging behind in diligence; aglow in the Spirit,
enthusiastically serving the Lord.
Romans 12:11 AMP

Fire. Aglow in the Spirit.

These words describe our third power emotion and one of my driving forces: enthusiasm. I love being around enthusiastic people. They give me juice. Fire and zeal for life are contagious.

Now before the introverts tune me out, I'm not speaking about a bubbly, outgoing personality. What I'm describing is deeper than a character trait. It's a spiritual force.

The word "*enthusiasm*" comes from the Greek word *entheos*. *En* means "in" and *theos* means "God." The Greeks coined the compound word when they could find no word to describe the fervor and spiritual fire they saw in first-century Christians. Something was different about these people, something indescribable. So Greek citizens labeled Christ-followers *entheos,* which literally means "one in whom God dwells."

It's my prayer that the unbelieving world will label me this way, but shouldn't this be the prayer of every Christian—to be identified as *one in whom God dwells*?

Enthusiasm, this spiritual fervor, is a gift to everyone who accepts Christ as Savior. Fueled by the indwelling of God's Holy Spirit, our lives should have the mark of uncommon enthusiasm, zeal, and energy for God, life, and people. Ralph Waldo Emerson has said:

Enthusiasm is one of the most powerful engines of success. When you do a thing, do it with all your might. Put your whole soul into it. Stamp it with your own personality. Be active, be energetic, be enthusiastic and faithful, and you will accomplish your object. Nothing great was ever achieved without enthusiasm.[31]

Indeed, enthusiasm is one of the most powerful engines of success. Enthusiasm is also integral to change. Enthusiasm lays the foundation for restructuring our thinking. Our passion helps us apply our minds and hearts to the fullest. As we unleash the Holy Spirit, we free our souls to become fully engaged. We must immerse our souls in the waters in which we swim.

Norman Vincent Peale states:

God will help you maintain enthusiasm. He will help you overcome all difficulties, all tragedies, all sorrows, all heartaches; He will give you victory. The word itself tells us that people with enthusiasm will be full of God and will, consequently, create a better world and have a better life individually. Enthusiasm makes life exciting and creative; enthusiasm helps a person accomplish things.[32]

Ultimately, Jesus called us to enthusiasm when he told us how we are to love: "Love the Lord your God with all your heart and with all your soul and with all your strength and with all your mind, and your neighbor as yourself" (Luke 10:27 ESV).

This integration of heart, soul, mind, and strength, bound together by the three-strand cord of God, defines wholehearted devotion—enthusiasm—and it gives us the winning edge as we journey through life.

So put on enthusiasm. Live with *all* your heart, soul, mind, and emotions fully engaged in the rhythms of life. Enjoy living with newfound fulfillment.

Declare

Lord, I confess that I've lived from moment to moment and task to task. Forgive me for not engaging fully in your world and your vision for my life. I commit to living with enthusiasm, with all my heart, soul, mind, and emotions engaged to glorify you, love you, and love others through you. Amen.

Meditate, Believe, Accept

I unleash my soul without fear, enthusiastic about life.

> And who do you think would [try to] hurt you if you become enthusiastic for doing what is right? (1 Peter 3:13 AUV)

I am redeemed, bursting with enthusiasm, and eager to do good deeds.

> Who gave Himself on our behalf that He might redeem us (purchase our freedom) from all iniquity and purify for Himself a people [to be peculiarly His own, people who are] eager and enthusiastic about [living a life that is good and filled with] beneficial deeds. (Titus 2:14 AMPC)

I have contagious enthusiasm; it stimulates others to live and give their best.

> For I am well acquainted with your willingness (your readiness and your eagerness to promote it) and I have proudly told about you to the people of Macedonia, saying that Achaia (most of Greece) has been prepared since last year for this contribution; and [consequently] your enthusiasm has stimulated the majority of them. (2 Corinthians 9:2 AMPC)

I live for God and enthusiastically serve him.

> Whatever you do, do it enthusiastically, as something done for the Lord and not for men. (Colossians 3:23 HCSB)

Confess

Lord, I confess that sorrow and negativity overshadow my zeal for life at times. I have allowed others to control my moods. But today I declare that I am free from the influence of moods and the problems of others. I live with enthusiasm because I am one in whom God dwells.

Affirm

I am enthusiastic about God, my life, others, and my work. I am one in whom God dwells.

Repeat "I live with enthusiasm, for God dwells in me" three times. Each time you read it, add special emphasis to the bolded word or words.

I live with enthusiasm, for God dwells in me.

I **live with enthusiasm**, for God dwells in me.

I live with enthusiasm, **for God dwells in me**.

Extra Memory Challenge

> Never lagging behind in diligence; aglow in the Spirit, enthusiastically serving the Lord. (Romans 12:11 AMP)

Explore

1. What does enthusiasm look like in your life?
2. What would be different for you if you chose to live with zeal and passion?
3. How can you guard your heart against negative environments?

Journal

Week 9

Day 57

Power Emotion 4: Joy
Today's Truth: I Put on Joy, and I Am Strengthened

Constantly rejoicing in hope.
Romans 12:12 amp

Jesus hardwired us for joy—for pleasure, happiness, contentment. Every person longs to find that space that satisfies their soul and enjoy a life filled with happy moments. Indeed, Jesus said he came to give us life and that more abundantly (John 10:10).

This is why we're all on a quest to find pleasure and satisfaction. We're built to enjoy life. Why then, are so many disenchanted people grappling with depression or living in unhappiness and emptiness? Are we looking for joy in all the wrong places?

I think so.

Where Is the Joy?

When I was five years old, I learned a song called "Joy." Maybe you learned it too. It went like this:

> I've got the joy, joy, joy, joy
> Down in my heart. (Where?)
> Down in my heart. (Where?)
> Down in my heart!
> I've got the joy, joy, joy, joy
> Down in my heart,
> Down in my heart to stay.

It was a catchy tune and fun to sing, and it communicated a message I still remember (dare I say it?) fifty years later.

This song taught me where joy comes from. We carry it with us down in our hearts—the spiritual part of our being. The world doesn't give it to us, and circumstances can't steal it away from us. Joy has no expiration date, and God gives us a never-ending supply. Sharing it with others doesn't deplete our supply—it makes it grow.

Joy is free but costly. Jesus paid the price for us to have it.

Joy can bubble up like a frolicking fountain, splashing contentment all around us, or it can be peaceful, like a quiet river, soothing us in difficult times.

Joy has many forms, but we can only find true joy through Jesus. It's given to us as a fruit of his Spirit as his deep abiding presence and love permeate our being.

We've been given the Holy Spirit to awaken our dead spirits. That's joy.

We've been justified and delighted in as adopted children of a heavenly Father. Joy.

We are coheirs with Jesus Christ. Joy.

We've been given his Holy Word, revealing the infinite riches of the mystery found in the gospel. Joy.

We've been given unlimited personal access to the King of the universe through prayer. Joy.

We've been set free from the bondage of slavery—from the pursuit of a better self, affirmation from others, fleeting pleasures in the world, and performance-based moral religion. Joy.[33]

Today we choose joy. We call it to spring up from our spirits. We embrace joy and allow it to fill our hearts with melodies. We refuse to allow the joy-suckers of stress, frustrated people, work, money, or other circumstances zap us of our joy. Today we bind our hearts to joy! "A joyful heart is good medicine, but a crushed spirit dries up the bones" (Proverbs 17:22 ESV).

Declare

I am an instrument of God's joy. I have joy bubbling in my soul to splash on others.

Meditate, Believe, Accept

I live each day filled with inexpressible joy.

> Though you have not seen him, you love him. Though you do not now see him, you believe in him and rejoice with joy that is inexpressible and filled with glory, obtaining the outcome of your faith, the salvation of your souls. (1 Peter 1:8–9 ESV)

Even when I'm going through tests and trials, I am filled with abundant joy.

> They are being tested by many troubles, and they are very poor. But they are also filled with abundant joy, which has overflowed in rich generosity. (2 Corinthians 8:2)

I'm on the path of life, and my joy is full.

> You make known to me the path of life; in your presence there is fullness of joy; at your right hand are pleasures forevermore. (Psalm 16:11 ESV)

I "put on" joy, for it is available within me.

> But the fruit of the Spirit is love, joy, peace, patience, kindness, goodness, faithfulness, gentleness, and self-control; against such things there is no law. (Galatians 5:22–23 NIV)

Even when I sorrow, I have deep abiding joy.

> Weeping may tarry for the night, but joy comes with the morning. (Psalm 30:5 ESV)

Confess

Lord, I confess that sometimes the joy-suckers get to me. I let people take my peace, and circumstances rob me of my joy. Today I put on joy. I wrap myself in an attitude of a victorious overcomer filled with joy, in Jesus's name.

Affirm

I will walk in God's pure joy, and nothing will move me out of my place of contentment and peace.

Repeat "I walk in God's joy" three times. Each time you read it, add special emphasis to the bolded word or words.

I walk in God's joy.

I **walk** in God's joy.

I walk **in God's joy**.

Extra Memory Challenge

> You make known to me the path of life; in your presence there is fullness of joy; at your right hand are pleasures forevermore. (Psalm 16:11 ESV)

Explore

1. Do you see yourself as a joyful person? Why or why not?
2. What joy-suckers drain you of life?
3. In what ways can you learn to guard your joy and stay at peace?

Journal

Week 9

Day 58

POWER EMOTION 5: PERSEVERANCE
TODAY'S TRUTH: THROUGH THE POWER OF GOD,
I PERSEVERE TO DO GOD'S WILL

Steadfast and patient in distress. . . .
Romans 12:12 AMP

You've made it to day 58 so you've demonstrated that you have perseverance. You want transformation of your mind and heart, and with the Word of God as your weapon of mass destruction against Satan's lies, you will achieve it. Continue to move forward in determined perseverance because God is making you mature and complete. You've got this.

"Let perseverance finish its work so that you may be mature and complete, not lacking anything" (James 1:4 NIV). Notice that this verse says perseverance has a work to finish. What's the work of perseverance? Well, for starters, perseverance is the emotion and attitude you create when you become determined, persistent, and steadfast, and when you decide to turn obstacles into opportunities. The work of perseverance starts when you enter any trial, testing, or situation that requires emotional muscle to stand firm. In other words, when adversity strikes, how long can you endure before you cry uncle? Perseverance or endurance says, "I will stand, for I can do all things through Christ, who is my strength."

Perseverance carves away the weakness in our souls that makes us quitters. It teaches us to direct our focus on the reward and not on the problem, just as Jesus fixed his eyes on the joy set before him and received power to endure the cross (Hebrews 12:2). We learn to reframe our challenges and recognize their potential for making us better, stronger, more mature, and compassionate. When

346

we persevere—when we stand up under our trial—our faith is perfected. And here's the good news: when we choose perseverance, we not only grow in depth of character, but we also receive the results we desire.

"You need to persevere so that when you have done the will of God, you will receive what he has promised" (Hebrews 10:36 NIV). Perseverance doesn't let us give up. It is the commander-in-chief within us that confronts our vulnerability head-on and bellows, "Give me ten more!" We're pushed to remain steadfast so we will win the prize.

We are not only called to endure, but we are to endure with joy: "Consider it pure joy, my brothers and sisters, whenever you face trials of many kinds" (James 1:2 NIV).

So the question is, how should we respond to adversity? Consider the following five steps:

1. **Listen to your inner dialogue.** Are your thoughts those of defeat? Change them quickly to align with God's Word.
2. **Analyze the situation.** Did I do something to create this situation that I can undo or correct? Act immediately.
3. **Recognize that you are *not* powerless.** You may not have chosen this trial, but you *can* choose how you go through it. Empower yourself quickly. You are not a victim.
4. **Set your mind and focus on the win, and then endure.** Remind yourself often of the outcomes you expect. Draw from Scripture the verses you need to stand on. (God never calls us to endure abuse, temptation, or sin. Flee those things—fast.)
5. **Sing.** Be joyful in your trial. Sheer grit may carry you through it, but Jesus gives you joy. Be joyful in all things.

Perseverance blesses us. It strengthens our minds, which keeps us from becoming weary in well doing. Because it drives us to reach our God-given potential and fulfill our God-given assignments, perseverance brings us joy, even when life seems to be going against us.

Today we bind our thoughts, wills, and emotions to perseverance. You *can* do *all* things through Christ (see Philippians 4:13). Kalpana Chawla, American astronaut, said, "The path from dreams to success does exist. May you have the vision to find it, the courage to get on to it, and the perseverance to follow it."[34]

Declare

I persevere with joy. Circumstances or fearful events do not move me. The journey does not weary me, and I am not impatient in waiting. I persevere. I press on. I do not quit, in Jesus's name.

Meditate, Believe, Accept

I am strengthened with power, prepared to endure and persevere with joy.

> Strengthened with all power, according to the might of his glory, for all endurance and perseverance with joy. (Colossians 1:11 WEB)

I receive my harvest because I do not give up.

> So let's not get tired of doing what is good. At just the right time we will reap a harvest of blessing if we don't give up. (Galatians 6:9)

I obey God's Word to persevere, and I do not fail in times of testing.

> Because you have obeyed my command to persevere, I will protect you from the great time of testing that will come upon the whole world to test those who belong to this world. (Revelation 3:10)

I am diligent and finish what I start.

But we want each of you to continue to be diligent to the very end, in order to give full assurance to your hope. (Hebrews 6:11 ISV)

So that you won't become lazy but will be imitators of those who inherit the promises through faith and perseverance. (Hebrews 6:12 HCSB)

I am strong in adversity. I persevere under trial.

Blessed is the one who perseveres under trial because, having stood the test, that person will receive the crown of life that the Lord has promised to those who love him. (James 1:12 NIV)

I persevere and gain a blessed life.

By your endurance you will gain your lives. (Luke 21:19 NET)

Confess

Lord, I confess there are times when I want to give up and quit. At times I'm weary and want to run from my problems. But today I choose perseverance. Teach me how to stand strong when I'm experiencing trials. I renounce a lazy spirit that would rather give up than press in. Today I endure.

Affirm

Through the power of the Spirit, I persevere in doing the will of God and standing firm in adversity and trials.

Repeat "I persevere and do not quit" three times. Each time you read it, add special emphasis to the bolded word or words.

I persevere and do not quit.

I **persevere** and do not quit.

I persevere and **do not quit**.

Extra Memory Challenge

Blessed is the one who perseveres under trial because, having stood the test, that person will receive the crown of life that the Lord has promised to those who love him. (James 1:12 NIV)

Explore

1. Are you waiting for the fulfillment of a promise? Explain the role of perseverance in this situation.
2. In what ways do you need to persevere now?
3. How can you draw from the character quality of persistence or perseverance when you feel weak?

Journal:

Week 9

Day 59

Power Emotion 6: Faith
Today's Truth: I Am a Man of Bold Faith

Devoted to prayer
[continually seeking wisdom, guidance, and strength].
Romans 12:12 AMP

You've done amazing work pursuing the goal of transformation. Today you've arrived at day 59. You're standing in new territory—the promised land, so to speak—the place where you can realize your divine purpose. You started this journey with the goal of transformation. The only thing left to do is to allow faith to rise and sustain you so you can claim the land and put down roots.

You're not the first person to ever stand on the edge of something great, something new and extraordinary. Other people of God have once stood here too. The only remaining requirement to possess this new territory and live out God's best is the *activation* of faith—the application of the concept of faith to your life.

Sadly, however, people often allow what they see to dictate what they believe. The children of Israel surveyed the promised land and decided it would be impossible to possess it. Why?

Doubt, fear, and mistrust of God's promises haunted them, so they shrank back in disbelief instead of "putting on" a renewed mind that said, "We certainly *can* possess this space! We can imagine ourselves living this amazing life. We can see this is God's will for us."

As we've learned in the Freedom Challenge, our state of mind determines the course of our lives. Proverbs 4:23 in the Good News Translation states it this way: "Be careful how you think; your life is shaped by your thoughts."

We must see and speak by faith first. No matter how dire circumstances may look, we must see the hope God promises through the eyes of faith.

Yes, it takes faith to possess a new victorious lifestyle, to be untied from unhealthy cords of bondage—lies that have trapped us in toxic living. In our efforts to break free, Satan will try to deceive us and pull us back into bondage. We need to speak by faith what we know is true—I'm free, I'm accepted, I'm loved, I'm enough—not what we feel or see. We possess new minds, so we must fill them with God's Word of truth. Any vacancy in our thought life will be filled by something, so choose your mental focus and your friends wisely and remain free.

Today, choose faith. Choose hope. Choose to believe.

"God . . . gives life to the dead, and calls the things that are not, as though they were" (Romans 4:17 WEB).

Declare

I am a man of faith. When my eyes behold a contradiction to what I believe, I will speak God's Word and trust him with my whole heart. I choose to live by faith, in Jesus's name.

Meditate, Believe, Accept

I live with confidence by faith in God.

> Faith shows the reality of what we hope for; it is the evidence of things we cannot see. (Hebrews 11:1)

I believe that what I hope for and what God promises will happen.

> But without faith no one can please God. We must believe that God is real and that he rewards everyone who searches for him. (Hebrews 11:6 CEV)

I do not worry. I have faith in God that everything will turn out for my good.

Don't be worried! Have faith in God and have faith in me. (John 14:1 CEV)

I am filled with joy. My faith keeps me in peace.

May God, the source of hope, fill you with all joy and peace by means of your faith in him, so that your hope will continue to grow by the power of the Holy Spirit. (Romans 15:13 GNT)

My faith comes from God's Word.

No one can have faith without hearing the message about Christ. (Romans 10:17 CEV)

I live by faith, and God is pleased and accepts me.

The good news tells how God accepts everyone who has faith, but only those who have faith. It is just as the Scriptures say, "The people God accepts because of their faith will live." (Romans 1:17 CEV)

Confess

Lord, I confess that at times I am a doubter, and I wonder if your Word is true. I feel uncertain about my life and sometimes about your goodness. I renounce my doubting spirit and confess that I trust in you, God. I choose faith.

Affirm

I will walk in faith and trust God because he accepts those who come to him with the faith of a child.

Repeat "I am a man of faith" three times. Each time you read it, add special emphasis to the bolded word or words.

I am a man of faith.

I **am** a man of faith.

I am **a man of faith**.

Extra Memory Challenge

> God . . . giveth life to the dead, and calleth the things
> that are not, as though they were. (Romans 4:17 ASV)

Explore

1. Describe a time when your faith was tested.
2. How will choosing faith and an outlook of hope improve your life?

Journal

Week 9

Day 60

POWER EMOTION 7: GENEROSITY

TODAY'S TRUTH: GOD CALLS ME TO CULTIVATE A GENEROUS SPIRIT

Contributing to the needs of God's people,
pursuing [the practice of] hospitality.
Romans 12:13 AMP

You did it! You made it to day 60. Let's take a minute and celebrate. Woo-hoo!

I'm proud of you for following through. Today you will learn about the last of the seven power emotions. This one holds the secret to a joyful and contented life and will keep you from the pit of pride and the grip of greed.

The Cure

Whenever I become sad or throw a pity party, the Holy Spirit gently reminds me, "Remember, Paul, it's not all about you!"

Wait, what? How can that be? It's hard for me accept that I can be self-centered and myopic. At these times, I need to apply the best antidote to cure my selfish condition.

Generosity.

Focusing on others helps me shift my priorities. I focus on others when I serve someone else and generously offer my time, talent, and treasure to advance someone else's cause other than my own. Nothing makes me more like Jesus than reaching out to others and lifting them up. We never truly give anything until we give of ourselves.

You haven't lived today until you've done something
for someone who cannot pay you back.
—John Bunyan[35]

A generous spirit is a grateful spirit. When we count our blessings, we take our eyes off ourselves—off our wants, our needs, our agendas—and awaken to the world around us. We experience life without entitlement. Our outward focus draws us to the condition of hurting humanity, and we become inspired to do something that can change the world.

A generous spirit crushes a scarcity mindset. When we choose to share our time, money, ideas, support, and resources, we discover there's plenty to go around. In God's economy, we find we're not depleted, but our life is abundant and overflowing with blessings. We gain, but the stingy and the hoarders find themselves with less and less.

Luke 6:38 says, "Give, and you will receive. Your gift will return to you in full—pressed down, shaken together to make room for more, running over, and poured into your lap. The amount you give will determine the amount you get back."

Some of Dawn's greatest moments in life have come because of her generosity. When she receives emails from people all over the world telling their testimonies of healing after reading her books, she gratefully rejoices that God gave her freedom from fear to tell her story. I have also shared my life, and as a result, other people found comfort and freedom through my gift of transparency. Giving has also brought me great joy.

Generosity breeds happiness, as well as other benefits. But don't take my word for it; believe the research. Much has been written about generosity and the benefits people receive from giving. Some of the benefits are:

- Better health

- Diminished depression
- Happier relationships
- Reduced stress

There truly is more joy in giving than in receiving.

Today, choose generosity.

Give with joy.

Be free from the clutches of greed and this world's me-first thinking.

Declare

I am a generous man. I share my time, talent, and treasures and still have more blessings than I can contain. I am grateful and content and look for ways I can contribute to others and this world.

Meditate, Believe, Accept

I share with those in need.

> If any of your fellow Israelites become poor and are unable to support themselves among you, help them as you would a foreigner and stranger, so they can continue to live among you. (Leviticus 25:35 NIV)

I live with open hands and an open and generous heart.

> But if there are any poor Israelites in your towns when you arrive in the land the Lord your God is giving you, do not be hard-hearted or tightfisted toward them. Instead, be generous and lend them whatever they need. (Deuteronomy 15:7–8)

I freely give, and I am prospered because of my generosity.

> Give freely and become more wealthy; be stingy and lose everything. The generous will prosper; those who

refresh others will themselves be refreshed. (Proverbs 11:24–25)

If you help the poor, you are lending to the Lord—and he will repay you! (Proverbs 19:17)

I am happier because I am generous.

You should remember the words of the Lord Jesus: "It is more blessed to give than to receive." (Acts 20:35)

Confess

Lord, I confess there are times when I'm ungrateful. I become blind to my blessings as I look upon what others have or what I don't yet have that I want. My entitled thinking can often prevent me from having the generous heart you would like me to have. Today I choose generosity, in Jesus's name.

Affirm

It is better to give than to receive.

Repeat "I choose generosity" three times. Each time you read it, add special emphasis to the bolded word.

I choose generosity.

I **choose** generosity.

I choose **generosity**.

Extra Memory Challenge

Give freely and become more wealthy; be stingy and lose everything. (Proverbs 11:24)

Explore

1. What resonates with you about living generously?
2. Do you believe you are fulfilling God's command to give?
3. What steps can you take to cultivate even more generosity?

Journal

CHAPTER 12

FREEDOM FOUND

*Christ has freed us so that we may enjoy the benefits of
freedom. Therefore, be firm in this freedom,
and don't become slaves again.*
Galatians 5:1 GW

You are changed. The anointed Word of God has liberated
you, but you must prepare yourself. Your old nature, like
mine, will want to resurrect itself, so don't be surprised when old
habits and attitudes try to make an appearance. Just remember to
follow God's direction in his Word: "Consider yourselves dead"
(Romans 6:11) and stand firm in your newfound freedom. "You
must think of yourselves as dead to the power of sin. But Christ
Jesus has given life to you, and you live for God" (Romans 6:11
CEV).

The Bible says we are to think of ourselves or consider ourselves
as dead to sin. Sin speaks to us, but we don't respond because our
old nature has died. We don't react because sin no longer has power
over us.

Because of this truth, we can stand firm in our freedom and
refuse to allow the cords of death to entangle us. We can shake off
cords of sin that are rooted in lies because sin and falsehood have
no power over us.

The Philippians 4:8 Test

Another way to remain in freedom is to take your thoughts captive and run them through the Philippians 4:8 test:

> And now, dear brothers and sisters, one final thing. Fix your thoughts on what is true, and honorable, and right, and pure, and lovely, and admirable. Think about things that are excellent and worthy of praise. (Philippians 4:8)

You're now skillful in challenging your thoughts and ideas, so evaluate the things that drift into *your* mind. The next time you're tempted to allow your mind to take a dive into the cesspool of toxic thoughts or to spew negative words, take a deep breath and exhale *and* submit those thoughts and words to the Philippians 4:8 test:

- Should I dwell on this thought or cast it down?
- Is this thought true?
- Does it bring honor?
- Is this thought accurate?
- Is it right and pure?
- Is it lovely and admirable?

When you filter your thoughts and behaviors through a biblical grid, you'll maintain your freedom and accomplish the goals and dreams God has set before you.

> So now the case is closed. There remains no accusing voice of condemnation against those who are joined in life-union with Jesus, the Anointed One. For the "law" of the Spirit of life flowing through the anointing of Jesus has liberated us from the "law" of sin and death. (Romans 8:1–2 TPT)

CHAPTER 13

FREEDOM TO SOAR

This chapter brings us back to where we began. Romans 12:2 introduced us to the concept of spiritual renewal and renovation, and here's where this process concludes: "Do not conform yourselves to the standards of this world, but let God transform you inwardly by a complete change of your mind" (Romans 12:2 GNT).

This *God-transformation* process has been working in you for the last several months, and by now, you should be experiencing significant, steady change. This is what transformation is—a complete metamorphosis. The Greek word used in this verse for "transform" is the word *metamorphoo*, a word with an explosive meaning. The first part of the word, *meta*, means "to change by being with." The second part of this compound word, *morphoo*, means "changing form in keeping with inner reality."

Can you see the picture Paul provides for us in Romans through the use of these words? We need a metamorphosis to keep on being transformed—growing, changing, and maturing so we look totally different from who we were when we started. Our former self surrenders to the new self as we are "changed by being with." This transformation happens when we spend time with God in his Word, just as you've been doing.

Dawn and I live near a botanical garden that features a display of tens of thousands of butterflies every spring. Visitors flock to Meijer Gardens to see caterpillars transform into butterflies. They hatch and fill an enclosed tropical garden with their breathtaking beauty. What we only recently learned was that in the process of metamorphosis from caterpillar to butterfly, a caterpillar completely dissolves while in the chrysalis before its physical state is rearranged into a captivating butterfly. What truly takes place during this process of dissolution and creation mystifies scientists and botanists.

When we combine the processes of *meta* and *morphoo*, we understand God's divine equation. Our changing form is "in keeping with an *inner reality.*" This inner reality is our true, original identity as created by God when he placed his spiritual DNA within us to reflect himself in his beauty and love in this world.

> Then God said, "Let us make mankind in our image, in our likeness, so that they may rule over the fish in the sea and the birds in the sky, over the livestock and all the wild animals, and over all the creatures that move along the ground." (Genesis 1:26 NIV)

When you spend time with Christ, you become more like him, and the transformation causes your outside—your attitude, your character, your countenance—to reflect the eternal, spiritual reality of who you are on the inside.

You, my friend, are like that winged creature. An amazing destiny awaits you. Don't quit. Struggle is part of growth. Stay in this process. Understand that you will feel weary at times as life continues to come at you hard. But encoded in you is the DNA of a successful, free, and glorious man.

This is your metamorphosis—your time to break free.

Soar.

ENDNOTES

1. "Sexual Abuse Survivor Story: Child Molestation Victim Letter." Klest Injury Law Firm, accessed May 24, 2020, https://www.chicagotriallaw.com/Sexual-Abuse-and-Assault/Open-Letter-to-a-Sexual-Abuse-Victim.shtml.

2. Caroline Leaf, *Switch On Your Brain: The Key to Peak Happiness, Thinking, and Health* (Grand Rapids: Baker Books, 2015), 80.

3. Passion Translation New Testament (2nd ed.). Savage, MN: BroadStreet Publishing Group, 2017.

4. Dawn Scott Damon, *The Freedom Challenge: 60 Days To Untie The Cords That Bind You* (Enumclaw, WA: (Redemption Press, 2019) 73.

5. Shelly Beach, The Silent Seduction of Self-Talk: Conforming Deadly Thought Patterns to the Word of God (Chicago: Moody Publishers, 2009), 27.

6. The Phrase Finder Online, origins of phrases. "Sticks and stones may break my bones." https://www.phrases.org.uk/meanings/sticks-and-stones-may-break-my-bones.html

7. Nathan Jones, "Now Showing: Epic Failure," *Faithlife Sermons*, March 9, 2018, https://sermons.faithlife.com/sermons/201502-rj-now-showing:-epic-failure.

8. Rick Warren, *Let Go, and Know God Is in Control, Daily Hope*, December 13, 2016, https://pastorrick.com/let-go-and-know-god-is-in-control/.

9. Mark Twain, Goodreads, accessed March 12, 2018, https://www.goodreads.com/quotes/14351-it-s-not-the-size-of-the-dog-in-the-fight.

10. J. R. R. Tolkien, Goodreads, accessed February 16, 2017, https://www.goodreads.com/quotes/96664-go-back-he-thought-no-good-at-all-go-sideways.

11. André Gide, Goodreads Quotable Quotes, accessed April 1, 2017, https://www.goodreads.com/quotes/4661-man-cannot-discover-new-oceans-unless-he-has-the-courage.

12. Mary Anne Radmacher, Goodreads Quotable Quotes, accessed October 19, 2020, https://www.goodreads.com/author/quotes/149829.Mary_Anne_Radmacher.

13. Robert B. Strimple, "The Fear of the Lord," Orthodox Presbyterian Church online, reprinted from New Horizons, March 2001, http://www.opc.org/new_horizons/NH01/03a.html

14. The Nelson Study Bible NKJV (Grand Rapids: Thomas Nelson, 1997), note on Psalm 128:1.

15. Marci G. Fox, "Give Up Worry by Recognizing It as a Bad Habit," *Psychology Today* online, January 28, 2011.

16. Guy Winch, "The Important Difference Between Sadness and Depression," Psychology Today, October 2, 2015, https://www.psychologytoday.com/us/blog/the-squeaky-wheel/201510/the-important-difference-between-sadness-and-depression.

17. Damon, *The Freedom Challenge: 60 Days To Untie The Cords That Bind You*, 214.

18. Rick Warren, "Forget Yourself, and Look to the Needs of Others," *Daily Hope*, June 11, 2014, http://purposedriven.com/

blogs/dailyhope/forget-yourself-and-look-to-the-needs-of-others/.

19. Harvard Health Publishing, "What Causes Depression?" updated April 11, 2017, https://www.health.harvard.edu/mind-and-mood/what-causes-depression.

20. Anthony Robbins, *Awaken the Giant Within* (NY: Simon & Schuster, 2007), Kindle.

21. Aristotle, BrainyQuote, accessed December 14, 2017, https://www.brainyquote.com/quotes/aristotle_138437.

22. Robert C. Solomon, *True to Our Feelings* (Oxford University Press, 2007), Kindle.

23. John Bunyan, *The Pilgrim's Progress* (Mineola, NY: Dover Publications Inc., 2003), Kindle. (Originally published in 1678.)

24. Sharon Ellison, as quoted by Linda Carroll, 12 Truths about Defensive Behavior, mgbmindfulness (website), https://www.mindbodygreen.com/0-17712/13/12-truths-about-defensive-behavior.html.

25. Stephen Arterburn, Fred Stoeker, and Mike Yorkey, Every Man's Battle: Winning the War on Sexual Temptation One Victory at a Time (WaterBrook, 2020), XX.

26. John Donne, "No Man Is an Island," Mediation XVII, *Devotions upon Emergent Occassions*, accessed October 19, 2920, https://web.cs.dal.ca/~johnston/poetry/island.html.

27. "Love." Merriam-Webster Learner's Dictionary Online, Merriam-Webster Incorporated, 2020. https://www.learnersdictionary.com/definition/love.

28. Martin Luther King, Jr., Strength to Love (New York: Simon and Schuster Pocket Books, 1964).

29. Ann Voskamp, AZQuotes.com, accessed August 3, 2018, https://www.azquotes.com/quote/1460133.

30. Thornton Wilder, The Woman of Andros (New York: Harper Collins, 2007), 149.

31. Ralph Waldo Emerson, Goodreads Quotable Quotes, accessed October 19, 2020, https://www.goodreads.com/quotes/294967-enthusiasm-is-one-of-the-most-powerful-engines-of-success.

32. Norman Vincent Peale, "Be Enthusiastic: Be Full of God," Guideposts, March 22, 2013, https://www.guideposts.org/faith-and-prayer/bible-resources/be-enthusiastic-be-full-of-god.

33. Matt Chandler, "The Secret to Finding True Joy," LifeWay, December 8, 2015,

www.lifeway.com/en/articles/bible-study-matt-chandler-recovering-redemption-pursue-joy.

34. Kalppana Chawla, as quoted in Study Adda, "6th class English: An Indian-American Woman in Space," accessed October 19, 2020, https://www.studyadda.com/ncert-solution/6th-english-an-indian-american-woman-in-space-kalpana-chawla_q1/189/25558.

35. John Bunyan, quoted by Jack Graham, "You Haven't Lived Today until You've Done Something for Someone Who Cannot Pay You Back," May 30, 2016, https://resources.jackgraham.org/resource-library/devotionals/you-havent-lived-today-until-youve-done-something-for-someone-who-cannot-pay-you-back.

COPYRIGHT PERMISSIONS

ESV
English Standard Version
Scripture quotations are from the ESV® Bible (The Holy Bible, English Standard Version®), copyright © 2001 by Crossway, a publishing ministry of Good News Publishers. Used by permission. All rights reserved.

EXB
The Expanded Bible
Scripture taken from The Expanded Bible. Copyright ©2011 by Thomas Nelson. Used by permission. All rights reserved.

GNT
Good News Translation®
Scripture quotations marked (GNT) are from the Good News Translation in Today's English Version- Second Edition Copyright © 1992 by American Bible Society. Used by permission.

GW
GOD'S WORD Translation
Scripture marked GW is taken from GOD'S WORD®, © 1995 God's Word to the Nations. Used by permission of Baker Publishing Group.

HCSB
Holman Christian Standard Bible®
Copyright © 1999, 2000, 2002, 2003, 2009 by Holman Bible Publishers. Used with permission by Holman Bible Publishers, Nashville, Tennessee. All rights reserved.

ISV
International Standard Version
The Holy Bible: International Standard Version. Release 2.0, Build 2015.02.09. Copyright © 1995-2014 by ISV Foundation. ALL RIGHTS RESERVED INTERNATIONALLY. Used by permission of Davidson Press, LLC.

KJ21

21st Century King James Version

MSG

The Message

NASB

New American Standard

NET

New English Translation

NCV

New Century Version

NIV

New International Version

NKJV

New King James Version

NLT
New Living Translation
Scripture taken from the New Living Translation, copyright © 1996, 2004, 2015 by Tyndale House Foundation. Used by permission of Tyndale House Publishers Inc., Carol Stream, Illinois 60188. All rights reserved.

NLV
New Living Version
Scripture quotations taken from the New Life Version© Christian Literature International.

TLB
The Living Bible
copyright © 1971 by Tyndale House Foundation. Used by permission of Tyndale House Publishers Inc., Carol Stream, Illinois 60188. All rights reserved.

TPT
Scripture quotations marked TPT are from The Passion Translation®. Copyright © 2017, 2018 by Passion & Fire Ministries, Inc. Used by permission. All rights reserved. ThePassionTranslation.com.

TSK
Treasury of Scripture Knowledge
Public Domain

Voice
Scripture taken from The Voice™. Copyright © 2008 by Ecclesia Bible Society. Used by permission. All rights reserved.

WNT
Weymouth New Testament
Public Domain

ORDER INFORMATION

REDEMPTION PRESS

To order additional copies of this book, please visit
www.redemption-press.com.
Also available on Amazon.com and BarnesandNoble.com
or by calling toll-free 1-844-2REDEEM.

CPSIA information can be obtained
at www.ICGtesting.com
Printed in the USA
BVHW030838060221
599516BV00008BA/138

9 781646 451104